Seven, Going Down

by

Dorothy Parker

ISBN 09551441-0-8
ISBN 978-0-9551441-0-3

The moral right of the author has been asserted.

Printed and bound in the UK by Antony Rowe,
Chippenham, Wiltshire.

Contents

'Lives of great men all remind us
We can make our lives sublime,
And, departing, leave behind us

.... Footprints on the sands of Time - - -'

(Longfellow)

'AHR   AYE

CHICKER   RYE

RONY   PONY

PING   PANG   PINY

ULLA   GULLA   GUSTA

ZING   ZANG   ZINY'

(chant of the Parker boys)

Acknowledgements

I wish to express my thanks to the author of *Discovering Essex in London*, Kenneth Neale, for points on the History of Wanstead and other facts on local history.

Also to the V.C.H., the Victorian County History, for details of Essex history.

Chapter One

Us

I remember her first in sunlight with the snakes. The early morning stillness, the silence, dazzling light, rustling leaves and Mamma's voice cementing the picture, and fear.

"Look at that carpet," she said, the conservatory carpet where we children sat and played. I looked at it fearfully, screwed-up eyes dazzled and saw sunbeams splinter to writhing snakes crossing the floor.

Snakes filled my mind. Early that morning Mamma had suffered a shock. Bending low to brush the carpet, with some difficulty because of her 'condition', one of Father's snakes had slowly slithered across the carpet barely missing the moving brush. A few piercing shrieks and the smelling salts had served to recover her. Now she gave vent to her feelings.

"Either those snakes go," she declared, "or I shall!"

Father loved pets. Mamma said it was because he had no brothers or sisters. Anything from a spider to a large stray dog was welcome. Father was also a law unto himself. If he chose to bring a mangy mongrel in for a spot of lunch, or a hedgehog in on a cold night, turning out the shoe cupboard to accommodate it, Mamma would make a mild protest on account of hygiene, and then calmly accept the situation. She knew that whatever she said would make no difference. Nobody was ever allowed to tell Father what he could or could not do. Nobody ever got their own way with him but this time with the snake episode it was different. Today Mamma had suffered a shock that gave Father no alternative but to give way. Mamma was six months pregnant and snakes hiding in the most unlikely places, like behind the books in the bookcase, even Father could not justify, and the snakes went.

Whenever Mamma was out of her usual sweet harmony with life, due to Father's 'ways', she would expound upon the virtues of her first husband, Giovanni Raggazone. As you can tell, he was an Italian. He was also handsome, wealthy and well educated. Through Mamma's discourses upon the subject, we knew as much, and sometimes it seemed, perhaps, more about Raggazone than we did about Father. This was not surprising as Father had no living relatives and knew little about his parents and nothing of his grandparents. Of course Mamma was discreet when Father was around, but alone with us children Mamma indulged in reminiscing. As we gathered around to listen, she rolled the pastry and captured our imagination. We heard all about Raggazone's gentlemanly behaviour. How we all admired him for speaking seven different languages. Mamma painted vivid pictures of herself sitting on Raggazone's knee, when he returned from a trip overseas; and of him pouring golden sovereigns into her lap as he called her by pet names, 'Saucy' and 'Blue Eyes'. He died, sadly, in the second year of their marriage and Mamma always mourned his loss. But his memory stayed evergreen with her because of his son, Mamma's first born. He was just over a year old when his Father died suddenly in Port Said and so was buried there.

Today, as I listened to Mamma relieving her feelings about the snakes which Father kept as pets, I shared her abhorrence, but then as her indignation with Father's 'ways' mounted, she began as always, to lament the losing of Raggazone. Soon the snakes receded and Raggazone took over. I looked up at Mamma and I too began to worry about the priority of Raggazone. I tugged at the blue velvet skirt, urgently. "Mamma," I interrupted, "Mamma."

Blue was Mamma's colour without a doubt, with her large blue eyes. The dress that she wore was all blue, cornflower blue. The skirt hung full and softly to the floor. Peeping from under the back were Mamma's shoes with the curved-out heels. The voluminous folds of skirt were easy to hide in if you were shy or nervous. Standing there clinging and listening to Mamma I completely forgot the snakes. The problem worried me I had thought about before, at times when Mamma discoursed upon Father's vices and Raggazone's virtues. In our house, Heaven loomed large in our thoughts and, Father apart, was important to us all as it was to Mamma. I tugged again at the sweeping skirt. "Mamma," I worried, "Mamma, who will you live with in Heaven, Raggazone or Father?" "Oh, we shall have to wait and see," she replied.

Now at the age of two I already knew that this answer was no answer. I pulled at the skirt again. "Mamma," I repeated, "who will you live with in Heaven, Father or Raggazone?" To my astonishment she did not give me the completely assured answer that we always expected. "That remains to be seen,"

3

was the unsatisfactory reply. Why was it that Mamma would not tell me the answer?

Mamma's discourses were a kind of intermezzo which she entwined between the babies' births, when no child was at the breast. Mamma made all her own clothes and so they suited her. She also made them to suit her 'condition' so that when she was 'expecting' we never noticed. She made her dresses to fall in soft folds from her high bosom; and from the base of her throat, a large bow followed the fall of her dress. Mamma was beautiful and her beauty and skill with her needle, completed a picture which captivated the eye, distracting the mind from her frequent 'interesting' condition. To use Mamma's parlance, the general effect was to 'take the dairy off'. In our house Mamma did not approve of crudities and so she had a saying for almost everything which turned crudities into niceties, such as 'It's an ill wind that blows nobody any good' and 'It never rains but it pours', sayings I puzzled over and never fully understood for years.

Mamma's striking appearance was due to a combination of things. Firstly she possessed a beautiful head of hair; thick shiny coppery chestnut tresses which hung so far down her back that she could sit on them. Usually it was all caught up behind and coiled on each side and held in place by tortoise shell combs, to surround her head like a fiery halo. Her cheeks bones were high and beautifully moulded so that with her finely-shaped eyebrows, they set off her great blue eyes. Her skin was extremely delicate and creamy with a subtle rosiness and the whole face enhanced by the crowning glory of her hair. But above all she wore a serene sweet expression a reflection of her inner calm and goodness. Mamma's portrait would have graced a Gainsborough canvas.

As the weather grew colder and the Autumn gave way to winter many people throughout Europe were hungry and cold. In this second year of the peace after the First World War, the great economic depression of the 1920s had begun. Hunger was the companion of the many. Illness was a thing to be dreaded as doctors had to be paid. Old Doctor Collins came to us. He was over eighty years old. Each of his visits cost three and sixpence and that included the medicine. Doctor Collins rode an old-fashioned bicycle. We would watch out for him from the sickroom window, Mamma's bedroom. We saw him coming slowly round the corner; how deliberately his feet moved up and down on the pedals. We watched as he propped his bike carefully against the kerb and, picking his bag off the back of his bike, walked up the black and white tiled path towards the front door. At this point, the owners of six or more pairs of eyes, retreated from the window and sped downstairs to appraise Mamma of his arrival. Anyone who was ill was always in Mamma's great four poster bed when the doctor arrived. By the time he had climbed the stairs, never hurrying, we had all dispersed to strategic points of the house, and the invalid, well aware of immediate investigation, was sitting up and feeling poorly but very important. We always felt tongue-tied as Doctor Collins carefully sat on the edge of the bed. As soon as our upper torso was exposed, he poked us in the chest with a bony finger. "Now what-is-the-matter-with-you?" he would enquire tediously as though pin-pointing the germ, a poke with each word. We never answered and he didn't expect us to, as by then he'd be looking at our tongue. At the last poke he would have decided on the answer and rising and turning to Mamma would instruct her about the

5

nt. His next question always made Mamma ... "Now who is going to pay me?" he'd demand, ...ng his stethoscope neatly in his black bag. And hearing the expected question Mamma would answer tartly, "Don't you worry about that!" as she led the way downstairs. Sometimes we owed the doctor the three and six for his first visit and Mamma would fret and worry if she wanted him to call again. You just had to pay it before he came again or he just didn't come. I suppose that he too was short of money and if you had no money you did not call the doctor.

By December 1920 the depression was affecting everyone. Father had no work; seven children to feed as well as Mamma and himself and a new baby expected before Christmas. Before the war he had a wholesale business in Billingsgate Market. On his discharge from the army, he could not get his pitch back. It was impossible to get back into the fish trade, and there was no other work to be found. With no income there was no money for fuel. The five elder boys whose ages ranged from six to thirteen, went to find sticks and wood for the kitchen range where all our food was cooked. This was an iron kitchen range or stove with a back boiler which heated all our water, and a long low oven at the side where Mamma baked everything, pies, roasts, cakes and bread. The range needed plenty of fuel to keep it going to cook for our family. Early in the morning at six o'clock, when all was still, I and Mamma found tiny twigs and sticks in the garden; then she bent low in the kitchen to get the fire going with paper and sticks so that the poranger and kettle could be put on the stove ready for the family breakfast.

Next to the kitchen was the dining room, linked by the hatchway in the wall and the short passage at the side where we often played. The dining room in summer, was light and airy with the French doors leading into the sunny conservatory outside. As Autumn set in and nights began to get chilly, we lit the oil lamps with the tall, polished glass shades. They stood on the long table where we dined, played, worked and read. Mamma sat there on darkening evenings. The lamps had been trimmed and the wicks adjusted to give their maximum brightness without smoking. There by the light of the lamp she sat; calm, busy and beautiful; sewing quietly; a piece of stitching in her hands; occasionally biting her thread; and as she finished each article taken from the pile in her needlework basket it was carefully folded and laid aside with others. A hum of talk filled the room, muted because of Father stretched comfortably before the fire, his feet, minus shoes, up on a stool. Mamma's face radiated contentment. Long shadows flickered about the room in the firelight as we moved. We had to play quietly and there were breathless games of 'Spillikins' where we fished out the picks, hammers, spades and shovels with tiny wooden-handled hooks. Afraid to breathe lest we disturb two from the tangled pile instead of one, and so miss a turn, yet trying to hook the highest numbers, we dexterously manipulated our tiny hooks, and at each capture the score was acclaimed and calculated. With five or six pairs of eyes watching inches away from one's hand, not a tremor was missed; nothing being allowed to move except whatever was being hooked out. How we loved those long evenings in the dining room. Father had innumerable packs of cards which he shared out among us for building. Tall Chinese pagodas grew under our nimble fingers; square blocks of shanty towns spread over the table cloth or carpet, collapsing down, just as everyone was declaring how clever you were to build so high, or to have covered such a space, by sheer lightness of touch.

When December came in the winter of 1920 the weather was bitter temperatures below freezing. A bed for Mamma was brought downstairs and fitted in the alcove by the fire in the dining room, ready for the new baby's arrival. The tall fire-guard encircled the fire, but how to keep a fire going with no money for fuel, was a problem. Father stuffed paper all around the French doors and Mamma's 'lying in' time was due.

Whenever Mamma was near her 'time', one of the boys was sent to fetch the housekeeper-cum-nurse who was going to look after us all. It was either Mother Cox or Mother Dix according to which one of them was free. This time it was Mother Dix. She came daily, arriving at about eight in the morning and leaving at about six in the evening. She had a great deal to do. She had to nurse Mamma; bath the baby and do all its washing; clean the house; see to the shopping; see to all the beds; cook for us all and as if Mamma and the baby were not enough there was all the family washing to be done, as well as the nappies. This had to be done in the wash house, out in the garden. It had to be done in the old stone copper with the fire to be lit underneath. This had to be kept going for hot water and if it was wet or the wind in the wrong quarter, the fire would not draw.

These surrogate mothers were wonderful women and did a magnificent job, but as we all missed dear Mamma so much, we hated these times when Mamma was at her 'lying in'. Our eldest brother, Roy, christened Alfredo Raggazone but known as Roy Parker at home and at school, referred to the stay of

8

either of these ladies of all work as 'looking after the tribe'. He didn't include himself as a member of the tribe. He was always rather superior, an attitude fostered by Mamma, and by us, as we regarded him with a certain amount of deference and awe.

Although all of us, except Roy, were born in our house, the advent of a new brother or sister always took us by surprise. Firstly Mamma's clothes suited and disguised her 'condition' so well. She cleverly made long draped gowns with soft ties and large bows just above the high bosoms, which completely set off her figure and beauty, so that any fulness merely made her look blooming. When a new baby's cry was heard early in the morning, we were awed and amazed.

"Did you hear that?" we asked each other. "Where has it come from?"

"I saw a nurse with a black bag," someone observed. Perhaps one of the boys had been sent to the nurses' home to ask a nurse to call that very day. "Why," we wondered aloud to each other, "did the baby not cry in the black bag?" Sometimes we did not know about the new baby until we were all marched in to Mamma's room to see it. The second reason we were surprised when a baby happened was our total preoccupation among ourselves with play and adventure. There was never a dull moment; Father saw to that.

Father and Mamma slept in a four poster bed with soft white muslim drapes at the head, hung on two carved posts which curved forward at the tops. The muslim went over the tops and down the sides. You could feel no draughts in that great bed and it was very quiet, as I found out once when I had the measles. The baby's cot was on the right hand side of the bed, Mamma's side. It was a delightful thing; a Moses basket made from intermeshed flat strips of metal. It swung from two hooks, one at the head and one at the foot, on a frame into which it could be lowered to lie like an acorn in its cup, but it usually swung. It was all painted white of course. Foamy drapes of muslin fell from the metal scroll which rose from the metal stand high above the baby's head; so that like Mamma's bed, there were no draughts. The whole thing was draped in a sweet fashion with pink or blue ribbons in frills and bows proclaiming the sex of the occupant. At the touch of a finger it swayed gently and silently to and fro and lulled the baby to sleep.

In December 1920 Father was unable to afford any help or nursing from either Mother Dix or Mother Cox, so he had to do everything himself. Having such a competent, wonderful wife, Father had never been put to the test of doing women's chores, and Mamma always dismissed his household capabilities as non-existent. Now he had to do everything. Everything was a great deal, especially for Father who was used to only giving orders. He now had to do all the nursing; making Mamma's gruel which was so good for making her milk; he washed the nappies; organised the shopping and food; cooked for us all; did all the washing and kept us all, seven children, quiet and occupied, clean and tidy.

This winter of 1920 must have been a hard time for him. With no work and no money Father had to cook with fuel found by the boys. The kitchen which before had been warm and cosy with bread and pies baking deliciously in the long, deep oven, was now icy – the range stone cold. Only a tiny fire was kept going in the dining room. Mamma's bed was made up in the alcove by the fire where the big brass fireguard tried to air the clothes. We children played and kept ourselves warm chasing about up and down the hall and passage. Father was good at thinking up quiet games which kept us busy. Flat building sticks of different lengths with notched edges which fitted together leaving gaps for windows and turrets made castles, where lead soldiers were positioned. Jigsaws, draughts, dominoes, snakes and ladders, cards and acting, made the hours swiftly fly and kept us all out of Mamma's way. If we needed to chase about then Father gave out balloons for us to head, with a farthing for the one who scored highest before it touched the floor.

As we chased about the house that December to keep warm, Olive was born. Without Mamma at the helm what a sad Christmas it was for us. No Christmas puddings to stir and wish in; no large sticky raisins to stone; no warm wet almonds to skin; no marzipan to taste; no smell of mince pies or stuffing; no tree to decorate; no stockings to hang and the worst thing of all no Father Christmas. There was no lying awake in the night listening for the dawn and the solitary cockerel's crow; no wild scramble in the darkness to discover our toys; no tangerines from our stockings to be peeled or nuts or sixpences to be found; no whistles or balloons to be blown. The house was cold and quiet and still. Only Mamma was happy. Father cossetted and protected her keeping the dining room as warm as he could with no money for coal.

Christmas morning came. Father had all of us seven children lined up by the long kitchen table. There was no fire in the kitchen range so it seemed bleak and miserable. Father was going to give us our Christmas presents. How cold I felt and how I missed Mamma. I stood by the table too small to see anything but the saucepans on the shelf below. "Youngest first," said Father and put his arms around me and picked me up to see over the table. With one hand he spread some things over the table and with the other he held me between himself and the table. The edge pressed against my chest; I felt lost, unhappy; I wanted to cry. "That is for you," Father said, and pointed to a tiny woolly lamb on wheels. The table pressed into me, I began to cry. "This is for you," said Father again and put the tiny lamb into my hand and put me down. I never forgot that Christmas without Mamma.

Mamma never forgot that Christmas either. She looked back on it with nostalgia. "We couldn't afford any help," she recalled. "We couldn't afford any nursing and so Father had to nurse me and do everything – everything. It was the best nursing I ever had!" she would declare. "It was the finest 'lying in' of them all!" And then she would go on to tell us of the miraculous Christmas present. With no money for fuel and Mamma needing extras for nursing care, in spite of all Father's efforts, life was comfortless and worrying and food scarce. Early December 1920 was bitter. The temperature an average of one and a half degrees below freezing over the first twelve days during which Olive had been born. Each morning Father made a trip to the chicken house with a hot mash of meal and vegetable peelings. He was over-joyed to find, one morning, that the old hen had laid three lovely brown eggs. This was not all. As Father was stuffing paper around the windows to keep out the cold and keep in any warmth, he saw a dark shape on the snow outside. He went out to investigate. It was a sack of coal fallen from a coal cart. As welcome as a sack of gold it was regarded as a great prize, a wonderful Christmas present. Never was coal more carefully used or appreciated – each nob a treasure.

"It was a miracle," said Father. "An act of God," said Mamma.

Although neither Mother Dix or Mother Cox came to help when Olive was born that winter, because there was no money to pay them, they came several times later when Mamma was at her 'lying in'. Whichever of them had been engaged came daily and we did not at all relish the idea of being looked after by either of these good ladies. Neither did we enjoy meals with Father without Mamma. They, Father, Mother Cox and Mother Dix, all had the same ways. Food was doled out on to our plates and we were expected to eat everything on our own plate, whatever it was. There was no such thing as choice; it was no use saying we did not like this or that, the answer to all our grumbles was always the same: "You'll eat when you are hungry."

The things we hated most were the potatoes. It was strange that Father, Mother Cox and Mother Dix were all the same with potatoes. They didn't believe in peeling them. They were scrubbed and boiled complete with spots and eyes. They were always boiling hot with steam getting into your eyes and up your nose and your fingers burning from the heat if you tried to take off the skin, so that you dropped the potato which fell apart. You still had to eat it and burnt your mouth while you were told off.

Tripe and onions was nearly as bad. We didn't like the look of it and said we hated it only to be told how good it was for us. We couldn't keep it still; it slithered about and wouldn't go on the fork. But we loved looking at the eels that Father brought home alive and put in a bowl in the sink. We could watch them and touch them as they snuggled around together. But the very idea of cutting them up and killing them horrified us so that we refused to eat what we were repeatedly told was a delicious, nourishing meal, and we were far too 'picksome'.

Another thing which became alien when Mamma was missing was the bread and butter. With Mamma, a crusty cottage loaf was held at chest height buttered and sliced thinly and expertly towards her. Father always nagged if he saw this as he declared it to be dangerous. "One day," he would bellow, "you will cut yourself in halves." But these slices were tempting and delicious. They bore no relation to the thick door-steps so uninviting, dumped on our plates in her absence. We must have been a great trial to Father, Mother Cox and Mother Dix, when it was their misfortune to give us meals.

Mother Cox and Mother Dix had to work very hard but luckily we were well behaved. There was no alternative as Father would not put up with disobedience, rudeness or ill manners. I cannot recall very much about Mother Dix except that she was smaller and quieter than Mother Cox, because she stopped working when I was four, when Joyce was born. Then, for the last time Mother Dix came to look after us. She arrived quietly, early in the morning wearing a long, black coat and bonnet. Buttons reached all the way down to her ankles which were covered by boots. We all stood around and watched as she undid the buttons and took off the coat. Silently she put on a long, white pinafore with starched frills on the shoulders. Then she took off her neat little black bonnet which had pleated silk all along the front like a Salvation Army bonnet and tied under the chin. She carefully put it up on top of the cupboard where we could not try it on. Then she sat on a chair and with a button hook, undid her boots which were buttoned at the sides. I remember her as tinier and quieter than Mother Cox; she seemed somehow remote, like a house-keeper. After tea, in the dusk, she would sit on a chair, exhausted no doubt, pulling on her small black boots and using the button book to do up the buttons. The lamp was not yet lit and the damp cool evening air got at our freshly-scrubbed cheeks. We were left all ready for bed but not yet undressed. We were waiting for Father to come in when Mother Dix would leave. Then he sent us all to say our prayers after Mamma by her bedside. We helped each other undo our back fastenings on our dresses and petticoats before climbing into our beds. I remember very little about Mother Dix and a great deal about Mother Cox as she was younger and lasted longer with us.

Mother Cox was noisy and well-built with a buxom bosom. I always felt wary of her bosom. Many times I was clutched to it, stifled, with my nose flattened against it. If you had a cold or sneezed she would pounce upon you like a cat upon a wasp. Whilst you were flattened and smothered face-first against her by one massive forearm, her other hand would be exploring the whereabouts of whatever it was that she used to wipe your nose. I always thought it was her apron but I was never able to see. She followed up the initial smothering with a few violent twists with the unseen object which almost screwed your nose off, and guaranteed that it would be red and sore until the next time, which, in the case of a cold, was at frequent intervals.

The next most hated thing after the potatoes and the sore nose was, for me, having my hair brushed. My hair, known as rat's tails to my brothers, was very fine and curly. Mother Cox had hair that was short straight and brown. It was scraped to one side and fastened in place by a brown slide. At the end of the day, Mother Cox would seat herself upon a chair in the kitchen doorway, by the sink, facing the garden. There, in the manner of the Cyclops, she awaited the approach of whichever member of the tribe happened near. As we returned one by one from whatever part of the house or garden we had been exploring in our games and activities, we were captured by a massive fore-arm. However, again like the Cyclops, Mother Cox had an eye problem – one of her eyes looked somewhere else. It didn't look at you. Because of this, she invariably held her head onto one side in order to look at you straight on. It explained why I always saw the brown slide facing me. Mother Cox's arms, although not tattooed were otherwise just like Popeye's arms. They were muscular, powerful and brawny, and always bare. They were the same colour as her face and legs, a reddish brown. A large apron, which seemed very short compared with the long starchy pinafore of Mother Dix against which we were never clasped, was wrapped around her waist and tied behind in a large sticking-out bow. Mother Cox's legs were just like her arms, very well developed and plainly to be seen as her girth took up her clothes. Each evening, as the time approached for her to leave us all, ready for bed, before returning to her own family, she would position herself upon the chair by the open doorway leading from the kitchen into the garden, to await the return of the flock. As we wandered in from the garden through the conservatory, she captured us, one by one. One by one we would be polished off. The nearest would be grabbed, scrubbed wet, eyes streaming with soap suds, and then scrubbed dry. A few violent twists of the nose which was by now, streaming in sympathy with the smarting eyes, and then for me, the real torture would begin. Wedged firmly between her knees which gripped us somewhere between the shins or the shoulders according to how big we were, our hair would be brushed. Armed with the punitive hair-brush which was wielded with force, Mother Cox looked down upon you, right-eyed, slide on, whilst the other unfortunate eye looked upwards in a squint. Taking long, powerful swipes with the brush she punished my scalp for producing such a scanty crop of hair. This way and that I squirmed and struggled, but there was no escape from those timber legs, which held you as though in a vice. "Keep still," I was admonished. "This will make your hair grow. Where-ever do all these knots come from?" as they were dragged out in clumps. My hair has never grown any thicker for all that stimulation.

Around the district our family was well-known, not only for its size but for its looks. Although Parker was our family name it was other people who were curiously nosey about us. Certain persons, knowing our route to and from school, waylayed us on our way home. We learnt to dodge them as we grew older. They asked us questions such as, "How many are there in your family now?" and the same people would repeat the same question only days later, or vary it with, "Are there still twelve children?" as though we were increasing the population week by week. Other questions followed. "Whereabouts do you come?" "Are you in the middle?" "What number are you?" as though we were in the army. This happened mostly if we were alone which wasn't often. Then I would say, "Seven going down and five going up", which used to worry me as it left one unaccounted for. But nobody seemed to notice that I was both number seven and five so that only made eleven and as nobody asked I never explained that one had died in the great 'Flue epidemic which swept away a multitude to add to the slaughter of the First World War.

People could not tell the difference between some of the boys and it was the same with us girls. In looks we were nearly all Anglo-Saxon like Mamma with our distinctive blue eyes, high cheek bones and fair skins. All the Anglo-Saxons in the family were flaxen-haired and people addressed us collectively as 'Snowball' or 'Blondie' according to whether we were boys or girls. Only two were like Father with his Mediterranean looks. Mamma liked to romanticise about his ancestry and whether his Father had Spanish forebears. Father certainly looked and acted with all the characteristics of someone of Middle East ancestry. His skin was olive pale, not swarthy, and his long hebraic nose and thick, black brows above dark hazel eyes together with his dynamic energy, attracted people to him. Above all, it was his ebullient vitality which captivated attention and he could gain the interest of anyone he chose when he wanted to. He held us all in the hollow of his hand, even Mamma, and counter-balanced the burdens of the tribe with a curiously mercurial force. The fact that most of us were pure Anglo-Saxon in looks, and quite unlike Father, seemed to always add a certain amount of piquancy to the interest of visitors.

It never ceased to surprise us how inquisitive people were about our doings. We were all healthy and attractive children with abounding energy. We were bubbling over and Mamma was always being asked what she fed us on and how she managed. She took everything in her stride; there was no fuss or bother. Neighbours came to her for advice and help with a thousand and one things. The most frequent question they asked, "How do you keep your children free from colds?" Then Mamma told them of the cough mixture she made which her mother had made before her; of the squares of camphor sewn in to the tops of our vests at the front, all through the winter. "Why haven't any of them had diphtheria?" and "Why don't they catch scarlet fever?" they worried, anxious to know where they went wrong. Mamma helped them as well as she could, knowing that everyone is different and what suits one may not suit another.

There were always more questions. "Where do you cook all your Christmas puddings?" and Mamma explained that she had to boil them all in the wash house copper because she made several large ones, there being so many of us. "How do you find time to cut their hair and make all their clothes?" they wondered. "You never seem to have the doctor in – why not?" "How do you make sloe wine and dandelion wine?" "How can I get a pea down from my boy's nose?" And the same parent later on: "Can you come, my boy's got his head stuck in the railings again." "What is the best thing for baby's wind?" This was the next most frequent question.

Sometimes Mamma was paid for doing some needlework like turning a skirt or coat; but she usually refused as she had little time, but she was relied upon for practical answers to innumerable questions, like the Oracle.

At the end of the First World War Mamma's days of being very hard up had begun. With Father no longer in the Fish Market and mass unemployment, the economic depression brought desperate times to us (along with thousands of others in London and millions all over the world). Mamma's skill with her needle earned her a little. Turning a garment took patience and time. The article had to be carefully unpicked, cleaned and pressed. Then it was painstakingly put back together with the old, faded right side turned to the inside. After a final press the garment looked almost new.

Aunt Dolly, her real name was Emaly which nobody ever used, lived in Battersea near Lavender Hill. Knowing how desperately short of money we were with eight children now and Father unable to find any employment, Aunt Dolly wrote to Mamma asking if she would visit her at Battersea to help her with some sewing. Mamma would not accept a gift of money my aunt knew, and so she asked Mamma to help her so that she could pay her for it. Very early in the morning Mamma and I went on the tube train to Vauxhall Station and then on a tram to Aunt Dolly's. Olive the baby was left at home with Father who looked after the family for the day. In the train I knelt on the seat with my face pressed close against the window. There against the glass I stayed watching the darkness of the London Underground as the train rocketed and thundered along. This was my first journey on the Underground and the noise and darkness was unforgettable.

Aunt Dolly had a tiny crowded living room where I climbed up on to a huge soft sofa. Cousin Jack came home to tea. How shy I was. This young man doted on his widowed mother whom he always addressed as 'Daw'. As soon as he spotted me the teasing started. With my face hidden among the sofa cushions, I tried to become invisible. Jack poked me in the back, laughing at my shyness. Tea time came. Like the proverbial ostrich I could not be prised from the sofa cushions where, head down, I sought escape. Eventually I was cajoled to sit at the table, precariously perched on the self-same cushions on top of a chair. I was hot and bothered. 'Please' and 'thank you' suddenly became a complete mystery. Jack was delighted when I said please instead of thank you and vice versa. He regarded all my efforts as hilarious. In front of me was a boiled egg in an egg cup. Someone had taken the top off and Jack was watching closely to see the fun. How difficult it was. How mortified I felt each time Jack exploded with laughter. The cushions wobbled. The spoon would not go into the egg: I couldn't see over the top of it. I tried to remember that it was sometimes "No, thank you" and sometimes "Yes, thank you", and sometimes "Yes please", and not to say, "No please". The whole of the tea time I was struggling with the egg and struggling to answer properly with everything the wrong way round, and Jack splitting his sides and hooting with laughter. I could hardly see over the table; the egg ran down the sides of the egg cup; my face was burning; I felt about to fall off the cushions; I longed to get down and hide under the table.

Emaly Brown, Mamma's mother, had died in the influenza epidemic in 1919 so my grandFather, George Brown, went to live in Battersea with Aunt Dolly, his eldest daughter, and left his home the Crabtree in Lower Beeding. He sat in a large easy chair with wooden arms; he sat as still as the chair itself. He was a little old countryman from Sussex, with white side whiskers known as mutton chops. His face shone like a rosy apple between his white whiskers which curled out by his high cheek bones enhancing his piercing blue eyes. He rested his arms along the wooden chair arms with his hands partly curled. Both of his little fingers were tightly tucked over against his palms. Years of village cricket, catching cricket balls, had injured the leaders of each little finger, so that he was quite unable to straighten either of them. When he washed he used a towelling face glove that Aunt Dolly had made, to avoid scratching his face. Mamma said that he was tiny at birth because he was grown to his mother's side, and, it was said, she never loved him because of the agony of his birth. He was born in the 'Old Crabtree Inn' in Lower Beeding, where his family ran a hostelry business. They supplied horses and coaches for transport and made the elm wood coffins when required. There was a great deal to do throughout the year.

When grandpa was born so small it was a matter of wonder. They put him into a pint pot and took him into the bar to show the customers how tiny he was. Now here at Aunt Dolly's I watched him shyly. His eyes were a vivid blue and, although he smoked a pipe, his eyes never wavered from your face. Even when he tapped out his pipe he kept his eyes on you. All his movements were slow and deliberate, quite unlike Father's.

Before we left Aunt Dolly's, Mamma sent me to where grandpa sat in his chair, to say goodbye. I stood in front of his knees and looked up at him. He puffed slowly and silently on his pipe and regarded me steadily, as though he were about to ask an important question. The white, curling whiskers framed the blue eyes. I felt the direct, steady, attentive gaze upon me; it imprinted the picture on my mind and made fast his image. My small thin legs were rivetted to the floor by the unescapable eyes. He took the stumpy pipe from his mouth, very slowly, and spoke. I have no remembrance of what he said. I was tongue-tied with shyness. Then he put his hand with the curled over fingers into his pocket and brought out two great, shining, golden pennies and laid one of them on each knee. I was covered with confusion and quite overcome. He took my hand and I picked up the pennies. I never saw him again; that was the last time as Mamma was not ever again to have the money for the fare to London.

When he and Emaly married Grandpa Brown left the 'Old Crabtree Inn' together with the family coaching and hostelry business, where he had worked hard but felt unappreciated, and took employment at nearby Lennard's Lee, on Lady Loder's estate. There at Chapel House in Plum Lane, he and Emaly had seven children, four boys and three girls with Mamma the youngest girl and Audie the youngest boy. For Mamma this was an epoch of peace and love. Wistfully she recalled her happy life in the country village with her mother and brothers and sisters, and once again she was there, helping her mother with her baking; skating on the frozen pond in winter; accompanying her mother to Chapel three times every Sunday or cycling to Horsham daily, where she worked as a young lady.

As Mamma's growing family played around her whilst she baked or sewed, we listened attentively, to the abounding romance of the far-away village which seemed to be a Never Never Land afar from the London–Essex border where we lived. In imagination we were there, going with her and her mother, taking goodies to the poorer villagers in their cottages. From mediaeval and Anglo-Saxon times, the well-to-do were accustomed to looking after the welfare of the poorer cottage folks, and Grandpa George Brown was the eldest son of the prosperous innkeeper at the 'Old Crabtree Inn'.

Emaly Brown, besides supplying the poorer folks with her home-made goodies, bread, preserves, broths, cakes and garments she made for their children, also acted as the village unpaid doctor. She practised homaeopathic cures and treatments; traditionally making all her own medicines from recipes handed down to her from her own mother. Unable to pay the local Doctor Dick, the folks round about sent for Emaly Brown. She brought the local babies into the world and was castigated by Doctor Dick grumbling that she 'did him out of his job'.

As a girl, Mamma described how she and her mother visited the cottagers with curative medicines, liniments and ointments; oxtail for the sick; jugged hare; brawn, bread, paté and linctus, whatever was needed and the people welcomed Emaly as 'Lady Brown' or 'Doctor Brown'. Mamma brought to life her days with her mother in Lower Beeding. Aggie, her sister, climbed high in the apple tree where she whistled like a blackbird and wouldn't come down. There she stayed at the bottom of the garden, high above Plum Lane, a freckled tom-boy mimicking the birds and we imagined the scuffling in her stronghold when one of her brothers was sent to drag her down. We could see Charlie, one of the brothers, playing his concertina and singing after his day's work in the gardens at Lennards Lee. We imagined the pheasant hanging from the hook on the door until it was ripe for cooking. Mamma pined for her home at Chapel House but was never to return there after my birth as she could not afford the fares with seven small children then. So she was heartbroken and fretted, never to reconcile herself when Emaly caught the flu in the great epidemic which swept the world, and having only grandfather with her at the time, also ill with flu, died early in 1919.

It was no wonder that Mamma inherited her mother's ways, constantly with her in her young days. Mamma said she was never allowed out of her mother's sight even in Chapel. And so, just as Emaly had been a source of help to the villagers, Mamma in turn was esteemed by our neighbours. Here, on the East London outskirts, a long way from Sussex, she passed on the wisdom acquired from her own mother. Proven skills now sadly almost lost in the hustle of modern times.

And so, far from Lennards Lee and Lower Beeding, in the still semi-rural outskirts of the great metropolis, we grew up under Mamma's patient guidance to be healthy and strong. Life was fun and exciting, full of both work and play and being well disciplined by Father, we thrived as Mamma was wont to say, "Like so many peas in a pod."

Chapter Two

Early Days

The early days were play days when we were very young. Long golden days blending fantasy and reality, it was all one and play governed our lives. The boys, being older, had to look after us girls. Mamma had five boys first and then five girls, finishing up with a boy and then a girl. 'Six of one and half a dozen of the other' was one of Mamma's frequent observations, especially when arguments arose between the boys and the girls.

The boys looked after us well but wherever they went I always wanted to go and it must have been a nuisance having a small girl tagging behind them everywhere; when they were climbing trees, jumping ditches, catching sticklebacks, and wading in muddy water up to their knees. I followed their every manoeuvre as they soaked their rolled-up trousers, tore their shirts on branches, cut their feet on broken jam jars in ponds, argued over cigarette cards, fought bullies and walked long distances home, worn out and starving hungry.

The Bonny Downs was one of their favourite haunts. It lay on the other side of the Barking Road where the River Roding ran into Barking Creek. This common land known as the Bonny Downs stretched beside the ruins of Barking Abbey, and bordered the Creek. We ran about along the ruined walls and swung high on the swings nearby.

Barking, reputed to be the oldest fishing port in the United Kingdom, was for a short while in the 18th and 19th centuries, a deep sea fishing port for London. The Barking fleet supplied London's fish, and the fishing smacks at the mouth of the River Roding, sailed up the Thames to Billingsgate. Fuel from northern coalfields was unloaded from colliers at the Creek and taken up the River Roding to Ilford.

In Pepys' day trees from the Royal Essex forests were cut for timber for the Fleet and rafted down from Barking Creek. Essex is noted for its hornbeam, as hard as oak, and provides one of Europe's main sources of this wood. As Essex lacks suitable stone for churches, it's chestnut, resistant to insects, was used instead.

The Venerable Bede described the establishment of Barking Abbey in A.D. 666 where the monks and nuns were ruled by an abbess, Ethelburga. Later it was a Benedictine nunnery. The abbess, appointed by the king, was the Queen of England. Danish invaders destroyed the abbey about A.D. 870. It was later refounded and William the Conqueror had his headquarters there whilst the great fortress, the Tower of London, was being built on land that belonged to Barking Abbey. Here at Barking Abbey, William took refuge for the following reason.

During his coronation ceremony on Christmas Day at Westminster Abbey, a serious riot broke out. When the Archbishop asked the nobles if they would have William as king, they acclaimed so loudly, the Norman soldiers outside, thinking the king was being attacked, rushed upon nearby English houses and set them alight. William abruptly stopped the ceremony, and feeling unsafe in London, where people were being massacred all around among their burning houses by his soldiers, escaped by a back door. He sailed down the Thames to Barking and there took refuge. He lay low there. Great earls, churchmen and thanes came to pay homage ubtil it was safe for him to return to London, where he continued to strengthen the fortress known as the Tower of London.

Barking Abbey flourished until Henry VIII dissolved the monasteries when it fell into disrepair.

Close to the Abbey ruins was Barking Creek, out of bounds for children. Here busy men were loading and unloading barges. Huge, flat-bottomed, they floated side by side, reeking of creosote and tar. We crept as close as we dare fascinated by the mystery of it all, until a shout sent us scampering away. The Creek ran into the nearby Roding.

The prospect of catching some tiddlers always attracted us. One chilly morning as soon as the rain had stopped, four of us went off to play. We were, Ralph, Stanley, Phyllis and me, aged eight, six, four and two. We chose to walk to the Bonny Downs carrying a couple of jam jars with string handles looped around their necks.

Our choice of the Downs was not without argument.

"The four of you can go out to play," said Mamma, seeing the rain had stopped, as she dressed the baby Olive, after her bath. We had all been fidgetting around the zinc bath which was on the hearth rug before the dining room fire.

"Where shall we go?"

"Let's go to Wanstead Flats and catch tiddlers," the boys agreed.

"No, it's too far," Phyllis and I complained.

"We can go on the tram," urged the boys. "Can we have the fares to Wanstead, Mamma?"

"No, you can all go to the Recreation Ground," declared Mamma, "that's not too far to walk."

None of us wanted to go to the Rec. It was boring unless the swings were open, which they weren't as it was not yet Summer.

"Well hurry up and go out or I shan't let you go," said Mamma, tired of us "fidgetting about indoors", as she put it. Nobody had any pocket money left for the fares so Wanstead was definitely out. But the idea of catching tiddlers was what we were interested in. When Ralph and Stanley found two jam jars and tied on string handles, that settled it. Fishing nets were a luxury we could not afford and we sometimes used instead, our hands, the jar or a piece of cloth or sacking.

We set off for the dawdle which took us past the rec. Roads were quiet then, the traffic mostly horse-drawn vehicles or bikes. A brewer's dray with a team of shire horses was the largest thing on the road. The horses were magnificent: well-cared for: all scarlet bows and ribbons on their braided manes: resplendent with polished harness and gleaming brasses. Bakery and dairy carts proclaimed their owners with colourful signs painted on their sides by craftsmen signwriters. Green grocery and coal carts were seldom up to the same standard, the former mostly poorer one-man businesses and the coalman a hired labourer.

Horses showed a great deal of neglect generally, and the exceptions were noticeable. I never saw a beribboned tail or polished brasses on a greengrocer's

horse and only rarely on a coal horse. The latter did a
vast amount of work pulling heavy loads in all
weathers and conditions. Too often in desperation,
in winter the whip was used, when the horse's iron-
shod hooves slid backwards down-hill on the cobbles.
Many a time we saw the carter throw aside the whip
and jump down to strain on the bridle alongside the
horse. He tried to pull the exhausted beast up a slope
of slush or ice, whilst his own hob-nails failed him; The
load behind, tugged them backwards, threatening to
topple off and often did. Sometimes the carter used his
whip and it was heartbreaking to see the horse slip and
struggle as he reared to pull the over-weight burden.

A fifteen minute walk or dawdle took us to the rec.,
where we walked through to the horse trough by the
end, where thirsty dogs and horses vied for a place to
drink with others of their kin. Close by, the main road
from London to Barking passes over the Roding. On
either side of the road bridge the brick balustrade had
a coping of tiles (about six to eight inches wide) to
throw off the rain. As we waited to cross the road to
the Downs a boy appeared on the other side. He
climbed on the balustrade and stood on the tiles.

We four crossed the road, hand in hand, and stood
near him watching. Above us on the parapet he looked
down with a mischievous and swashbuckling air. He
seemed about eleven years old with rough rosy cheeks
and black, curly hair. He was well-built and had about
him the confidence and style of the circus as he began
his balancing advance along the coping above the
river. The sloping, weathered tiles shone with the
recent rain. His breeches, in the manner of the day,
were strapped and buckled beneath the knees. We
were mesmerised by his daring. He showed no fear.
With four small children as audience he travelled the

thirty feet or so, walking steadily, balancing carefully, until he had crossed the river. Once across, he gave us a cavalier smile, hopped down on the river side and disappeared.

For a few minutes we stood there. He had made an indelible impression. It was the artificial leg, the wooden peg around which one leg of his breeches was strapped, that awed us. His left leg was missing!

We ran over the bridge and scrambled down the muddy bank to the river. After the rain the banks were slippery and the river, usually shallow here, now fast-moving. We hunted about looking for a spot where we could get closer to the water to see the fish. These sticklebacks were magnets to us. We spent long hours trudging to their haunts and long days trying to outwit them into capture. Soon, one of the boys spotted a slight wavering. Were they elusive tails of fish, lurking there in the shadows? Greatly excited, the hunt was on.

"Quick, here's one. Where's the jam-jar?"

"Got it. Missed it. It's got away."

All this from Ralph and Stanley induced in me a fever-pitch of excitement, until at last, "Quick, there's two, get one in yours," impelled me to action.

Being the smallest I could see only arms, legs and bodies between me and the fish; so, rather like the Mole when he decided to throw caution to the winds and sieze the sculls from the Rat, I pushed through a small space between the backs, arms and legs, and unable to stop-slid down the muddy bank, and was up to my neck in water in a twinkling.

The children clutched my clothes and dragged me out. A horse-drawn gypsy caravam, hitherto unnoticed, stood in the field. I found myself inside it, a tiny home perched on two huge, wooden wheels. Shiny copper pans and painted china clung everywhere, held in place like a painted picture. I saw it all in a state of trance as my clothes were stripped away, and wearing nothing but a woollen shawl, I was handed to Ralph to be carried home.

Mamma bemoaned the loss of my clothes. She was upset. She had made them all.

"I'll never see them again," she declared. "They were all from my own needle." How mortified we all felt.

"Hand embroidered, every one of them," she wailed, "the petticoats, dress and the pinafore. *And* there were Uncle William's pink shoes!" We were reduced to silence. Uncle William, never seen by us, a relation of Mammas who lived in Lewes, Sussex, made all our boots and shoes.

We wore layers of clothes in winter and spring. A flannel petticoat gathered on a yoke: a fine cambric white petticoat, trimmed and embroidered: a fitted dress made especially for the wearer with a pinafore over the top to keep it clean: a vest and liberty bodice of course was worn beneath, but at this time of the year, we all wore combinations, coms. to us as well, over our vests. These were like miniature workmen's overalls with tops and bottoms all in one. The seat at the back unbuttoned to drop down when one needed to use the toilet. No wonder we all kept free of colds especially as a tablet of camphor in a muslim bag was always tacked onto the tops of our vests at the neck in front, to keep cold germs away.

"I might as well say goodbye to all those clothes of Dorothy's," Mamma told us four miscreants, making us all feel very sorry about it.

Some days later a knock came at the front door. There stood a buxom, colourful, well-wrapped gypsy woman. Over her arm was a large basket with brightly coloured articles overlying the top.

"Good morning, ma'am," she said, and so saying turned back the scarves and ribbons to reveal my missing clothes. All were folded neatly, washed and pressed. They were all there, every layer of them. On the top, clean and visible, were Uncle William's pink shoes, made especially for me.

Mamma always had a soft spot for gypsies after that, and many who called with pegs to sell, made from the hedgerows, or flowers, real, or hand-made from wood shavings brightly coloured, left with gifts of clothing for their own large families, or food or a little money. Mamma was as impressed by the gypsy, clean, honest and reliable in an emergency, as she was by Violet Pinder, Mamma's one and only good nurse-maid.

On these trips with my brothers we sometimes went over the Holloway Fields. They were fairly near; just where all the houses ended at the bottom of the road. The Holloway Fields were not nearly as inviting as a trip to the Bonny Downs, by the Roding. They were mainly used by allotment holders growing vegetables. The ditches between became full of frogs and tadpoles in Spring, but never any fish.

The main attraction for the boys was in jumping the ditches criss-crossing in different directions, but beyond the powers of my small legs.

One day we saw some carrots poking their coloured heads with dainty plumes above the soil. It was a forgone conclusion that we would pull one up. We were about to rub it clean when there was a great shout. Racing towards us was an irate gentleman, like an Indian warrior on the warpath. We were terrified. Grabbing me up in his arms, Ralph began to jump the ditches as he had never jumped them before. Jolting up and down against him, my knees, already scabbed from tumbles, scrambles and climbs, were rubbed raw as we made our escape across the ditches and fields. It was a painful escape.

My knees were a sore problem in every sense. The long holidays spent chasing about with the boys, falling over, scrambling through undergrowth and up trees, never allowed them to heal.

"You fall over matchsticks," Mamma declared, sighing as she tied yet another bandage around my knee. Not yet three, I believed this, and taking it as a literal truth, anxiously searched for these perilous objects as I ran about; but seldom saw any to avoid.

As I ran fast to keep up with my brothers, no matter how careful I was, I still fell over. Finally I was taken to Doctor Collins. I was small and skinny. He stared at my spindly legs. Not only my legs but my buttocks were covered with wounds which never healed. As fast as nature provided its healing protective scab, another collision knocked it off and the wounds bled profusely. Doctor Collins was a wise man.

"She is knock-kneed," he pronounced. "You must keep her in bed until all the sores are healed."

I felt I was being punished and was desperately unhappy as Mamma took me into the smallest bedroom in the middle of the day. Choking back tears, I was presented to a small bed enclosed by rails and a short ladder to climb up into it.

How long and lonely and fretful the day was. Nobody wanted to stay with me. All the long Summer's day I heard them playing together out in the garden. Used to being active from morning till night, I was now a prisoner. The time seemed interminable before anyone came. Then it was Gilbert.

Gilbert was Mamma's first-born from Father. Always full of fun and excitement, he inspected the situation, trying to cheer me up. When he ran out of the room I felt worse than ever. Soon he was back with a book. Opening the gate on the bed, he put a large book on my lap. Bubbling over with enthusiasm, he turned the pages, showing me all the well-loved characters from the nursery rhymes that Mamma chanted as she bathed the baby or sat at her sewing.

Sitting there on the step beside me, Gilbert read the words to me, pointing out the pictures as he went through the book. Everything was exactly as the rhymes said: the cat playing the fiddle: the cow leaping over an amazed moon: the goose climbing the stairs: the old woman with her broom, chasing the children as they slid down the toe of the great shoe, and all the others. There they were, all inside. I began to recite: 'Old King Cole': 'The Crooked Man': 'Jack and Jill': my knees and imprisonment forgotten. I was breathless with excitement and so was Gilbert.

Nine years older than me, he must have been eleven or twelve when he read those words to me that day. Words that I knew by heart and which were alongside their pictures. As I recited, 'There was an old woman tossed up in a basket, seventeen times as high as the moon', Gilbert's eyes shone.

"Now you can read," he encouraged, urging me on to travel through the book. His enthusiasm was so infectious as he watched me turning the pages and reciting the familiar words, that I began to enjoy myself in my cot, believing I could read.

He soon brought me another book which he read to me. It was *Grimm's Fairy Tales* and how I longed to be able to read that one as well. And so began a love of reading that sprang from Mamma's nursery rhymes. Like the Great King Alfred, we learned at our mother's knee: in litanies of, 'This Little Piggy' at bath time and 'Gentle Jesus' at bed time, together with 'Wee Willie Winkie' crying through the lock who fixed in all our minds that 'past eight o'clock' was indeed late for bed.

When the boys were at school, Phyllis and I, not yet old enough, spent long days in the garden. We were the eldest girls and our favourite game for a while was Violet and John. Phyllis was Violet and I was John. Although two years younger I had to be tough and brave and it was all very real.

We played mostly in the garden when we weren't with the boys. The weather made little difference as we spent a lot of time in the wash house, where we went to sea. There in the wash house we had a wonderful ship where I was always captain. Sitting on the large wooden mangle which took us over the seas, we had every kind of adventure to be had on ships. Turning the big iron wheel, I guided our way through stormy seas; violent storms almost capsized us; evil pirates were everywhere. As we travelled to far away places we were forced to land where dangerous crocodiles and unknown monsters had to be avoided. Jumping overboard it was fatal not to land on an island or into a small boat that had come to our rescue.

In these pre-school days for Phyllis and me, all was quiet and still at home with Mamma busy somewhere indoors, and the hours flew by until she called us in for lunch. Running indoors I demanded anxiously, "Can Violet come to lunch Mamma?"

"Yes, my dear," she replied.

"What are we going to have Mamma?"

"Cold meat, potatoes and peas," whereupon I ran to tell Phyllis the good news that she could come to lunch and we were having peas.

The garden was full of giants and fairies just as real as Violet and John.

When the wash house was in use once a week, on Thursdays, and became full of scrubbing soap and steam, steam which rose from the boiling copper when the heavy wooden lid was lifted, and deadened all sound and blocked everything from view, even Mamma, then we played at the bottom of the garden. Here the Virginia Creeper trailed down over the wooden fence, in autumn ribbons of scarlet and gold. The old brown fence was clothed then in wondrous colour. Varied lengths of every hue hung there. We festooned ourselves with scarlet girdles and head bands. It seemed shameful to pull it down off the fence where it looked so beautiful.

On the other side of the fence lived a witch. We whispered fearfully as we pulled off leafy trailers and tip-toed away with our booty in one hand and a wand in the other. Round Father's rose beds we wandered, catching the dark velvet pollen dust from the tiger lilies as we passed. Among the Indian corn we rambled, tall-plumed above us, whilst beneath, a few hens scratched round about, searching for any solitary grain with beak claw and eye.

Phyllis was always the princess so I had to be prince, brave, unafraid of giants and robbers. I was often called 'cry baby' so I tried to be a stoic about constant knee injuries, which led to the nick-name of 'tomboy' instead.

Directly behind the wash house, where there was little sun, grew a tall slim Lombardy poplar tree. It was difficult to get near enough to climb it so close it grew against next-door's fence. On hot summer days caterpillars would drop down, progeny of the Hawk Moth.

Nearby was the hen house. During the day the hens scratched about along the paths and among the maize roots, their strong claws showering stones and dirt around. From the kitchen doorway Mamma called to us, her voice came sweet and lilting through the conservatory.

"Phyllis – Dorothy, come and feed the chickens."

We ran to take the shallow pan of corn from Mamma, then stepped back carefully into the garden, holding it high above our heads; sharing the bird's excitement as we shook the maize seed and the sound of its rattling brought the hens rallying around. They streaked towards us, mobbing our feet and legs. We couldn't move. It was almost impossible to scatter the seed with chickens flying up over each other to get at it. How quickly they rushed to peck it all up. In the evening they had a hot meal of vegetable peelings mixed with meal. The hot mash gave off a lovely smell like roasting hops.

As soon as a hen began to cackle Mamma sent us to look in the nest box which was on the outside of the hen house. We lifted the lid and waited till the hen got up off the nest and went into the hen house or the run, leaving behind a sweet-smelling, warm egg or two lying in the clean, dry straw of the nest box. Carefully, in cupped hands, we carried the eggs in to Mamma.

Sometimes we had a broody hen and Mamma would allow it a clutch of our chicken's eggs to sit on for we usually kept a cockerel to Father and guard the hens.

In three weeks, continuous, squeeky cheeps announced the chicks had hatched. Very soon, in a matter of minutes, they were all out and about, out of their shells, pecking specks of grit here and there, drying out into balls of yellow down with a piece of shell, perhaps, not yet cast, still adhering.

Meanwhile the mother hen, freed from her incubating duties, was making the dirt fly, as she too pecked and scratched in the earth with the chicks scattering and scuttling away from a clawful of flying grit.

Getting under the feet of another hen earned the chicks a warning peck; then they scooted back for safety to their mother. After a while, the mother hen, selecting a warm dust patch in a sunny spot, scratched a shallow hollow, smoothing it against her breast and called her chicks softly in a downy cluck. Some flew immediately and hid among the feathers about her body, but the laggards, like loitering children, hung about to investigate this or that. Then the hen changed her tone and an urgent 'cluck' brought the lingerers flying to her, tiny wings outstretched, their feet miniature windmills.

Soon they were all invisible, snuggled among the warm down of her feathers. There in their cosy, secret places, they all dozed off, mother as well. With both eyes closed over she sat there, red comb flopping in the sun. Now and then a small fluffy ball popped up on her shoulder or peeped out from among her breast feathers, yellow against the brown; and then, lazily, she would open one eye, blink her eyelid, and close it again as the tiny head, lured instinctively back to its cosy place, vanished from view.

There they stayed, close in the warmth of her down until she suddenly rose, tumbling them all out like dandelion puffs, when they instantly picked themselves up to dart about again, pecking impulsively and following her in zig-zag runs until she settled down in another patch of warm dust, then they bedded down once more among her feathers until the performance was repeated all over again.

Opposite the chicken house William Pear trees grew. Along the fence beneath grew Summer Jasmine, where, in late Summer, great, juicy, yellow, heavy pears dropped and squashed upon the ground and in the warm twilight, the heavy, sweet scent of the jasmine filled the air and wafted towards the house. Then we children pulled the white starry flowers out from their pointed green cups and sipped the nectar from their tiny tubular stems. How sweet it was. No wonder the insects seek it.

Lying about on the ground under the maize, were old, tough corn roots, left there for the chickens to peck. One day, as Phyllis and I played in the garden, we heard a knocking at the front door. Nobody was in the house. Phyllis looked at me. I knew she expected me to open the front door.

"John," she whispered, "it's a giant!"

Trying to look brave I needed a weapon. There was a root of Indian corn lying on the ground. I looked but could see nothing else with which to fight a giant. I used both hands to pick it up. It was heavy. I struggled it along, through the conservatory, through the kitchen and along the hall to the front door. Trying to feel brave I wrestled with the latch as I held the root against me. Very afraid, I felt the door being pushed as the latch released it. There stood Ralph, quite calm and peaceful, staring at me clutching the corn root, nearly as big as I was.

"We thought you were a giant," I said, overcome with relief. He gave me a very ungiant-like look and walked past me and the root into the house.

A variety of cats came to stay with us – all strays. There was the 'Old Cat' which lasted many years; a couple of 'Fluffs' and several that just passed through on their way, "turning up from nowhere", as Mamma put it, for relatively short stays. Some were categorised as delinquent on account of bad habits or behaviour and were put beyond the pale and – "Disappeared into thin air," explained Mamma when we asked their whereabouts.

One feline visitor, no doubt unnerved by all the attention unexpectedly thrust upon it, sprang about the dining room, and after a couple of circuits from bookcase to serving hatch via the sewing machine, needlework basket, chairs and table, landed on the mantelpiece on top of the chiming clock, Father's treasured time-piece. This usually stationary machine promptly deposited itself on the floor with the cat, the chimes all going together. The strangled sounds coming from the hole in the top of the clock sent the cat flying; and one more cat went on it's way.

Then there was the cat which took to snoozing on the bookcase shelf, which ran the width of the bookcase, just below the top cupboard. One hot summer's day, a newly hatched nest of fleas leaped into being at the back of the shelf, the cat's favourite spot. It was its spot no longer! The cat, like the hedgehogs was declared *persona non grata*.

The 'Fluffs', possessing the best coats, became dishevelled and knotted, rolling about in the dust with other cats. They needed to be brushed and growled like dogs and fought to escape from the brush. (I knew exactly how they felt with memories of Mother Cox wrestling with my tangled mane.) It was always a losing battle trying to groom them and we watched them in the garden, heaving up fur-balls and grass, with their battered ears twitching in sympathy. All most of us got from them in return for hugs, were scratches.

The rabbit was the only pet that scratched me. I worried Mamma. "Let me take the rabbit out of the hutch. Please can it run in the garden?"

"Yes," said Mamma, eventually, but you must watch it very carefully."

I did. But then suddenly, it was gone! Out I had to go, knocking at all the neighbours doors. There was little encouragement.

"Please can I come into your garden to look for our rabbit?" The replies were all of a piece, daunting.

"What is a rabbit doing running loose?"

"Why don't you look after your rabbit?"

"You shouldn't have a rabbit unless you have a rabbit hutch."

"There's no rabbit here, try someone else," and so on.

At last I found it in a garden where it 'couldn't be', under some foliage, busy nibbling which the woman described as "Pecking my lettuce". By this time I was very hot, bothered and flustered, more by the coals of wrath heaped on my head immediately my mission was explained, than by anything else.

I walked warily towards the rabbit. It studied me with those outsize eyes which can see in all directions, and went on nibbling. As soon as I bent nearer it was off. Round and round the garden we went, advice being delivered freely by the woman from the back door. At length, somehow or other I had it but knew nothing about handling rabbits. Its strength was unforseen; its back legs with long claws, formidable. Clutching it close against me, we wrestled our way through the woman's house, and back up the street, home.

"Don't ask me again, *ever*, if you can let it out," observed Mamma, as she bathed my lacerated arms and legs and I sat in the kitchen with the front of my dress ripped to shreds.

It seemed I was forever in a 'pickle' as Mamma put it.

"Oh Dorothy, Dorothy Dean," sang Mamma,

"Oh, Dorothy where have you been?" or

"Dorothy, Dorothy Dean, not fit to be seen."

I didn't like to hear this about me from Mamma. I took it literally like 'falling over matchsticks' and crept away to hide my mortification in the wash house where I sat on the ship and turned the wheel and became a sailor.

Various accidents befell us all from time to time. Always running, one day I ran into the low latch on the kitchen door; it cut me just above my eye. Once again I was taken to see Doctor Collins. Standing between his knees, I was held fast as he stitched the wound, slowly, carefully and firmly, tugging the flesh with the catgut. "She has just missed her eye," he observed severely, as though the latch and I had conspired together to miss the target.

An unfortunate cyclist bumped into me one day as I ran out in front of him. It was at the corner of the street close to our home. Mamma was busy with the lunch and opened the door to an agitated young man, holding me by the arm covered in mud. My white starched broderie anglaise round the armholes of my pinafore was now starched brown with mud. Everybody crowded round to see if I was hurt. The cyclist,

44

distraught, repeating his explanations and apologies; the family eyeing me for injuries and finding only mud from the gutter, brought everything to an anticlimax. Reprimanded by Mamma for running out without asking and sensing the general feeling of disappointment, I decided to cry which soon brought the matter to an end. Because I was always 'in a pickle' Mamma named me 'Gyppo'.

My sailing days on the mangle caused a lot of argument with Mamma. I was forever telling her that I was going to be a sailor.

"Girls can't be sailors," Mamma said.

"Why not?" I demanded over and over again.

"They just can't," she answered when I pressed her.

"But why not Mamma?"

Mamma made me a dress with a sailor collar. How I loved it. Two rows of blue ribbon went all round the square, white collar.

"Look at Doll in her sailor's suit," teased Graham.

Horatio Nelson, small and delicate, went to sea at the age of twelve. He never overcame sea-sickness but neither did he ever lose his love for the sea. It was a compulsion which I understood as I thought of running away to sea many times, disguised as a boy.

The hours sailing in the wash house became lonely when Phyllis went to school. I found a playmate of my own age next door. We sat on the ground in our back gardens and played through a hole at the bottom of the wooden fence. We carried on long conversations bent over and eyeing each other like birds looking for worms. Sometimes he had temper tantrums with his Mamma and I felt shocked; but we were able to push our toys back and forth through the fence and play games.

Leslie's Father had made him a small wooden bicycle. It had two wheels. It was just the right size. How I envied him, watching him through the hole in the fence as he rode about the garden.

Diphtheria infection came to the district again. Dreaded by all parents of young children, there being no vaccine for it then. This time it struck Leslie. All through one night we all worried about him: Joyce too was ill, but in the morning Leslie was dead.

Now the bike was given to me. It travelled round with me in our garden and no longer did I haunt the hole in the fence, to watch Leslie on it next door. Early in the morning, before the sun was up, I was chasing along the pavement on the two-wheeled bike. It was high summer and all was still. No traders were about. Sometimes I thought of Leslie and how lucky we were that Joyce had recovered. But the joy overcame all other feelings and the cool, fresh morning air swept past and I felt I was travelling like the wind.

When that bike was gone I was left with a bike compulsion. Each birthday and Christmas I dreamed I had a new bike. One summer I woke early in the morning remembering I had a new bike for my birthday. It was in the hall, leaning against the wall. I flew downstairs but it was gone. My birthday present was nowhere to be seen. My desperate searching revealed that it was all a dream. Unable to speak when Mamma said, "You must have been dreaming," no-one knew how I longed for that bicycle.

Our house was second from the corner. Around this corner and living on the next one was a small boy. He was different because he went to a boarding school and dressed accordingly. He wore a starched Eton collar under a short cut-away dark jacket. His grey knickerbockers, buckled beneath the knees, were always neat and tidy. His stockings and shoes were spotless and above all, his speech was perfect; being called 'Gyppo' by Mamma made me appreciate the appearance of this immaculate friend. But what I really appreciated was his go-cart. Kenneth's go-cart could be worked either by pedals or by a rachet with a T-shaped handle which was pushed up and down, using both hands. Proudly I took him home. Father was impressed by his speech. He was invited to tea.

Tea in our house meant a table loaded with many courses to be eaten separately or together. The reason for this was Mamma's cooking; always on a large scale, there were invariably left-overs to be eaten, pieces of pies, portions of tarts, a batter of sausages and baked potatoes, bread pudding and so on.

The day that Kenneth came must have been one of Mamma's baking days. This day at tea time, on the large table there were goodies to cope for all ages and appetites; for those at work needing dinner and those of lesser importance requiring only their tea.

This day the table was covered by food. Shepherd's pie, vegetables, Cornish Pasties, sausage rolls, salads, fruit pies, rice pudding, jelly, cakes, bread pudding, bread and butter, various tarts – some cut, some uncut, and all the odds and ends that needed 'finishing up' from the pantry, which was a large walk-in one, had been placed on the table somewhere. Every part of the table cloth, except for a space round the edge, was occupied by food of some sort.

We all took our places at the table, Kenneth being positioned at the far end near Mamma. Well dressed and well spoken, he was viewed both by Father and me, at the other end, with some deference. Father, with his eye on everybody, kept strict control at the table and we all had no option but to behave ourselves. Nobody started on their food until we were all served and Father gave permission.

Kenneth was offered food and at first all went well, but soon he began to be demoralised by the large choice of dishes. You did not ask for anything else until you had finished what you already had, was the rule in our house. But it soon became apparent that Kenneth was not going to finish anything. Demanding one thing after another, taking a bite or two from each as though he were engaged as a food taster, he appeared to be anxious lest he might let something escape his notice. Suddenly he scrambled down from his chair, climbing back up where he knelt, the better to survey the board.

The bemused family focussed him with disbelieving eyes as he pointed excitedly at this and that, after a bite or two, pointing at something else. This and that were passed to him as he stuffed bits and pieces of first one thing and then another, into his mouth. The final *coup de grace* was executed on the rice pudding. Kneeling up high, he spotted it at the far end of the table.

"I want that," he declared, leaning over the table and pointing to make clear his demand.

There was an expectant silence, we all waited for Father to explode. Watched by us all, Mamma served the pudding and passed it to him. With all our faces registering disbelief, he fixed himself indelibly in our memories, by climbing down, again, off his chair, without permission, running out of the room into the garden, leaving the rice pudding quite untouched, together with a litter of unfinished portions of food in a clutter of plates, behind him.

When Phyllis and I wandered about hand in hand, things were not at all like our jaunts with our brothers.

Instead of paddling about in ponds and scrambling about in trees or undergrowth, we wandered as though in a dream.

One summer of drought found us rambling about willy-nilly, helping each other up and down unmade lanes and rough roads, in and out of cart ruts, cut deep, iron-hard and branding us with their baking heat.

Awed by deep cracks opened up in the clay, we went on and on like nomads in the Sahara, as though hypnotised by the heat, until at last we came upon a great wide road, throwing the hotness back at the sun in a shimmering sheet from its wide expanse. This was the main highway to London, the Barking Road, slumbering in the sun, not yet awakened to the ribbon of vehicles that would daily thread its surface, like soldier ants, never ending.

We turned along the hot pavement for a while until we saw a little cottage with a small wicker gate beside it and cool trees. An old woman was sitting on a low chair, sunning herself, beneath a large straw hat. As soon as Phyllis saw her she knew. Her hand tightened on mine.

"She's a witch," she whispered, "let's run."

Swiftly we ran past, hand in hand, but fascinated by the fears in our imagination, we had to go back. Dashing past as fast as possible, neither the flowers on her hat nor the welcoming smile, gave us the courage to pass again.

That was a very hot day. We found our way home somehow, negotiating warily the unpaved ground, the cart ruts and hard-baked earth deeply cracked by long drought, so punishing to my sore knees.

Wet days and winter days were usually spent playing in the dining room or the passage to the kitchen, depending upon what we were doing. At times, when Father was out, we played with all the books from the bookcase; that was, all those we could reach.

The bookcase was very large with two glass doors above a large cupboard. In between was the long shelf, the width of the bookcase. We could unlock the glass doors if we climbed up on the shelf. In the cupboard at the bottom, also with two large doors, the biggest and heaviest books were kept. We dragged them all out onto the floor on wet days. There in our starched and frilled layers of petticoats and pinafores, we sat on the floor together with the boys in their breeches and homespuns, among the books, exhorting each other to look at this and that, but the favourite with us all we called the *Olden Days Book*. This was a large volume of Hogarth's etchings and the story of the 'Rake's Progress' and of Hogarth's life and times.

It was the people in the pictures that fascinated us. The wrong-doers having their knees beaten flat as they lay with bent legs, strapped to wheels. How sorry we felt for the baby being dropped into the basement area by its drunken mother with the legend on the wall behind:

'Drunk for a penny;
Dead drunk for tuppence;
Clean straw for nothing'.

The picture was entitled 'Gin Lane'. We did not know that William Hogarth's exposure in his pictures of the England of his day; of the squalid life of the poor; the empty, degenerate daily life in wealthy households; eventually changed, not only the false art world, but helped change the society of the times.

There we knelt and stared at the book which we imagined, must be depicting the end of the World.

Hogarth never had a more searching audience, every detail noted, to be recalled each time his book was pulled from the bookcase cupboard.

After looking at all the books that interested us we crawled into the cupboard and played at Mothers and Fathers. Our visitors called on us by knocking with the heavy brass handles on the drawer above which spanned the bookcase beneath the shelf. 'Rat tat a tat tat' they went; first on one and then the other. We entertained in the manner of Mamma and Father.

"Good evening, George. We've come for the evening."

"Hallo, I suppose you want to play whist?"

"Yes. We want to play cards."

"So you want to play cards, but I'm afraid we are going to play Mah Jong."

Sometimes we chose that the caller should be unwelcome. The knocker at the bookcase would get the reply from inside,

"I'm sorry, Annie Alcock, but we are not in." Arguments arose as to who should be inside and who should be visitors come to play Mah Jong, Father's favourite game. These two brass handles, one at each end of the long drawer, made a resounding knock and were the bane of Father's life. After a short time in which we used the knockers for one of our games, if Father were home he would suddenly raise his voice, which Mamma said, "could be heard a mile away". That was enough to send us all scurrying off to play somewhere else as Father's voice, developed in Billingsgate Market, was more than enough.

When Mamma was cleaning the floor all the chairs were put on top of the table. We made the most of it. Up on the chairs we all climbed and played buses. The ticket collector came round with his bicycle bell and gave out tickets. There was much getting off and on so that we had to take care that the seats did not fall out of the bus. Then it was time to climb down; the game was over and we had to help Mamma put them all back in place all round the walls and at the table.

On wet, busy days, Mamma allowed us to play freely as long as we didn't argue or squabble. The dining room table turned upside down made a very roomy ship. Inside the table with several passengers, a great deal of organising went on that led to misunderstandings. When Phyllis and I went to sea in the wash house, we knew exactly what was about to happen, exactly the way we wanted. Orders now in the table caused crew and passengers to abandon ship capriciously until we turned the table back again to play something else.

Now it was a cliff. Two of us were on the top and the rest below, hidden by the tablecloth, huddled together. The dragons hanging over the cliff edge, tried to touch the rest, so that once touched by a finger tip, you were turned to dragons. As the victims shrieked and screamed with horror, the dragons hung over the edge of the table, clutching at the tablecloth, hanging almost to the floor, and hanging on with their legs until Mamma packed us all off to play at something else.

The weather did not imprison us for there were infinite variations in our games and so many things to do. We acted, dressing up from the contents of Mamma's big linen basket which was large enough to make a bed on top. It was large and covered with black rexine with a cane-looped handle which fastened over another loop to keep it shut. In earlier days it had held all Mamma's linen, her new sheets, table cloths, serviettes, towels and pillow cases, all monogrammed with G.R. in flowing script. Now it was filled with a conglomeration from the years. Remnants from Mamma's sewing and all manner of oddments were tucked inside. If we wanted a scarf or tie, some material for a doll's dress or a rag to clean a bike, Mamma's answer was always the same.

"Go and look in the linen basket."

It was filled to the top with pieces of every description and discarded clothes. There was a finely chequered pair of Raggazone's trousers: spare corsets from pregnancies needing a stay or two: long whale bones from old dresses and stays, which we tried to break but found them too flexible: embroidered blouses and dresses with tucks and gathers and fine inlets of lace: pieces of soft, golden seal skin fur, so smooth when we stroked them over our skin: jigsaws of lace large enough for veils dragged tight over our faces: ribbons and bows and broken fans: but the star attraction was Mamma's feather boa.

We all wore it in turns trailing it along the passage behind us. Made from ostrich feathers it was very long. Wound around our necks it trailed the bedrooms and around the house with swords and daggers tucked in our belts in case of giants. One of grandma Emaly Brown's tiny blouses became my prince's blouse. All brown satin, inlet with creamy lace; big puffed sleeves that reached only to the elbow where a neat pleated frill adorned the edge. This was just my size and I wore it for parties and doing the Highland Fling.

If Mamma were out we threw everything out of the basket on to the bedroom floor and climbed inside quite comfortably, two at a time. Luckily nobody ever thought of putting the loops over and the tags across, or we would have imprisoned. And it was air-tight with its black rexine cover.

The boys sometimes lit a candle and burnt a cork in the flame; then they gave each other black moustaches and became pirates, robbers or detectives. They made excellent newspaper hats like Napolean's or Nelson's, and swords that looked very real as they appeared to go through your body as the roll of paper telescoped inside itself. Grasping the ends of our paper weapons, we ran about stabbing each other and dying. Mamma's tailor's dummy stood there, watching us, a silent, unfriendly, buxom lady with a menacing air enhanced in the gloom before the lamps were lit. Ever since it gave Mamma a terrible fright one day, no-one ever touched it. It met her in the dark at the top of the stairs and she nearly fell down backwards.

Besides acting we did acrobatics, standing on our heads and cartwheeling as far as we could in a confined space. The boys tried Cossack dancing, squatting on their haunches with folded arms, but it was too difficult for us girls; our legs were not strong enough. We all practised our own form of Yoga which we knew then as being double-jointed. Contorted in weird positions, we screwed ourselves in place to see who could stay there longest. The smallest swung on the iron bar beneath the length of the dining room table, and we all slid down the bannisters. We rowed about the floor in pairs. Sitting on our partner's feet and grasping each other's shoulders, we propelled ourselves along by small movements of our feet. We had to decide which direction we would take, to know who would push and who would pull. It took practice as the rocking movements required to make any progress backwards or forwards, sent us rolling over sideways.

The table legs came in for their share in our activities. The boys spent long hours tying each other to the table legs which we girls did not find much fun. Our fingers were not as strong as their's. The ropes gripped the strong, curved legs of the table and the boys tied each other with knots, double knots and multi-knots dependent upon the adroitness of the victim at escaping. They were equally proud of escaping as of contriving unknottable knots. We girls were seldom cajoled into this activity as we knew all too well that we could never escape.

Some of the boys' games we enjoyed and became quite skilful at playing. Five Stones was one such game. In the first round it was easy with its, Onesy, Twosy, Threesy, Foursy, Creeps, Cracks, No cracks, Little Titch and Big Titch. If we got through that lot it was made more difficult as the repeat was played without moving the stones from where they fell. What followed I can't remember as we girls probably never progressed further. Boys could be seen round about, playing, sitting on the ground in groups wherever there was a flat surface. I believe the third round was a repeat with no stones being allowed to crack together.

Cigarette cards were plenty of fun. We not only swapped them for anything tradeable with family or friends, but used them for games. We skated them into cardboard tunnels stood against the walls, and knocked down small screws standing on their heads, by skimming the cards along with a flick of the wrist, from a distance. Hide and seek was a last resort, usually when our parents were out. Then we climbed up on the wash house roof; lay on bookshelves where books should have been; climbed on the mangle under an old sheet disguised as a bundle of washing; blacked our faces and stood still in the cellar, crawled under beds and behind arm-chairs, and generally made ourselves invisible with a great deal of forbearance at having to keep still for so long. The better you were at hiding, the longer you had to stay there until at last, unable to bear it any longer, a moment was seized to reappear without revealing the hiding place.

Most of the boxed games, draughts, chess, ludo, snakes and ladders and so on, were kept in the bookcase cupboard and were dished out in a flash, when Father became tired of our noise, when we couldn't go out, and he was in.

On the very top shelf of the bookcase one small, fat red book was often hauled out for general inspection. It was anatomical. To get at it involved climbing up on to the long middle shelf to open the big glass door, then kneeling down whilst the doors were swung open about your ears. The red book was put down on the floor with all the others that we were in the habit of looking at. Sitting and kneeling on the floor surrounded by books, we turned the pages showing diagrams of the unborn baby. It was not very interesting and it seemed strange for a baby to be sucking its thumb in such an odd position. We knew the book was on the top shelf to be out of our way and so we wanted to see it. But the 'Olden Day's Book' and the 'end of the world' seemed far more interesting.

Lots of the games we played in the garden could also be played indoors on wet days. They could be played quietly, and had to be, if Father were there. 'Peep behind the curtain'; 'Statues'; 'Up Jenkins'; 'Hunt the thimble'; and many others in similar vein were our occupation and kept us busy and out of mischief. 'Please we've come to learn the trade' was favourite. It was mostly mime. We advanced in line chanting together.

"Please we've come to learn the trade."

"What to do?"

"To eat plum pudding as fast as you."

"Set to work and do it."

We then started the mime of whatever trade we had thought up until the Master standing in front of us all, deemed one of us good enough for him or her to guess correctly the trade being mimed. Then that apprentice mimer took the place of the master and stood out in front. We never tired of this and skipped back and forth repeating the formula for the game.

If Father were in high spirits we skipped about as he played the piano, and as his hands flew lightly over the keys we charged the 'musical chairs' with furious shovings and pushings, or musical bumps which raised the dust all over the ornaments as we thundered up and down on the carpet. Playing by ear and dancing up and down on the high piano stool in rhythm, Father changed the tempo now and then to fool us, thoroughly enjoying our disgruntled thuds at the wrong moments.

As Mamma made all our clothes when we were small and was "always able to use her needle" as she put it, even until we were in our teens, we were always finely dressed. At bedtime we were put into small white nighties with embroidered collars and knelt on our beds to say prayers, with our eyes tightly closed, repeating after Mamma. We looked and felt like little angels. Mamma told us a story we knew by heart and kissing us goodnight, went downstairs.

If it were early evening on a summer's day we sometimes sang for hours with frequent calls for drinks of water. Sometimes we went to sleep after inventing stories between us. But quite often, full of energy and wide awake, we stripped the bed ready for a swing in the sheets. Standing on the bed two of us held the sheet, one at each end and a third lay in the middle for the swing, then we changed about to have turns. Up high we were swung often screaming with excitement.

Meanwhile downstairs, Mamma and Father were oblivious to these goings on as they were busy playing Mahjong or Whist with their friends, shut in the front room amid a hubbub of chat, cigar smoke and an argument or two. For some reason Mamma never found out and years later when I was busy with hockey, swimming, gymnastics and homework and things of that sort, I told her about our nocturnal jinks.

"Nonsense," said Mamma, "if you had done anything like that, I would have known."

This was not the worst of our goings on. One day the boys decided to have a wrestling match and charge the spectators an entry fee.

As our parents entertained a great deal they, in turn, were invited back by their friends. Of course 'the tribe' never went on these evening visits which were mainly Whist and Mahjong parties. So when one of these social evenings occurred and the boys were left in charge, they thought up a wrestling match. Father, always a keep-fit enthusiast, was going through a phase of weight lifting at the time and training the boys to wrestle with him.

On this evening all their friends had been primed about the show. It was proposed that I aged three who should have been in bed, would stand at the front door taking the money.

It was a penny each to enter, quite a lot in those days. The big dining room table was the venue for the match. I stood at the open door taking the pennies from the boys who were chattering excitedly. They were all between about eight and twelve and rushed to the seats in the dining room. Soon it was full of spectators sitting on the floor by the walls of the room, on the long stool and all the chairs.

As soon as all the children were installed, my brothers, waiting in the passage clad only in their red bathing drawers, entered the room like gladiators. On top of the long table, at eye level for me, they wrestled. Over and over they rolled tied together in knots like those they practised on the table legs below. I felt apprehensive; it all seemed very rough; I was afraid they would come crashing down on the floor. As soon as one pair climbed down, puffing and hot, another pair climbed up and took their place greeted with cheers and whistles. How the children shouted and clapped. To me it all seemed very unreal almost like one of my nightmares. It was long past my bedtime. Wee Willie Winkie would certainly not have approved but the boys and their friends had a rip-roaring time and the boys made some money and their friends made a lot of noise.

In later years Mamma's reaction to my account of this was the same as to my tale of the swings in the sheets.

"Nonsense my dear. You children never did anything like that. I should have known if you had".

The long play days in our own Never Never Land were filled to the brim with the magic of childhood. Everything was fun. All the paraphernalia of wash day with the fire roaring away beneath the stone copper and Mamma fishing out bundles of steaming clothes on to the zinc wash board above: when we were so small we could climb into anything: when the housework and furniture were woven into games: and Father's books were sat on, stood on, and pored over: and Mamma's face could be seem at the wash house window all day Thursday as we tip-toed round the roses and lilies as fairies: when cats and chickens, robbers and giants followed us among the maze and the milkman and coalman sent calls over the house tops; and Violet and John were as real as the family: when trooping about after the boys, and on the wooden mangle 'ship', the cellar like Aladdin's cave, and Mamma's linen basket with all the dressing-up things, all filled the days which seemed endless, with Mamma piloting us all in the proper direction whilst Father appeared and disappeared like a shooting star.

This endless time of childhood where every day was full of happiness and care, was a blue print for Life. As Emaly Brown had cared for her own large family and the villagers, so Mamma cared for us with the wisdom and love caught from her, so that we ran about and grew to be strong and thrived like the chicks in the garden, without a care in the world.

Chapter Three

Infants School

As all of us attended the same Infants School, the teachers had a time of it with the 'variations upon the genes'. We all went through the same classes and through the hands of most of the same teachers, sometimes to our advantage and sometimes the opposite.

The very first class in the Infants, nowadays referred to as the reception class but known to us then as the 'Babies', was dreaded by the latest of us about to fly the nest and start school. We had been well-primed for it by the older ones as to what to expect and what we were 'in for'. By the age of five, that at which the law decreed we started school, Mamma always had two or three other younger children tying her down at home, so that we were taken to school for the first few days by our siblings. These, of course, had their own friends, and it was not long before the initial trotting along together ceased, and one found oneself alone to cope with the long streets, crossing the roads and any small boys who felt inclined to cat-call and tease. These traumas were added to the enigma of the Bell which called us in or sent us forth with no clear indication as to time;

whether we were to go home or not. It was all confusing.

At first the bell meant running out; running until I reached home to tell Mamma all about it. My mistake was impressed upon me so that the next time it happened, the realisation dawned upon me when I was half-way home that I had once more left the mêlée prematurely. Suddenly the situation was fraught with peril. As I passed quiet alleyways between the streets, I trod softly, tip-toeing, aware that retribution in the shape of giants or policemen would seek me out. If only I could be invisible. How anxiously I looked for a companion to share my fear, but there was none. They were all safe, inside the school playground where I longed to be.

The next day, Mamma said, "Take a picture book to look at in the playground and stay with the other children." I chose a favourite of the boys', it was *Jack the Giant Killer* I trotted into school with it under my arm.

Miss Morgan was the teacher of the Babies' Class. She was plump and stocky and middle-aged. She always wore a loose, long-sleeved overall with green flowers and big pockets in front. Her voice was a deep rumble and, as we were all over-awed and quiet, she never needed to raise it. Her hair was greyish, curly and grizzled; it never moved or became untidy. She moved about silently in flat shoes among the low tables at which we were wedged together like a jig-saw that had only us keeping it apart.

I had heard all about Miss Morgan from the six older than me who had all been with her in the 'Babies'. She was firm and unsmiling and helped us with our shoes and coats and gloves. "Old Miss Morgan plays the organ", chanted my brothers as I set off to make her acquantance that first week. The reality of our meeting brought no musical thoughts into my head. Some of the family now ensconced in other rooms, unseen, about the school, had spent a lot of time in her classroom and had endured a great deal of grumbling so that she appeared to me as the troll-like figure in the fairy tale: a giant dwarf whose voice like the troll's from under the bridge seemed deep and menacing.

Accordingly, when *Jack the Giant Killer* was snatched away from under my arm and stuffed firmly behind the cupboard, I did not protest, it was just what I had been led to expect. Neither did I mention it at home to my brothers as I knew they would not be at all pleased to learn that 'Old Miss Morgan' had captured *Jack the Giant Killer*.

Miss Morgan's room was crowded; there was hardly room to move in the maze of tables at which we were all conglomerated; there we were firmly secured, with a pin and a small piece of cloth about five inches square in front of each of us. We spent a lot of time tediously working on this piece of material. There were no children moving about even if there had been room for it. Miss Morgan watched over us as we dragged the point of the pin adroitly through the edge of the square, unravelling a thread at a time. Very carefully round and round we went, amassing a small pile of coloured threads. When the cloth was finally disintegrated, the situation was not ameliorated. There was always another piece to be plucked with the pin. No doubt this training in manual dexterity paved the way for writing skills later, and the ravellings were, I believe, justly used to stuff pin cushions where they held the self-same pins firmly in place.

There was unanimous disrelish of sitting close to Miss Morgan where she grumbled at your every movement. But I found myself at the front, right under her nose. She sat next to the cupboard behind which *Jack the Giant Killer* had vanished, so that I had constant vague yearnings to rescue it and make it mine again.

The next class I went in to was totally different. It was a revelation like coming out of a tunnel. I remember the teacher as 'Catherine'. She was fast-moving, darting about the room, slim and dark with her hair caught up in a bun perched on the back of her head as though about to take off. She wore a long skirt and blouse tucked in and we chattered excitedly as she marshalled us into our seats.

The first morning she marked the register as we all watched appreciatively, feeling important and so much older than when we had walked hand in hand into the 'Babies'. She made no comments about me or the family as Miss Morgan had. We each had a desk and I sat there stroking the top and the edges but no-one interrupted Miss Catherine. She lifted the lid of her desk and put the register away. Then she rose and flitted about the room among us, opening all our desks. As the lids of the desks stood up we found that each was a small black-board underneath. Whereas in Miss Morgan's we had been so crowded that our things had to be put on the floor under the tables, we now each had a desk where the things inside could kept safely unlike the debris made under the crowded tables.

Miss Catherine's was a treat. We each had a piece of chalk. A large apple was drawn on the teacher's blackboard with a large round 'a' beside it. It was so much like the apple that I was impressed. Soon Miss Catherine came to admire my 'a' and the apple I had drawn. The children were invited to see it. It seemed no time at all before I discovered that 'cupboard' meant what it said although it was in two halves on the cupboard doors and that between really meant between, although similary halved.

Later during that school year, the Infants performed a commemorative tableau in honour of the pioneer aviator Alan Cobham, later knighted by King George V. He flew the 16,000 miles return route to the Cape for the first time, subsequently appearing in a series on television called 'The Flying Years'. He also flew to Melbourne and back, flying 28,000 miles in 320 hours. He alighted on the Thames by the Houses of Parliament by attaching floats to his trusted old machine.

He was knighted not only for his record flights, but for survey flights he made to discover about air currents, storm tracks, weather of mountain ranges and possible landing grounds. He was the pioneer of refuelling in the air. He was the first Briton to fly a light plane, with only a six horse power engine, across the Channel to Brussels in the King's Cup Race of 1924.

It must have been 1924 when dressed in a Union Jack I danced in the tableau. The importance of it all remains, but what we did I forget. But all around the Infants were pictures from magazines and newspapers, and all around our classroom were our own pictures in a frieze. Streamers and decorations decorated the hall where we performed in his honour. How wonderful it seemed that a small aeroplane could travel all that way over land and sea across the world and back.

Soon it was time to leave Miss Catherine and the little blackboard desks to enter Miss Everett's class. This lady had helped in the education of most of the family to date so that I knew her too by word of mouth before we met. She was energetic, possessed a deep resonant voice and a moustache. Nothing escaped her notice which was sometimes mortifying, as when for instance, you needed a handkerchief. She had the forceful habit of focussing the attention of the whole class upon you, so that you wished desperately that either she, or you, could disappear through the floor.

One day she began to read to us a wonderful story about an army that sprang out from the earth. Each day for about a week, the hazardous twists and turns in the story kept us rivetted to Miss Everett and her voice. Suddenly, sadly, it was finished.

"Now, children," intoned Miss Everett resoundingly in her bass voice, "I wonder if anyone can think of the name of the story?"

Many suggestions came from all over the room, but to each one, Miss Everett, who was thoroughly enjoying the secret known only to her, shook her head and dismissed them all as quite wrong. I raised my arm. With an imperious wave of her hand, Miss Everett invited me to speak. I answered with my guess.

"Speak up, Dorothy," ordered Miss Everett.

"The Dragon's Teeth," I repeated.

Miss Everett was startled.

"Come here Dorothy," she said, "and stand in front of the class. Yes, you are right, "The Dragon's Teeth". For being so clever you can tell the story all over again to the class". I stood out in front and relived the story once again. There, in front of my peers, I shared it with them. I have never found that story since.

This, I believe, started me off into the bad habit of retelling events to the teachers; events about our family life about which the teachers had and insatiable curiosity. Miss Everett had started me off as a raconteur. Whereas I had been first out of school in the 'Babies', now merely six months later, I was last. Each lunch-time, instead of running off home with the other children, I stood around the hall fire blazing away there in the now very empty large hall, with the big fire-guard as tall as I was, among a semi-circle of Infant teachers. There we stood, thawing ourselves, and there they plied me with questions about life in our family. They wanted to know all about 'Us'. Their curiosity was everlasting and I was delighted to be able to answer them. It was always cold in the large classrooms with only a small coal fire at the front near the teacher's desk, and plenty of draughts taking any heat out under the door. Now with my back to the great hall fire, I became beautifully warm and my every word was received with a keen attention that was gratifying. I was never lost for an answer. I was always able to think up something to satisfy them, yet seemed to stimulate their relish for more information. One answer was never sufficient. My explanations were not adequate; they whetted their appetites for more. Their insatiable thirst for knowledge about 'Us' flattered my young ego and I was pleased to keep them happy. When I stated as a fact that Mamma says, "As fast as Father does one job, he makes twenty others," they professed to be mystified.

"Whatever does she mean by that?" they cried with one voice. I regarded them with surprise. Anyone knew what that meant as I explained to them.

"It means," I informed them patiently, "that Father made far more work when he was helping, so that he was no help at all."

"How does your mother always know what the weather will be?" they wanted to know. Again I looked at them in amazement.

"Every morning Mamma studies the sky and the sky tells her," I told them all.

"But how does the sky tell her?" they went on.

"She is a country woman and knows all about the winds, the weather and the sky," I told them, following up with sayings that Mamma was always quoting such as:

"The South wind brings wet weather,

The North wind wet and cold together;

The West wind always brings us rain,

The East wind blows it back again."

I followed these sayings with snatches of rhymes and nursery rhymes that foretold weather which Mamma chanted as the weather changed, my inspiration primed by their curiosity. Although at a loss to know it's meaning I recited:

"If the Ash is out before the Oak, the Summer will be a soak.

If the Oak is out before the Ash, the Summer will be a splash."

In addition to weather forecasts from Mamma, Father's doings, Mamma's baking days, her sewing sessions for us all, the teacher's wanted to know the most trivial things.

"How did we manage on bath nights?"

Thereupon I quoted Mamma once more who, when we complained that we didn't want to share a bath, replied, "You must fit in like spoons and face the same way." The teachers probably conjured up pictures of the whole family wedged in the bath like sardines in a tin.

They quizzed me on all aspects of our family life and I always found an answer making it sound as exciting as possible as they were so eager to know. I didn't tell Mamma, but I don't think Father would have minded, especially as they were so interested in him, and I think I must have been like him in some ways.

Miss Everett was the prime instigator of these heart to hearts round the hall fire. With her deep bass voice and forceful whiskery face, she and I held the floor as she prompted me to share the family secrets as spokesman for the house-hold which had a member in almost every class in the school. Primed with questions, I thought up answers with verbatim quotes from Mamma who repeated herself with old country sayings, proverbs and wise remarks from the Bible. They tripped neatly off my tongue as we were nurtured from the cradle with her own beatitudes distilled from her own mother's wisdom and the reverence for the lives in their small village. Mamma fed us an ongoing daily song as lyrical as the Song of Hiawatha. Morals that Aesop told in his fables, were condensed into epigrams in a phrase or sentence and it was this wisdom that the teachers were intrigued by and left me curious as to why they did not know these things for themselves.

When I arrived home late at lunch-time, Mamma had no idea that I had been having my half hour upon the stage, on the mat, by the fire-guard, keeping all the Infant teachers acquainted with a day by day account of, not only Father's doings which they were particularly interested in, but of all our family doings. It was a wonder that I got home at all as their curiosity knew no bounds; and as the 'tribe' was familiar to them all, I enjoyed spilling the 'beans' and they listened attentively to every word.

One day I felt very guilty at not running straight home as Stanley was ill in bed. All of a fidget to escape I finally darted from the hall, running home as fast as possible. With my eyes fixed on the ground to avoid treading on any lines in the pavement, I spelt out the words as I ran, a letter with each step. P O O R S T A N L E Y. Over and over again I spelled it out as it would be lucky. I did it all the way home and flew indoors breathless.

"Yes," said Mamma, in answer to my anxious question, he is better and will soon be up." I knew it would work.

After Miss Everett's class we went into Miss Card's. This was the top class in the Infants. The room was like a lecture theatre with the desks rising up towards the back on platform steps. I sat next to Edmund, a small thin quiet boy wearing spectacles balanced on a pointed nose. He was not very much like the other boys; much too matter of fact and serious, rather like a small grandFather. He never joined in with the games the long rope tied to the rain pipe in the playground, which we jumped over, or snaked or skipped through. He seemed as if he were already grown up.

By now Gilbert my eldest brother had started work. He brought home small samples of preserved fruit for Mamma. Lots of children took things to school for Christmas which they gave to Miss Card. I decided to take one of the sample boxes of preserved fruit. It was very small and I don't suppose that Mamma missed it. I gave it to Miss Card. Miss Card had a penknife. She sat at a very high desk on a platform. Very slowly and carefully she cut the candied peel into fine thin strips. I jumped down from the platform steps and joined the other children who were busy enjoying themselves, crawling under desks and hopping up and down the platform steps of the gangway. This was not the usual better behaviour, but Miss Card was very busy with the penknife, enjoying herself and in a good mood, which we noted immediately and reacted accordingly. Whilst she was busy trying to cut a piece for everyone I felt happy and important in the reflected glory of the misappropiated peel that was taking our teacher so long to dissect, there being so little of it.

Edmund sat quietly in his place, airing his expectations of probable Christmas presents. Briefly I sat next to him to listen. Scornfully he rejected the idea that he should hang up his stocking. My attention was divided between Edmund's expectations and the imminent distribution of the candied peel. Suddenly I was shocked to hear Edmund saying, "There is no Father Christmas." I couldn't believe my ears. I remonstrated with him. I tried to explain that he always came down the chimney but Edmund sat there with a silly grin on his face and refused to be saved from his ignorance. I ran out to Miss Card and looking up at her, implored her to come and tell Edmund about Father Christmas. Miss Card's face wore a strange look as she just went on separating all the tiny, sticky pieces of peel from each other.

"He's a silly boy," she said, "take no notice of him." I felt sorry for Edmund but Miss Card didn't seem to care.

Over all these teachers was the Headmistress, Miss Underhill. Her name always seemed significant as though it were chosen to fit her. She had an enormous bosom and because of it, you couldn't see her face when you were near and looked up. She also had her hair drawn back in a bun and was always in the large hall where we went to skip and dance to the piano over the large wooden floor. She it was who was custodian of the bell at play times.

Somewhere in the Infants came Miss Palmer. I was never in her class but she attracted me like the Star over Bethlehem attracted the Wise men. It was not Miss Palmer that mesmerised me, it was her apple. Whenever she was on playground duty I followed her about as she produced an apple from her bag hanging from her wrist, and with a penknife began to peel it. I jigged about and around her, dancing up and down at her elbow, waiting for the piece that was for me. One day I watched as she peeled the apple very slowly. She seemed to be concentrating on keeping the peel unbroken. Slowly it spiralled down, swaying tantalisingly still attached to the fruit. I was in a fever of impatience. Playtime was almost over. I wanted to say, "Hurry up." My agitation mounted. Would she ever let the peel free of the apple? Why were teachers so slow? The bell would soon appear at the door in the hands of Miss Underhill. Playtime would then be over and we should all have to run inside. Suddenly the peel was being offered to me on the end of the penknife. Simultaneously the bell was clanging that we must all run inside. I joined the others and ran. I don't know what happened to the peel but I didn't follow the apple any more, although, these days, one would perhaps consider that it was the best part of the apple that I was offered.

One of these Infant teachers helped us each to make a shoulder bag. I believe it was Miss Morgan the teacher of the 'Babies'. It was made from two pieces of calico or strong cotton, material sewn together and had a bright flowery pattern which was like Miss Morgan's overall. It was closed by a flap of material which folded over the top to be fastened with a loop over a button. The long strip of material sewn to the top at each side enabled it to be worn across the shoulder like a satchel. Proudly I wore it home and was allowed to keep it on through tea. Soon afterwards a knock came at the front door. Phyllis was sent to answer it. Engrossed in my bag, I followed her. A man stood there asking for Mamma.

"I am sorry she is not at home," said Phyllis.

Feeling very important with my shoulder bag I spoke up.

"Oh yes she is," I contradicted.

"No she is not," said Phyllis firmly.

"Yes, she is," I insisted, puzzled at Phyllis' stupidity. The man looked from one to the other of us. I settled it.

"Mamma," I called, "there is a man to see you."

Mamma was soon at the door where I received a tap on my bottom.

"Go up to your room," Mamma commanded. "How many times have I told you to say gentleman!"

I went upstairs unhappy and bewildered. I couldn't understand why I was sent up to my bedroom when it was Phyllis who had been wrong. I took off my shoulder bag and put it on the bed beside me. The new calico had a lovely smell. The large flowers on the cream background looked beautiful with the afternoon sun lighting them through the window. I looked at it but didn't want to open it or wear it now. All the joy was gone and it brought me no solace.

Poor Mamma in her constant battle, to use her words, of "Robbing Peter to pay Paul," had been caught out. Engrossed in my shoulder bag I had unwittingly let the 'cat out of the bag'.

Whilst in the Infants, running to and from school alone, boys could be a nuisance. Hair ribbons were snatched off and hair pulled. One day on my way home a group of boys snatched my hat and threw it over a wall. I ran home upset and Mamma was in high dudgeon. The next morning she accompanied me to school and together we mounted the many flights of stairs which took us to the top story, to the 'Big Boys'.

Mr. Harris, the headmaster, small and dapper, straight-backed with neat moustache, listened quietly to Mamma and then rang the bell for the whole of the 'Big Boys' to assemble in the hall. Doorways all around opened and boys of all sizes came streaming out. I spotted Ralph carrying Alfie Palmer on his back as though pick-a-back was his friend's only means of locomotion. Soon the hall was full of lines of boys silently assembled for this special occasion. Mr. Harris standing on the platform by his desk, cane in hand, regarded them severely.

"I want the boy who threw this girl's hat over a wall to raise his hand," he said looking them over from one end of the hall to the other.

I felt very sorry to be there and the cause of all this upheaval. Suddenly a boy raised his hand. He was summoned forward and ordered to raise first one hand and then the other where he received the cane. I am sure I felt as badly as he did, but Mamma considered that it was no more than he deserved.

Memories of days in the Infants are linked to those teachers, Miss Morgan who never played the organ; Miss Catherine and the little blackboard desks, darting about the room with her 'bun' like a full stop behind her; Miss Everett and The Dragon's Teeth; Miss Card with the candied peel, disregarding Edmund's barren existence without Father Christmas; and Miss Palmer sauntering about the playground taking a whole playtime to peel her apple. And in the background was Miss Underhill, custodian of the hall and the bell as unapproachable as a balloon as she was invisible from the chest upwards.

Each year as the Farnborough International Air Show takes place, described as Britain's largest outdoor exhibition, I think back to the Infant School celebration for Sir Alan Cobham's achievements in the early 1920's. His son Michael Cobham, chairman of the Flight Refuelling Group, calls Farnborough, "an outstanding and unique event in the aeronautical calendar". But nothing will match the outstanding achievements of his Father in the early pioneer days.

This was the only important event I remember in those early school days and I still feel proud that I wore the Union Jack to dance on that occasion although all else in the celebration has become lost in the mists of time.

Chapter Four

The Juniors

The best thing about going up into the Juniors was that now we were old enough to go swimming. Every Wednesday we were in a state of nervous excitement. Every Wednesday we sang the hymn 'Fight the Good Fight'. The strains from the music of the piano and the voices raised to drown it, competing in volume swelling the sound, evoked the Wednesday morning nostalgia – it was swimming day – and images of the baths drifted into our minds with the music. We were all filled with a restless energy, aching to be on the way to the baths, to get started on the weekly crocodile jog-trot to the pool.

Outside the hall, we lined up with our towels and costumes jostling in a mob of all possible arrangements to sort ourselves into pairs, until the teacher suddenly descended like a magnet on iron filings, and instantly we were all in position, the permutations and arguments of seconds before frozen, and we were aligned ready for departure.

The only thing that really mattered now, was getting there as soon as possible so as not to miss a second at the baths. We travelled at the fastest walk possible without running and the teacher's calls to

"Slow down!" fell on deaf ears as we hustled her along with us.

On our route was the house of a girl whose Father was a policeman. On Wednesday mornings he was at home looking down at us over his garden wall as we trooped by. He was tall and kind and friendly. He stopped his gardening to gaze at us as we greeted him and acknowledged our calls with a deep word or two from beneath his long straggly moustache, his eyes twinkling as we all rushed past like lemmings towards the sea.

At the baths, we were out of our clothes in a flash and lined up along the edge of the pool. The lady instructor had a loud, hoarse voice like a coalman. When the last shivering junior was ready, she blew her whistle and we entered the water in a dozen different different ways. Boys were usually soon in. They chose their favourite way. They bombed the water and generously shared it with as many of those still dry as possible; flung themselves in backwards; dived; waited patiently to 'bomb' their friends; took a run to enter as near the other side as possible; showed off jumping in the deep-end holding their noses, or joined the girls on the steps going one down and two up until helped with a shove from those behind. This took only a few seconds and reluctant laggards were shouted in by the instructress.

The pool was now a cauldron of organised uproar with the noise from a hundred throats, twice doubled in volume, as if in some deep underground cavern. We pushed and choked our way about the water, struggling to imitate the frog in movements that we had all tried out painfully, on our desk tops the day before. Chlorinated water forced itself down our throats, up our noses and into our ears. We choked and coughed against a background of a long, deafening, echoing din.

The instructress had a long, hooked pole which was her ally in the combat. Promising candidates found themselves hooked by the shoulder strap and dragged along through the water. As we progressed to completing a few strokes, we were exhorted by the booming voice, to exert ourselves to stay longer afloat and to try to reach the hovering hook, now held a few inches in front of our noses, ready to be clutched before we sank. However, when we missed the pole and disappeared choking beneath the surface, we were dragged out on the hook by our costumes, like so much dangling frog-spawn. Always too soon, a loud blast on the whistle, repeated ferociously, brought us all out into the changing room. There we stood, shivering together, jostling elbows, standing on each other's clothes and rubbing our numbed extremities wrinkled by chlorine, whilst we competed in chattering our teeth.

Eddie Almand lived opposite us with his brother Sammy and his mum and dad. He was about eleven. He lent me his water wings. As soon as school finished I ran all the way to the baths. All day long at school the time dragged as I thought of once more being in the baths with the water wings. They were a wonderful help unlike the hooked pole. They went across the chest and under the arms where they ballooned out behind as you floated on the water. Soon I was able to swim and do the back stroke.

One day the water wings disappeared and were nowhere to be found. From then on they haunted me. From the day they vanished I watched Eddie Almand's house carefully, afraid and anxious that he would ask for the missing water wings. If I saw any of his family I ran back indoors as fast as possible. This went on for some weeks. One day Stanley brought Eddie into our house. I only had time to hide behind an armchair. It wasn't long before I was discovered.

"What are you doing there, Doll?" asked Stanley, puzzled.

Doubly hot with shame at my cowardice together with losing the water wings, I confessed. To my astonishment, Eddie did not seem interested in the loss of his water wings.

"Oh, that's all right," he said mildly. If only I had owned up before, how many weeks of worry I would have been saved.

We juniors, ever full of energy, had such an insatiable appetite for events so that our 'cups brimmed over' with all the excitement of the adventure of life. After a hectic day at school where we would be all afidget to be back once more at the swimming pool, we raced along to the baths. Never pausing, we ran all the way, afraid it might be too crowded to get in, and soon were once again in the water with the would-be swimmers, throwing our limbs about, chins thrust upwards with contorted faces, struggling with the force of gravity that pulled us down and destroyed our efforts to propel our bodies along without sinking. The pool was packed and barely two strokes could be made before we were in collision with other bodies, jumped on or halted by a diver rising from beneath. It was a constant battle for a space to swim and any small clear area was promptly filled by a body flying from the pool side. It was all rather like the 'Dodgems' at the fair. At each collision we seized up like the cars do. But we were swallowing water and gasping for breath before taking two more strokes towards the next impact.

A whistle told us our 'time was up' and we were all turfed out, ejected to make room for the queue outside, waiting on a hot summer's day to get in.

But all our Herculean struggles, far from wearing us out, were a stimulus which galvanised us into further activity as we made for the library next door. We avid readers among the Juniors, now dived in there. Wet bundles from the pool were dropped about here and there on the parquet floor as we raced around the shelves, summoning each other to share each important discovery until we had to choose. Then it seemed, we were all after the same books; but 'top priorities' were all 'out' as we discovered from scrambling up the shelves, on a toe-hold, out of sight of the librarian. From our perches we passed this information down in loud whispers, our voices hoarse from struggles in the chlorinated pool next door. Finally all swapping about was over, our books were stamped by the thankful librarian, and now noisy, like chorussing cicadas, we swooped through the swing doorway, down the wide steps into the main highway with our prizes clutched among our swimming things, to race all the way home without stopping, accelerated by magnificent appetites.

The first favourite library books were Viking sagas. These tales of 'Finn and his Warrior Band', took me on thrilling and heroic adventures, mighty expeditions of bravery and daring. The series finished with the death of Finn. How sad it was. In later years I searched for these stories of Finn in vain. Like 'The Dragon's Teeth', they were nowhere to be found.

The death of Finn was brought about by the treachery of one of his warriors. Seated around on the great circle of council stones, which can be seen to this day in the Scandinavian forests, Finn and the council debate the fate of the traitor. He is sentenced to death. Traditionally, he is to be beheaded by the Warrior Chief. He is taken to where Finn sits on the great Chief's stone. His head is laid across Finn's thigh. With one mighty blow Finn severs the head from the body but it is an unlucky strike. The strength of the blow and the sharpness of the sword send part of the blade into Finn's own thigh. His great femoral artery is severed together with the traitor's head, and within two minutes, in spite of all the warriors can do, Finn has bled to death.

With the death of Finn and the end of the sagas, I went on to other immortal stories, *Treasure Island* and *Coral Island* and the one which was the 'hit' just at that time, *Alan a Dale*.

Intermingled with the library books, the grisly paper backs of my brothers fascinated me. Purloined books were smuggled up to bed. By the light of the candle I sat with the book on my knees, reading and reading, fascinated by horror, Phyllis and Olive fast asleep beside me, reading *The Face in the Night*. Chapter after chapter kept me riveted to the book, until – 'The body fell out of the cupboard; his throat was slit from ear to ear', was enough. The book was closed and under the pillow but now the candle had to be blown out. With the candle lighting the page, gloom had been confined to the corners. That puff on the candle flame brought darkness; it swallowed me. Dr. Fu Manchu's evil men made their presence felt. They advanced from the corners. Vivid words and phrases flashed through my mind peopling the room, recurring over and over again so that, afraid to sleep I dozed into nightmares from which I awoke fitfully, only to dream again.

Roy was also a bookworm and belonged to a shilling library. He was eleven years older than me, and at work, and his taste in books superior to the paperbacks of my other brothers, which was to be expected as it was a kind of book club he had joined.

At intervals, he turned out his cupboard where he kept all his treasures including wine gums, but was curiously loath to give away anything he no longer wanted, no doubt preferring not to see his old books being scribbled in and scattered about among the large number of his smaller brothers and sisters. He often threw out a large pile of things, putting them in the rubbish bin.

Seeing Roy taking the stairs three and four at a time and descending with his arms full of redundant belongings, I hovered unobtrusively knowing well his aversion to the 'tribe' handling his personal effects, especially the small fry like me.

As soon as he had departed to join his friends for cricket or an outing to a cribbage party, I dived on his discarded goods. Piles of books which had been valuable possessions until this moment, locked in his cupboard, were now by the rubbish – free for the taking. The arms full of books which had so recently descended the stairs from Roy's room, now went back upstairs into my room. Up and down I went with everything practically that he had committed to waste. Half-used note-books, carbon paper, a few paper clips, stubs of pencils, order pads from the silver smiths where he worked, all were resurrected and with piles of books reascended the stairs, as I staggered up and down until everything with scribbling space and anything readable was safely stowed in a box or two, under my bed. Roy knew nothing of all this and he never found out as he lived on a different plane to the small fry among us, and we didn't exactly 'hob-nob'. With his 'superior' ways, he would not have approved and my actions would have been condemned with the rubbish.

In the following weeks, after each reclamation, I read in turn *Silas Marner*, *The Mill on the Floss*, lots of Edgar Wallace, Edgar Rice-Burroughs, Victor Hugo, Rider Haggard, H. G. Wells, Conan Doyle, Wilkie Collins, Baroness Orczy and many others including Dickens. The very fact that Roy was unaware that I had fished out and kept, all his discarded trash, made the whole operation much more interesting. The *Last of the Mohicans*, *Micah Clark* and *Tarzan*, always remind me of lanky Roy, his arms full of books, long-legged and bandy, streaking up and down the staircase between his bedroom cupboard and the dustbin, to rid the house of his redundant belongings, and of me, unnoticed, waiting in anticipation to reclaim it all as soon as his back disappeared through the front door.

In the early Juniors we had Miss Hopkinson. This old-fashioned-looking lady with puffed out cheeks rather like a rabbit, was kind and quiet. She was cross-eyed which was noticeable even through her glasses. Her brown hair was worn in an untidy bun and she was always dressed in brown, the brown of beech leaves, with very long skirts.

The classroom blackboard was large and rested on two wooden pegs on a tall easel. One day, for some inexplicable reason, the heavy wooden easel suddenly folded up and we were presented with the spectacle of our teacher sitting on the floor, legs and feet spread-eagled, glasses awry, beneath the blackboard and easel. Whilst she sat there dazed, we all shrieked at first with laughter. It wasn't that we were not sorry for her, we were, and we felt worried but it was an immediate reaction to burst into laughter as when someone slips on a banana skin. She was a kind and dedicated teacher and must have thought us very cruel, whereas, in reality we loved her.

One October morning she took us all on the tram to Wanstead Park for a nature ramble. We each had a small note-book and pencil. We alighted from the tram at the terminus by the ponds on the Flats. Then we walked the long Avenue which led to Wanstead Park. Just inside the gates there was a choice of paths. Straight ahead led towards the boating lake on the left and on to the cricket field and the woods; the path to the right wandered along under tall trees by the park fence and a stream – straggling alongside the path, overhung with trees and bushes. It was always dank under these trees and the stagnant stream had areas of pondscum, the bright green duck weed which provides oxygen for the pond creatures below. We chose the right hand path and followed the stream.

Following Miss Hopkinson, we strung along excitedly finding the things she had told us to look for. Above us, the tall trees were letting go their few remaining Autumn leaves. Acorns and conkers lay hiding in the grass. Some small fat acorns sat in their cups like miniature pipes with twig stems. A few conkers were still in armour, their sturdy spikes on their thick green overcoats, quite undamaged in spite of the impact with the ground as they fell from the tree high above. Cones lay about; some tightly closed, guarding their seeds still unripened, others, from earlier fructification, wide open – the seeds either eaten or buried awaiting germination. Twigs were collected. We were shown how to recognise them, their buds clearly seen now they were bare of leaves. We learned the horse-shoe scar of the chestnut; the tightly-rolled pointed cigar of the beech bud, the black rounded bud of the ash and quickly learned the prickly scarlet-berried hawthorne and the thorny dog rose with its bright, fleshy, orange haws which fed the birds.

We scrambled about and found hands-full of sycamore seeds to throw high in the aim and watch them spiralling down. We climbed about in the hazel hedges and found a cob nut or two that the squirrels had missed. We found the North by the green moss on the tree trunks and blackbird feathers patched with white. We froze to watch a swan in the reeds by the water's edge, and we had to put it into our note-books which we didn't want to do as it spoilt the fun.

No-one fell into the pondscum and Miss Hopkinson guided us all back to the gates and up the long Wanstead Park Avenue with our note-books and specimens of twigs and feathers, acorns and conkers, berries and seed cones, all the way back to the tram terminus, where we scrambled madly aboard with that interminable energy unflagging in the young.

Once back in our classroom, we filled it with evidence of our outing and then endeavoured to do the same with our note-books.

The dank smell of Autumn, leaves baring the trees, fruits and twigs underfoot, bring a pang of nostalgia, bred in a copse by a sluggish stream, with Miss Hopkinson, so many years ago.

Junior school life was not all fun and a bed of roses as I recall. There was the time we were suffering the trauma of long division. This introduction to it was a lengthy enigma there up on the black-board, As morning 'play' approached, the teacher wrote a sum on the board for us to follow with her, step by step.

"Now children," she said, "you must each of you get this sum right before you can go out to play," with which she turned the board around to face the wall.

The sum being so recent in my mind, I soon had it completed. Out to the front I ran to show her my book. To my amazement she looked very annoyed.

"How did you manage to get this right so quickly?" she wanted to know.

I was non-plussed. Dumbfounded, I could not answer. After looking all over my book, I was allowed out to play. It seemed strange that the teacher did not understand that I could remember the answer which she had shown us, so that I did not need to work it all out again.

There was the time a man sat on his bike outside the school and caused a great commotion. Seeing the crowd there I ran to see what was happening and then ran into school. During the first lesson of the afternoon, a note was passed to me.

"Did you see the man on the bike? What was he doing?"

The class was very unsettled and the teacher cross.

Another note came on my desk.

"What was the man on the bike doing?"

I scribbled back. "He was sitting on the bike with his dickie out."

The teacher came and picked up the note. I was banned from the room and sent to await the headmistress by her desk. Feeling that I had committed some dreadful crime, I cried bitterly.

It was a long time before the headmistress came to her desk in the big, cold hall where I waited. By that time I was drenched in misery, unable to speak. That patient, white-haired, elderly lady, took both my hands in hers and calmed me down. Miss Mobray, tall and slender, her head always shaking slightly, showed her wisdom and depth of understanding that day. I heard no more about the affair at school but at home Mamma was furious.

"Come with me," said Mamma, and off we went to see the teacher concerned who lived close by. But in spite of repeated knocking at her door we never obtained an answer, so the matter was left.

Looking back, it seems that the younger teacher, still living with her parents, was out of her depth and had no idea how to deal with a small child in this situation, whereas the older woman, also a spinster, had the wisdom to understand that I did not know what the terrible crime was that I had witnessed or the implications of the danger involved. She understood the agony of mind I was in as a result of the teacher's action, and promptly gave me all the reassurance and sympathy needed to banish my terror. I only hope that she was able to instil a little common sense into the teacher as well.

That teacher, together with her parents, was living close to us for a short while only and was never part of the community, which was a kaleidoscope of colourful characters about whom we felt we knew quite a lot.

There was little Miss Hough, pronounced Huff, who passed back and forth in front of our house. She took short, quick, silent steps as though she were on wheels. This dear lady had an affliction. Her head twisted itself to one side, always to the right, so that to acknowledge you, which she always did being a well-bred lady, was easy for her when she was going 'up' the road and we were on her right. But if she were going 'down' the road back home, being very genteel, she would acknowledge us with a sweet smile and a

"Good morning", or "afternoon" or "evening", by turning her head manually using both hands.

We suffered with her, watching fascinated, from our perches on the railings outside, as she drew parallel, knowing the exact moment when she would take hold of her hat and with both hands, turn her head to face us and smile her greetings. As she glided by, her head was already reasserting itself in its customary position, and she kept her hands on her hat as camouflage, for her own benefit, to cover her embarassment.

She was never without her hat trimmed with flowers or a ribbon, and beneath, her bright ginger hair was always neat and impeccable, like her clothes, and we suspected that it was a wig. She floated by frequently, coming and going like an apparition; always begloved; the well-trimmed hat close over her red hair; a chiffon scarf floating out behind.

Miss Hough had an elderly mother and they lived together just four houses away from ours. All the people 'down' the road from us passed by our house to get to the shops, so that we observed their comings and goings as a matter of course.

Miss Hough's mother occasionally sauntered by alone. Dressed all in black, her diminutive figure seemed swept along by her layers of skirts standing out from her waist. They almost swept the pavement but small elastic-sided boots could just be seen beneath, taking her along. Her neat black bonnet, tuckered and beribboned, was tied at the side in a bow. The front stood up high like mother Dix's our nursemaid, the silk gathered and pleated, framing her smiling face.

As soon as she saw us children, she stopped to smile at us all and have a little rest. No words passed between us but when she had looked at each one of us, off she went. Occasionally she was to be seen walking past, arm in arm with her daughter, on the right-hand of course. They fluttered past like two small birds, smiling gently, but shy and reserved; the handicapped Miss Hough and her mother – like a Dresden doll clothed all in black.

There were usually four or five of us standing or sitting on the iron, black-painted railings at the front of our house, so that most passers-by saw us and smiled and we smiled back and sometimes greeted them. We knew exactly who would smile or speak and who wouldn't.

One who never did was Mr. Pike the butcher. Dashing along in his heavy boots, chin thrust forward, he was a brawny, bulky figure. Looking neither to left nor right, he rushed by, his feet gobbling the pavement, as he hastened to the shop in the High Street where he worked. His elbows stuck out helping to propel him along as though he were about to take off, and sometimes his white apron could be seen, showing below his coat as he hurried past as though he were late for an execution. A pair of waxed moustaches projected on either side of his face like two sharp skewers and his face was reddish (like the meat in his shop), enhanced by his greying-white hair. People worked hard and late, and between ten and eleven o'clock on a Saturday night, Mr. Pike could be found outside the butcher's booming out,

"Buy! Buy! Buy! – Buy! Buy! Buy! – Buy! Buy! Buy!" to any late shoppers who might be dawdling around hoping for a bargain.

During our Junior School days, Mr. Rowe a retired chemist had been one of the genial neighbours, observing us with his twinkling blue eyes as he approached us where we played on the pavement with our hoops, balls, tops and skipping ropes. He always had a friendly word for us as we stood aside for him to pass along the pavement with his heavy, rubber-ended stick. He was distinguished, strongly built and always well-dressed. His wife we saw occasionally, slim elegant and superior, always carrying a rolled-up umbrella and never without hat and gloves. The only time she spoke to us was when our eldest brother, Gilbert, was killed, and as the accident happened on the corner, close to our house, all those near by felt involved.

Many years after our school days were over, whilst we were teen-agers, Mr. Rowe appeared on our doorstep asking for Father. He was still a forthright, impressive, bearded figure, but now older and greyer and grizzled. His wife was ill, he said, and he asked Father if he could arrange for her to be taken to hospital.

Father left his evening meal on the table and accompanied Mr. Rowe back home. Father had a shock. Downstairs, in conditions of squalor, lay Mrs Rowe, unrecognisable as the elegant lady with the umbrella. In indescribably miserable conditions, she lay dying. Mr. Rowe of the strong weather-beaten appearance, twinkling blue eyes and robust physique, had become almost a recluse and had apparently lived that way for years.

Little Miss Hough, living next-door to them, told Father in an awed whisper,

"After a quarrel over a woman some thirty years earlier, Mr. and Mrs. Rowe never spoke to each other!"

As a result, nothing in the house had been done and practically the whole house had become disused. A few cracked cups lay in the kitchen sink. On the back of a bedroom door upstairs hung the remains of a dressing gown, now reduced to a dusty grey cobweb. We wondered how long Mrs. Rowe, detached, aloof and ladylike, had lain in this appalling state.

Nobody in the street had known anything of their affairs except Miss Hough and she told no-one until now when she told Father. Neither Mr. nor Mrs. Rowe, had mounted the stairs for years. In the downstairs rooms, heavy expensive books were stacked from floor to ceiling, all appeared to be theological books. The fine mahogany bookcase remained in fine condition, untouched by the decay around it. Mr. Rowe had allowed no-one in, not even the doctor until now, when he realised that Mrs. Rowe was about to die.

Father prevailed upon him to go into care after much talking had to be done. At that time, Father was employed as a Relieving Officer so that he knew the steps to take. Mr. Rowe gave over his affairs for Father to sort out. He discovered there were two sons, one a compositor, but they had disassociated themselves from their parents some years before. It all seemed unreal and terribly sad.

Further down the road lived Jack Alcock who was still working in the fish market. He and Father were great friends still from their days together at the great Billingsgate Fish Market. Jack was very kind and as Father was at this time unemployed (it was the 1920s) Jack decided to treat the four smallest of us children, to a show at East Ham Palace. He did it in style. Mama was expecting Olive. It was December and very cold. Ralph, Stanley, Phyllis and myself, the youngest, were to have a box to ourselves which he had taken for us.

We were full of excitement and at home, could hardly eat our tea, before we left for the evening performance.

It was near Christmas. Neither Phyllis nor I were old enough for school. In the cold night it seemed wrong to be going out. Stanley and Ralph were very excited and hustled us through our tea. Then off we all four of us went.

Going out of the house as the evening was darkening, seemed to be all wrong; it seemed very late; the air was chill; I didn't want to go and felt I would not enjoy it.

We hurried to the Palace and I ran to keep up with the others. The box was large and the seats seemed a long way from the edge. It was strange sitting there with no people in front of us, but we could walk about to look more closely at the stage. It had been impressed upon us that we were very lucky and felt dutifully awed, but I have no recollection of the show and was too young to enjoy it, really.

Jack Alcock was a good friend to Father, not only playing whist and mahjong with him and Mamma through many a night, but fetching home from the market the shellfish that Father loved and could no longer afford whilst out of work – shellfish for the whole family, for which he would take nothing.

When Jack died painfully of lung cancer, refusing all medicine and doctors because he had become fanatically religious, Father was deeply upset and no-one else outside the family was invited in to play whist and mahjong like Annie and Jack Alcock had been. Nobody else took Jack's place.

Our neighbours on the pear tree side, were the Bulls. Mr. Bull had been a lighter-man on the Thames.

"Not in the same class as the previous occupier who had bought his house at the same time as we did," said Mamma. "He was a gentleman, a Major."

However, Jim Bull was tall and would have made a good cowboy and I remember now he looked very like Gary Cooper. Mr. and Mrs. Bull wanted children desperately but none came. I heard her confiding in Mamma over the garden fence.

"It's not fair," said Mamma. "Why can't life be more equitable so that everyone has their fair share?" And I heard her telling Mrs. Bull that Father said "he had only to put his trousers on the bed for her to be 'in the family way' ". I wondered what Father's trousers had to do with having a family?

The Bulls had a large, curly, Airedale dog, gentle and quiet like Mr. Bull, who was also tall, strong and kind. One day I met the Airedale who seemed to be going for a walk on its own, near the park. I was worried. To me, being small, it was a long way from home. I held it by the collar. If only I had a piece of string to lead it home, but I had none. There was only one thing for it – I must carry it home. For a thin little child the dog was terribly heavy. It was as much as I could do to get my arms around its body. What a weight it was to lift! Luckily the dog was still and patient. I staggered along slowly, stopping for frequent rests, sitting on people's railings and holding the dog's collar. The Airedale put up with it obediently.

Finally I turned the corner into our road. We were the second house from the corner and Mr. Bull's was the third. Would I be able to get there without putting the dog down again?

Worried that the dog might run off at the last moment; agitated by concern with the dog's safety; breathless and exhausted; I finally struggled along the path to the Bull's front door. Afraid to put it down lest it run off, I pressed against the bell. Mrs. Bull looked out. To my great surprise she didn't look at all worried or even thankful at having her dog delivered. But in my mind I could see that the dog was thankful. As soon as he saw the open door, he bounded inside in a flash.

One day the Sunday School took my class and a few others, on an outing to Southend. I am not sure which church I was going to at the time and no-one else in the family came. I must have been one of the youngest there as I remember very little about the sand or sea and I thought the boys very badly behaved.

After a trip to the beach, we all trooped up the stairs into Garon's restaurant in Southend High Street. There we saw tables laden with food, end to end, in the long elegant room the size of a banquetting hall which it probably was. A fine assortment of cakes and pasties, sausage rolls and sandwiches, jellies and biscuits was laid out on the white table cloths.

The boys made a dash for the tables and after some shuffling around and moving about, we were all finally settled in a place at a table. Whilst the adults brought fruit drinks for us, we helped ourselves to the food in front of us. Soon the children were reaching over each other and the tables, grabbing sandwiches and cakes here and there until finally, in the mad scramble to be the fastest eater, which seemed to be going on among the boys, all the food had vanished except for plates of buns left all along the tables. In the twinkling of an eye these became ammunition being projected all about the room, between the tables. Sticky missiles were flying around in all directions.

As I have no recollection of any of us paddling or even playing on the beach, I suppose the boys took their frustrations out on the buns with a spontaneous declaration of war between the tables. In a matter of seconds it was all over, there being nothing left on the tables but the table cloths.

When four of us went to learn the piano we were thrilled. This didn't last long. As soon as Father began to nag us to do our piano practice, I no longer enjoyed it.

The piano teacher was long suffering and severe it seemed to me. Those who had not done their piano practice had their fingers banged on the piano keys each time they played a wrong note.

Ralph, Stanley, Phyllis and I were the four. We had twenty minutes each and sat and waited for each other in the hall of her house. The teacher had suffered from Polio and had to wear a high boot. The poor lady was grumpy and no doubt tired of having small children to teach who hated to practice.

We were about five, seven, nine and eleven with Ralph in charge, being the eldest. He always managed to find a ha'penny in his pocket which was spent on a coconut bar which he shared between us. It was always a coconut bar as we liked them better than other sweets.

After we had all had our twenty gruelling minutes, we dawdled home to tea. Then the ha'penny was produced, which, after the usual cogitations, we agreed should be spent on the coconut bar.

Outside the shop we stood against the window dividing the crisp toffee-nut bar into four. With our allocated portion, we each disposed of it in our own way. Each piece was either being slowly licked, gripped by two sticky fingers and a thumb; or nibbled tentatively, the paper wrapped around tightly to restrict the inroads of sharp teeth; or dissolving en bloc inside the mouth against a bulging cheek, or hidden away – hoarded in a pocket to be eaten later, probably after tea.

Whatever was happening to the coconut bar, there we stood happily free from care with the lesson over for the time being. We stood outside the shop and gazed in. The low window through which the smallest children could see, was a colourful feast. The eyes wandered over tangles of liquorice braid, jumbles of lollipops, boxes of leaking sherbert dabs, lashings of farthing strips, tiers of tall jars through which striped candy, pear drops, humbugs, post toasties, sugared almonds, brittle nut toffee and all sorts and colours of sweets, could be seen waiting to be bought and devoured. We stood and gazed, slowly savouring the delicious morsel of Ralph's coconut bar and conjecturing among us as to what we could have bought with the ha'penny instead.

Finally the sweet was gone, the interlude over, and we moved away to meander across roads where horses were trotting briskly with empty carts, after their day's work; along quiet streets of houses whose occupants were indoors about their tea, hastening only with guesses as to what Mamma would have waiting for us indoors.

It was not long before the piano teacher 'dropped' Ralph and me and only Stanley and Phyllis continued and went on to play duets. Stan had a natural ear for music and being much better than anyone else among us, became the family pianist which brought him into great demand at our frequent parties.

Several of us continued to play by 'ear' as Father did, but only Roy learned the violin. He was extraordinarily unmusical so that the neighbours complained about his practising, likening it to torturing a cat. They complained perpetually until, after weeks of hostility between Mamma and the neighbours, an agreement was made. It was arranged that poor Roy would practise only between six and seven in the morning.

The hardship of the 1920s, forced Mamma to try to recover money and property due to her and Roy, from Raggazone's estate in Italy near by Lago Maggiore. Her letters were sent to the British Embassy where they were translated for her and sent on to the Raggazone family in northern Italy. Father knew nothing of this as he was dead against Roy being anything but a Parker and wanted Mamma to have no reconnection with the Italians.

At this time, Gilbert had brought a small spaniel home for Mamma which unexpectedly, as it had been sold as a male, produced five pups to look after and find homes for.

One morning Mamma spent some time collecting papers and writing a long letter, which were sealed in a large envelope for me to take to the post office to be registered.

I set off with the letter and the five puppies of assorted genders and unknown paternity, on a tangle of leads. With these brindle and variegated puppies, I wandered along towards the post office.

The puppies took all my attention. They were too young to walk more than a few yards. In short spurts they dashed about in opposite directions and then sat down – refusing to budge. It took all my time unravelling their leads and picking up those who only wanted to sit down. It was difficult trying to hold more than one whilst half-dragging the rest along out of bushes and gateways. I'll never know how I got them all back home.

On my return, flustered and exhausted, Mamma asked me for the receipt for the registered letter. Try as I might, I could remember nothing about the letter. I had no recollection of the post-master or of putting it into the letter box. Mamma was furious with me. I felt ashamed of myself knowing how important it was as we were desperately short of money. The only blessing was that Father knew nothing about my carelessness. He was far too proud and far too jealous to help Mamma claim anything from Italy and so it was kept secret from him.

Because of the constant planning and scheming that Mamma was compelled to practise, to feed and clothe us all in the long depression, we were well aware of the importance of every last farthing, to us all. Out of this was born a game we girls played in bed. It was mostly Phyllis and I and was called 'The Bare Family'. This imaginary family were entirely without anything whatever, and night after night we played at furnishing the items they needed to survive. We took it in turns to care for them. For weeks and months we told each other their story. We had to decide what we could spare for them, for their clothes and food. They were just as real to us as (when we played) Violet and John (see chapter 2) and how seriously we took all the planning and worry.

When it started, I cannot remember, but we looked forward to this story which went on night after night, with every twist and turn that we could devise, until we fell asleep. As soon as we had said our prayers and Mamma had tucked us in and kissed us 'Good night', we snuggled down in bed and asked each other,

"What shall we play tonight?"

"I know. Let's help the 'Bare Family'."

Then would begin all the essential life saving steps that we could think up; which clothes we could spare for them; how much we could spend on their food and what it should be. Could we afford to give them a treat? And so we went on until one or other of us fell asleep and the other fell asleep talking and it was forgotten until the next night when the saga continued.

When the kitchen range was given up as dangerous, all the hot water pipes being furred up, and Father afraid they might overheat and explode with no money to have it all renewed, the hot water from the wash-house was used for our baths instead. The water was heated in the stone copper* over the boiler fire and carried upstairs in buckets.

At some time in the Juniors I started to help Mamma to carry the hot water upstairs. From carrying up the bath water I started to help bath the 'kids'. I had a double incentive. Firstly I did it because I could have the first bath and the clean water and topped it up for the 'kids' with extra buckets of hot water, two at a time. I also bathed the 'kids' two at a time, as by now, I was about eleven years old and there were four younger than me. In the bath they sat, as Mamma put it, 'like spoons', all facing the same way. The second incentive was that, as soon as Father realised that I would help Mamma in this way regularly, he gave me extra pocket money.

In winter we lit an oil stove to heat the bathroom.

After their baths, I brushed and combed the children's hair. The curly ones were curled around a

---

* **Stone copper**. Fire beneath bricks which heated a copper tub holding the washing in water.

finger, but tighter curls were produced by strips of rag wrapped around several strands of hair, rolled up and tied in knots. These combed out into long ringlets when untied.

One bath night a celluloid comb fell on top of the oil stove. In a second it melted and burst into flames. I snatched up a wet face flannel and flung it onto the flames as I pulled the towels and nighties away. The soaking wet flannel soon put out the flames. That was the only memorable incident about those Friday bath nights that I can recall.

This was all happening in the 1920s and at one time, both Father and Graham, Father's second eldest son, were unemployed. Graham, about eighteen years old, was very quiet, but Father wasn't satisfied until he provoked him into an argument. Poor Graham found it all very trying one lunch time and, on impulse, picked up his plateful of stew to throw over Father. Unfortunately the plate slipped. It flew across the table with its contents, hitting Father on the head. Blood trickled down! We were all shocked and silent. Graham went out and enlisted in the Grenadier Guards. When he returned and told Father, he too was ashamed, feeling responsible. Father went to get him released but it was too late. Graham had taken the King's shilling.

He was installed in the barracks in Caterham for training. Gilbert, one year older than Graham, took us all there to see him. It was Graham's first Sunday at Caterham.

Gilbert had an old Studebaker. The car was huge but there were lots of us. We all jostled to get in.

"Come on, Doll," said Father, "be a good girl and sit down there."

Down there was the floor at the back of the car. I saw all the others being squeezed together on seats and laps where they could see out of the windows. How I hated that journey, Sitting on the floor I could see nothing but legs and feet. I was very unpopular. I was in the way of several feet. I knew just how dogs feel people tread on them and then blame the dog.

The day was blustery and cold. It was April and the weather was bad. After a picnic all together some-where near Caterham, photos were taken with Graham in his new uniform and of all of us, by Gilbert, the family entrepreneur. Then we sadly said good-bye to Graham, the very first to leave home. How sorry Father must have felt as he hated any of us to be away from home at any time. He liked to think of us all in his charge but now Graham was to be away for three years. He went off to Egypt where he boxed for the battalion and made a name for himself, finally becoming a physical training instructor.

Wet days indoors meant playing at something quietly. This didn't mean being inactive; there was the dining room table to be tipped on its side for libraries. The wide side piece was used to stack the books on and the edge of the table top projected far enough to keep the books from slipping off. We stood on chairs to see over the top for now the side was the top and the width of the table, was the height. Writing out names of Father's books, cutting up paper tickets and climbing up and down to change books for our customers, books which were up aloft on the table side, occupied us for quite a while until it was time to put them all back in the bookcase when arguments began, and we were sent off to play elsewhere.

There was always the conservatory to play in which was ideal for 'shops' when a missing window pane became handy for serving groceries through. Standing on stools we passed the goods to the customers via the space where the glass should have been. Packets of Persil, cartons of Lifebuoy soap, Dolly Dips, Reckitts's Blue, Robin starch, caustic soda, Vim, porridge oats, all packaged and new, together with pot menders, clothes pegs, tins of all sorts – Vaseline, pilchards, salmon, sardines, golden syrup and condensed milk plus boxes of long macaroni and tea, which had all been dragged out of the cupboard below the kitchen dresser and stacked on the ledges beneath the windows of the conservatory.

It sounds as if we were stocked up for a siege, but the truth was that the food was gone in days and needed a purseful of money to replenish it, which Mamma seldom had. But she was an excellent manager and made a 'muckle out of a mickle'.

How lovely all the fresh packets smelled. We were fascinated by the newness of everything; all unopened, new from the shop. There were no baked beans, crisps or corn flakes as the first two had not been invented and the third was only just about to cross the Atlantic. Mamma didn't mind us playing with all the packets and tins, as she put it, "I know it cannot hurt, and it keeps them all quiet and busy."

The mountain of supplies which shrank so rapidly as the week progressed, was restored by the next avalanche of goods brought home in the kit-bag, baskets and pram. Then Mamma checked the list against the goods. Out came the avoirdupois, the heavy scales; chops bacon, tomatoes or anything that Mamma suspected may be short of weight due to shop-keepers' previous peccadilloes, was checked together with the prices; every farthing had to be accurate, or back we were sent to the shop for it to be put right, before we could go out to play.

Now, playing at shops, we had a good idea of the worth of everything, not in price alone, but as a family commodity and respected it all accordingly.

Busy at the sink, Mamma helped us with the prices, patiently answering a multitude of questions and steering us through any hiccups in the proceedings, until lunch was ready and we put everything back into the cupboard.

We loved 'dressing up' and Father often persuaded us to sing or recite the things learnt at school. On Empire Day, the Juniors performed various national dances. Four of us were taught the Highland Fling. Dressed up in a kilt, white socks and black slippers, I enjoyed performing this energetic dance. At home Father was delighted to watch as I skipped about the room in this Scottish dance. At parties and at Christmas it was, "Come on Doll – heel toe, toe heel," from Father.

I didn't need much persuasion, I loved it. I had no kilt, but in my black gym knickers and stockings, topped by Emaly Brown's blouse, my prince's blouse, I flung myself into the routine of the dance, whilst Father clapped a fast rhythm.

It always struck me as strange to be called 'Doll'. Firstly as the family called me 'tom boy' and Mamma called me 'Gyppo', and secondly because I almost never was given a doll. I didn't complain as I supposed I was expected to be a tom boy and it meant I did not get involved with quarrels over dolls as my sisters sometimes did. But when, one Christmas I was given two identical small attache cases, I felt aggrieved. But deciding to be like the Stoics I said nothing.

The two top classes in the Juniors were in a shared room. A partition divided the two lots of desks but the folding door was never used. The two teachers, both very easy-going, had no problems.

First I was in Miss Knight's class. She had light brown hair. It was curly and wavy and there were always stray wisps over her forehead, which she was continually brushing away, so that the front of her hair became covered with chalk. She was so easy-going that we tormented her. One day she lost patience with me. I was called out to be hit with the wooden pointer. I held out my hand for Miss Knight to carry out my punishment, but I began to laugh. This set Miss Knight off laughing as well. Soon all the class joined in. I dropped my hand and was sent back to my seat without being punished. There, appreciating the humanity of my teacher, I behaved myself.

It was not long before I was in the other class on the other side of the room, with Miss Lilian Jackson.

Miss Lilian Jackson became a milestone in my life. From her I learnt that patience and kindness and encouragement are the greatest educators and nothing else can compare. I might say she changed the course of my life.

She was young and slim with the short, neat black hair curved round her cheek bones in the manner of the twenties. She was understanding, matter of fact, and completely calm, so that I did all the things, she wanted us to do and did them well. Now I took pride in working well for Miss Jackson. There was no need to play about to make the children laugh. The lessons became fun as round and round the two classes we went, trying to win the spelling 'bee'. When either Miss Knight or Miss Jackson, gave me the prize for winning, I ran home with it with great pride. It was a tattered old book without a cover, but it was full of wonderful stories, *Uncle Arthur's Bedtime Stories*. I can recall the thrill with which I took it from one of those two teachers as a reward for being the last survivor in the spelling 'bee'.

That year I came top of the class and was presented with a dictionary by the silver-haired Miss Mowbray.

All too soon it was scholarship time. Mamma went to see Miss Mowbray. I stood there with Mamma and listened.

"I am afraid it will be a waste of time to put her with the scholarship group," she told Mamma. The scholarship group had done extra maths.

I was shocked. I couldn't believe my ears. Out in the playground I related what had happened to my gang who had been waiting to hear all about it as none of them were going to enter. Our gang was called 'The Black Death'. They stood around me loyally, like the warriors in Finn's Band.

"You go and show her," they exhorted.

"What a cheek," declared Audrey, whose other name I forget, standing there, freckled and pigtailed, her back always so straight even when she skipped. "You pass and show her." The others, in a small tight bunch around me, echoed her words, urging me to go in for it, saying they knew I could pass and to do it just to 'show them'. I looked at these small girls, mostly bigger than I was, and felt strong and inspired like Finn on his Council Stone, and made up my mind to do just that, to try to pass the scholarship. Even Gracie Boyle who I remember as a bit of a ruffian and banged my head against the wall because she wasn't in the gang, agreed with them all and urged me to 'show them'. I resolved I would try to pass and 'show' all my friends.

The day of the scholarship tests came. I went into the room at a strange school like a gladiator, anxious and worried, knowing that I was not expected to emerge victorious, but determined to do so.

The first exam was Dictation. Soon I was a sentence behind. I felt agitated – I could no longer keep up. Suddenly I heard a voice in the next room. It was saying exactly the same as the man in our room – but it was one sentence behind. Clutching at the sentence I wrote it down but the man in our room was now once again, one sentence ahead. Then I heard the missing sentence coming faintly through the wall. Closing my ears against our examiner, I kept pace until the end with the unseen voice echoing his words. Writing as quickly as I could I wrote down the echo and managed to complete the extract in time for it to be collected with those from my room.

We now had 'Composition'. I read the choice of titles. Only the 'Parrot' appealed to me as I felt that a parrot could have many adventures. With all the books I had read that mostly belonged to my brothers, there had been a great deal about crooks, robbers and thieves. I found myself writing a story about a parrot who terrified a burglar so that he was caught. It meant writing and writing as fast as possible to try to finish in time, like the Dictation.

After 'play' we had the Arithmetic paper which was very difficult as I had no idea how to set about the problems. Only children chosen to sit the scholarship, had been set this work at school. It was all entirely strange to me and I could do only the sums which were straight forward but none of the problems. There may have been a fourth paper but I cannot recall it.

At the top of every sheet we wrote our names and it was stressed that the names written must be correct. This posed a problem.

Each time one of 'Us' was about to be born, Father occupied himself in the final stages of the waiting, with our 'birthday book'. Into this he wrote the string of names he had finally chosen for the next boy or girl about to appear on the family scene. On my birthday he had written, Kathleen, Dorothy, Mildred, the last being, as Mamma later informed me when I voiced my dislike, the name of a prominent figure in the First World War.

Father never attended christenings, being anti-religion, and I emerged from mine with Dorothy Kathleen Mildred, duly written on my birth certificate. However, as most young children were never allowed to see legal documents, I never saw Dorothy entered as my first 'given' name and assumed that Dorothy and Doll at home were just preferred. Together with my brothers and sisters, I read the 'birthday book' with its verses and quotations and our names, many times so that it was registered in my mind that my correct name was Kathleen (called Dorothy).

Now at the first important step in my life, I looked at the official sheet of paper on which I was scribbling, writing against time, the clock on the wall being all-important, and crossed out the Dorothy and wrote Kathleen. Agitated, I forgot each time I started a new sheet of paper and had to alter my name to Kathleen.

The day came at school when Miss Mobray read out the names of all those who had been successful candidates. One by one we stood up from where we sat, on the floor of the big hall. One by one she checked over the names and and each in turn sat down. Finally I only, was left standing.

"And where is Kathleen Parker?" demanded Miss Mowbray. I put up my hand, feeling that I must be invisible to Miss Mowbray.

"Oh no!", declared the headmistress, "you are Dorothy Parker."

I tried to explain, standing alone like a shipwreck in a sea of classes, seated cross-legged closely over the floor. I tried to explain to the whole school listening with upturned faces, about the 'birthday book'.

Miss Mowbray listened in apparent disbelief springing from her lack of faith in my ability to pass the scholarship. At last she waved me to sit down.

Then she went through the list of names of those who had done well enough to go to the Grammar School. Once more we went through the business of being called to stand and once more Dorothy Parker stood up in place of Kathleen Parker. Miss Mowbray said nothing more but neither did she smile or look pleased as she had for the others.

Later when I left the Grammar School as Kathleen Parker, I went through the same rigmarole in reverse. Now we discovered that the elusive birth certificate declared that Mamma had christened me Dorothy Kathleen but that all my certificates were for Kathleen Dorothy. I had to sign documents stating which name I was going to use and give specimen signatures to reinforce my identity. After six years of writing Kathleen Dorothy I stuck to that but it has caused many problems with passports and official documents and I found I was using first one name and then the other and my friends came in two lots, the Dorothys from home and the Kathleens from school and each declared that I looked nothing like the other name when they heard it as they did not associate with me. As for Father, he disassociated himself from it all and stated that I chose to call myself Kathleen on the day of the scholarship.

Leaving the Juniors and going to Grammar School was the end of an era. At first I continued to live in a world of phantasy and adventure but gradually the magic of the Juniors melted away and a new life took over. Romance and imagination were pushed into the background by the pressures of homework and sports – gymnastics, swimming and team games, tennis and competitions, and the 'Black Death' was replaced by a new gang of friends, the 'Secret Seven', with its own magazine.

Chapter Five

Meal Times

As the family expanded, the dining room table had to be expanded too. Father fixed a leaf at the end by the French doors, which could be raised and lowered as needed. This was the end where Father sat at the head of the table. We each had our own place. I always sat next to Father on his right.

When Mamma announced the meal to be ready, Father sent one of us to call everybody in to take their places. We all trouped into the dining room as hungry as hunters, and scrambled around and over the chairs to sit down in our places.

Out in the kitchen, Father and Mamma were waiting at the long wooden kitchen table, to 'dish up' our dinners and serve them through the serving hatch.

When all scrambling about was at an end and all were seated, the serving would begin. Usually Roy, the eldest, treated deferentially by Father and so by us all, was served first and then the two or three youngest. Next to be served were those who went to work and then the next younger ones, and so, in this way, the middle of the family came last.

Father dominated the scene as he carved the meat upon the long table which ran almost the length of the kitchen, whilst Mamma 'dished up' the vegetables. As each plate was filled it was passed through the hatch by Father with, "That's Ron's," or "Pass that to Evelyn" or, "Whose was the dinner I just served?"

Whilst we awaited our food, the boys, Gilbert, Graham, Ralph and Stanley, hungry and impatient, would start to rock the long stool which they all shared. It was against the wall just beneath the serving hatch, so that Father could not see the four eldest boys who were closest to him. But eventually, when a large hole in the wall suddenly appeared, Father saw to it that their rocking came to an end.

As the plates were filled and passed through the hatchway, Father kept a check on who was to be served next, keeping a balance between the younger and the older. Constantly peering through into the dining room, he assured himself that plates were passed to whom directed; that our conduct was exactly as it should be; and noted who was still to be served. At last he stayed, framed by the hatchway gripping the carving knife and fork in mid air as he demanded like a Rembrandt portrait come to life,

"Is there anyone without their dinner?"

Being number seven had its drawbacks and meal times was one of them. Often, in answer to Father's, "Is anyone still waiting to be served?" I had to call back, "Me."

"Me. Me," echoed Father. "Who is me?"

Full of fury that I had been forgotten again I could hardly bring myself to utter, "Dorothy" as I struggled with my injured feelings. But Father rode roughshod over all this. Always inclined to put you in the wrong he had the last word.

"Why didn't you say so?" he demanded facetiously, as though that would have made the slightest difference to being forgotten.

At last both our parents joined us all at the table, where, after he had cast an eye over us to make sure no-one had, we were given permission to start eating. Father, being agnostic, discouraged 'Grace'. Any complaint about not wanting some portion of food was bulldozed into silence as Father insisted we ate everything.

Sitting next to Father was a great trial to me as I hated any fat. If I left a piece I had to sit at the table until it was gone. If Phyllis had a chance she ate it for me. Known as 'Skinny Liz' to the boys, Phyllis was indeed thin and pernickerty about food, but she loved fat. Whenever we had a chance we swapped our fat and lean meat, but for some strange reason to do with self discipline, Father would not allow this. On school days, when Father was not there, we swapped our fat and lean as the rest chorussed between mouthfuls, "Jack Spratt could eat no fat, his wife could eat no lean, And so betwixt the two of them, they licked their platters clean".

When all thirteen of us were sitting around the table at week-ends it was difficult to impossible to leave one's place at the table during the meal, and we were given permission to do so only if it was urgent. From my seat next to Father at the head of the table by the French doors, it was a terrible job to 'get down'. After Father had reluctantly granted permission, the only way to leave was by crawling underneath. Getting below the table was only the start of a tricky foot and leg, the latter both wooden and human, obstacle course.

In the gloom beneath the table there was a forest of knees, legs, boots and shoes. I manoeuvred this way and that trying to find an opening to get out, like a dog trapped in a rabbit warren. No doubt some of the feet were being made deliberately obstructive so that I felt booby-trapped by boots and shoes, their owners enjoying the fun going on unseen by Father as I tried to push between legs and chairs. Grumbles arose.

"Be careful. I can't move *my* chair."

"Trust Dorothy; go somewhere else."

And Father becoming irritated by the remarks and the length of time I had been out of sight would add severely, "Be quick. What are you doing under there? Why aren't you out yet? Why didn't you think of it before you came to the dining table?"

Emerging from beneath the other end of the draped table cloth clothed in unanimous disgrace, I beat a hasty retreat to the toilet.

In the short time that I was away, the family had perhaps started their second course. I seemed to have become even more unpopular. Obstructions seemed to have multiplied. Grumbles resumed.

"Can't you get in somewhere else?"

"Do you mind, I am trying to eat."

"You are a nuisance."

And as Father became furious at my complaint that,

"I can't get in under the table," I was told in Father's Billingsgate bark, "Go back the same way that you got out!"

I was blamed for jogged elbows, spilt food and Father's bad humour, and finally, with the help of a shoe and a gentle push here and there, in the twilight zone beneath the long table cloth, I finally climbed back onto my chair and once more in place at Father's right hand side. I was lectured at length on thoughtlessness, as, under his eagle eye I hastened to catch up on my meal, dreading the encounter with any piece of fat. That journey under the table, was not repeated often I must say.

I clearly remember undergoing this obstacle course of twenty two legs, four table legs, twenty two feet, thirteen chairs packed closely together, one of them a high-chair which was wedged as close to the table as possible, near Mamma; knees and shins, trousers, boots and shoes all tightly close together in a fortress below the table, whilst above, the owners, unseen, were busily engaged in battle, with their knives and forks. All noisily in combat with hunger. It was this battle that sharpened their resentment with my interruptions and resulted in the battle below.

Although Father's wishes were treated with a respect that was positively daunting and discipline accompanied all meals with Father, he didn't always quell us completely. Joyce loved greens and celery. Father encouraged us to dip our celery into syrup as he had a very 'sweet tooth' and regarded sugar as a necessary form of energy. Joyce would ask, "Is there any more celery?" when she meant lettuce. And when she wanted more celery she called it lettuce. This so exasperated Father that one day he started to use his Billingsgate voice to shout:

"Remember, lettuce leaves and celery sticks! Lettuce leaves and celery sticks! Lettuce leaves and celery sticks!" Then he paused to reprimand another of us to hold our knife correctly and resumed his shouting:

"Lettuce sticks and celery leaves," he boomed. "Lettuce sticks and celery leaves! Lettuce sticks and celery leaves!"

We tried hard not to laugh. First one of us girls and then another started to giggle. The boys were more cautious.

"Go and stand in the corner," shouted Father, sending first one and then another of us. Soon all four corners had giggling girls facing the wall. Father had no idea what we all found so amusing and as he always did all the talking, we all kept quiet. If we didn't we were in for long lectures and it was simpler to be like Mamma and let him think we were all in agreement with him and not 'tempt providence' as Mamma put it.

One day at dinner, somebody thoughtlessly asked:

"Mamma. What does G.R. stand for on the serviettes?"

There was a shocked silence. Knowing how much Mamma had loved Raggazone, whose monogrammed serviettes these had been, and how much Father resented the thought, I quickly answered,

"George Robey, of course," and everybody laughed and no more was said.

In those days before television dominated households, people sat down together at the table. We always sat down to 'proper' meals with the table set out correctly. White table cloths with linen table napkins washed and starched by Mamma for the older ones and Father, were the order of the day. There were no snacks before meals; crisps had not been invented and sweets were not allowed before meals. We were expected to come to the table with a good appetite, and we did.

In these hard times all through the 1920s, Mamma's skill in managing and cooking, triumphed over shortages. We had every vegetable; artichokes, swedes, turnips, broccoli, curly kale, and with potatoes served in every way imaginable. There were rich soups from the stock pot which accommodated marrow bones, sawn-up aitch bones, bony chops and chicken carcasses and anything in which there was goodness which could be rendered into soup. Using the large stock pot extract, Mamma was able to conjure up rich soups, adding pulped tomatoes, lentils, peas, pearl barley or chopped vegetables, and make rich sauces for pies.

One night in bed, we were all awakened by the sound of Father's deep voice intoning between a frightful hissing noise he was making. Then we heard him banging his bedroom door to and fro as he hissed. Burglars, we decided, had broken in and Father was trying to scare them away. We knew better than to stir out of bed to enquire but were all agog next morning as to the cause of the middle of the night commotion. During the previous evening, Mamma had set on the iron stove, a saucepan full of marrow bones to simmer. It was forgotten and was left on the stove still simmering. By two o'clock in the morning, it had boiled dry and was soon emitting thick black smoke. In the middle of the night, Father awoke and rushed downstairs to find out where all the smoke was coming from. He threw the completely burnt-out saucepan into the garden and then opening all the doors and windows, returned upstairs where we heard him banging his bedroom door to and fro and making a loud hissing noise as he tried to blow the smoke out of his lungs and out of his bedroom.

As Father did not encourage us to be religious, we never said 'Grace' when he was there, and gradually Mamma stopped keeping it up. When Father was not there eating with us, a quite different sort of discipline was in force. Mamma, quiet, watchful, calm and patient, heard all about our likes and dislikes, which she knew as well as we did ourselves, wisely steering us all this way and that through the meal. Ron would say:

"I don't want any dinner today, can I have extra dumplings instead?"

After a plateful of seven or eight dumplings, Ron who was very quiet spoke up again.

"I think I could eat my dinner now."

After this had happened once or twice, we all urged Mamma not to let him have a plateful of dumplings first. As he was the youngest boy, born long after all the other boys, Mamma was inclined to spoil him. But he was not the only one who took advantage of Father's absence during a meal, as I knew full well the relief at having Phyllis to eat my fat meat for me.

Poor Joyce sat next to Roy with his aristocratic ways which was unfortunate for her. Roy, was normally very quiet but could become so exasperated over trifles, that he almost exploded. One day, hearing lettuce referred to as celery and celery as lettuce, he began to fidget with annoyance. Joyce, as I have said before, also loved sprouts and greens which were in dishes on the table. Roy, as the eldest, rather fancied himself as deputy Father on occasions. At some time during this meal, feeling irritable, he anticipated Joyce's request for another helping and shouted out, making us all jump,

"ANY MORE GREENS?" before Joyce could open her mouth. We all stared at reserved Roy in great surprise much to his discomfort.

All through the meal we were busy enjoying our food asking for this and that to be passed along the table to us. Roy was at the opposite end of the table to where I sat. The table was very long. Roy did his share of passing condiments and dishes for a while then suddenly he lost all patience and self control.

"This is the FEAST OF THE PASSOVER," he yelled, banging the mint sauce down in front of somebody half the length of the table away. He could do this as he was six feet or more tall and had very long arms and legs which earned him the name of 'Sticks', which I appreciated only when I saw him playing cricket one day; his long white-trousered legs streaking along the crease, devouring it in a few strides.

At midday lunch when Father was not there, Mamma spiced our meals with her country sayings. To quieten our chatter so that we would eat our food in time to return to school, she declared:

"Every time a sheep baas it loses a bite," to be repeated urgently as the clock hands crept round nearing the time when we would hear the school bell ringing. We didn't like being compared with sheep and were quiet for a while until an argument began. Arguments were unheard of in Father's presence. Appealing to Mamma for support we were sprinkled with well known phrases from Mamma's stock-pot of wisdom.

"It's six of one and half a dozen of the other," was a standard remark when we appealed for her to support us against the boys. But when we protested that the boys had said this or that she lost patience and uttered her judgement which filled us with chagrin.

"I'd rather have twenty boys any day than one girl." How we hated to hear that. It soon stopped our tales. Then the boys feeling 'cock-a-hoop' as Mamma put it, said something to annoy us and Mamma declared:

"I'd rather have twenty girls than one boy, any day."

Then we were all putting on our hats and coats to hurry back to school two streets away, and pulling faces at the boys to get our own back. The school bell measured out the seconds as we continued to argue as to whether Mamma's final remarks had been in the favour of the boys or the girls. Then we ran out of the house and along the road, a long straggly crocodile of all the Parker children currently at school; the longest legged ones right away in front and the smallest, like me, running too, searching the pavement for pitfalls, running to reach the playground before the bell ceased to call us, feeling very full and dreading to find an empty playground.

The table in the front room was Edwardian, an oval veneered with walnut. It could be tipped up to stand vertically on its four, heavy, carved legs and clawed feet radiating beneath a pedestal. We often sat underneath the table on the carved knees of the legs and played or read. This table was for special occasions and for guests; for us to sit at times for Sunday dinner; for Mahjong and Whist parties; for meals at Christmas and to hold the large punch bowl when the table was put into the hall.

How we hated going to bed when Father and Mamma were entertaining. Lying in bed, especially in the Summer, we could hear laughter and chatter, the sounds of doors opening and shutting and food being carried through the hall from the kitchen.

First one and then another would creep out of bed and part way down the stairs to peep between the bannisters to see it all. Soon, as our numbers on the staircase increased, we were spotted.

"Go back to bed at once," we were admonished, and feeling very left out we crept back to bed to play at story telling, or continued the 'Bare Family' saga until we fell asleep.

Of course there were those among us who, to use today's parlance, pushed their luck. Finding that Father was in a good humour they disobeyed and begging to be allowed to stay up for 'just a little while', succeeded, and Father, busy entertaining his friends could hardly be cross with them with visitors there. Then Mamma came and whispered to me to go to bed with the younger ones saying:

"Do go to bed with them, Doll, just to please me, there's a good girl." And feeling full of disappointment that Olive, younger than I, should stay up with Phyllis who was always determined to have her own way, I went to bed with the young ones to please Mamma, knowing she was worried by the children and further worried with the guests there.

Whenever we sat around the oval front room table we felt duly impressed, whether it was Sunday or any other time. Although much smaller than the dining room table, we fitted around it quite well. Nobody complained about elbow room and anyway, we behaved well with Father there, which he always was on these special occasions. We all sat there in the front room, surrounded by antiques for which we had a great respect inculcated in us by both our parents, and the fact that we spent a lot of time dusting them all.

We were always ravenous by the time midday dinner was served on Sundays, and had developed enormous appetites. Father loved nothing better than to know that we were all hungry as he liked to pile up our plates and see us eat everything. As he passed the dinners out he would ask:

"Is that enough. Do you think you could eat some more of this?" or that, pointing at it with the carving fork.

Unable to press us to more than a huge plate full of everything, he would relinquish his hold on the plate with,

"There's plenty more. Come back if you have room?"

Mamma's pie dishes were the largest I have ever seen in a house. Although Mamma had only Mrs. Beeton's cookery book which she said was for those with a fortune to spend on food, she never used it as she had no need; she carried all her knowledge of cooking, in her head. She seldom weighed anything; it was all guesswork she told us. But it was more than that. It was the ways of Emaly Brown, born and bred in the country in the days when folks used the countryside resources; when the collecting of the bullace, the blueberries, the crab apples and black-berries, dandelions and elderberries, nettles and herbs, to make into pies and preserves, wines and herbal teas, medicines and ointments, was the accepted practice. These were the long days when there was plenty of time for Chapel three times on a Sunday, and visiting needy folk a matter of custom.

Mamma baked twice weekly to fill the larder, from the old iron kitchen range with the shiny black-leaded top with the kettle sitting there, singing away, before the pipes became furred up and we had the black iron electric cooker. Putting things away in the pantry which was our term for the Larder, often needed Mamma's help as it was usually almost full already. A mouse would sometimes be suspected to have taken up residence or had been seen to scuttle away behind a bottle of wine, or the huge bread crock. Great excitement would follow. Everything was dragged out onto the kitchen floor. The huge bread crock was too heavy to lift, so its contents were removed and it was left there to be hunted around. Open-topped like a giant's bowl, no wonder mice came in to have a nibble at a fresh crusty loaf.

The things to be dragged out seemed interminable and still no sign of the mouse. By now, the cat had been found and shut in the kitchen among the turmoil. But cats are remarkably detached creatures and refuse to be dragged into a scene not of their own choosing. They are independent actors doing what they want to do when it suits them. When we went into the room to see what progress had been made by the cat in the capture, the cat darted out in a flash and disappeared. Yet the same vanishing cat brought dead mice in and left them repulsively dead in the most awkward spots under our feet, with a nonchalance showing equal disdain for both humans and mice.

After the abortive mouse hunt all the things had to be replaced in the pantry, all very boring now with no mouse there. For days afterwards we were examining food to see if the mouse had returned as Mamma could not bear the thought of a mouse among the food. But those mice were wily and kept away for a long period until we had forgotten, when the whole schemozzle started all over again as soon as evidence of their presence was suspected.

Mamma used the huge bread crock to brew her wines. I can't remember where the bread was put at these times. Perhaps we had another one. As Mamma examined the contents to see if it were still working we hung around to look over the top. Pieces of bread floated about on the top among a thick crusty scum, frothing at the edges. If Mamma thought it needed a boost she threw in a handful of sugar or raisins to accelerate the process. We watched the yeasty mixture with abhorrence as we didn't like the smell. Mamma's wines were sparkling, clear and varied. People refused to believe that they were made from rhubarb, parsnips, beetroot, plums, dandelions or anything else that was in berry or in season and edible.

Refrigerators and freezers were not yet on the map for ordinary people and only butchers, fishmongers and ice-cream merchants were identified with ice. Instead, baking and preserving were the order of the day and Mamma did a great deal of both. In the country as a girl, she and her brothers had gathered the blackberries and cranberries, bullace and blueberries, sloes and damsons, crabapples and quinces, nettles and elderberries, for her own mother to make into jellies and preserves and wines. Now, on the London outskirts, she did the same for us, using what ever there was to hand and sending us to collect blackberries when there were any.

"You live like Lords and Ladies and eat like fighting cocks," she declared.

Truly enough, Cornish pasties, jam tarts, rice puddings, shepherd's pie, with pies of rhubarb, apple, gooseberry, plum, puddings of every description and cakes large and small, were all eaten in succession to be replaced at the next baking. Appearing and disappearing at half-weekly intervals, nothing was wasted and 'never went begging' as Mamma put it. Into the big steamer went the steak and kidney pudding, like a large football wrapped in a cloth the four corners knotted over the top, and how delicious it smelled when it came out. We stood around watching as Mamma hooked out the pudding, with the aid of two large carving forks, on to a large meat dish, where the boiling hot lump, round and steaming was lowered. Then peering through the steam, she pulled the knots apart with the prongs of the forks. The cloth was peeled back and the knife went into the gleaming, shiny, dumpling crust showing the rich contents, and the steam gave off a wonderful smell of steak and kidney. Then a gravy from the stockpot, thickened and brown, was poured in to the top and we were sent to sit at our places by Mamma if this were a school day lunch and Father was not there. Otherwise we would have all been regimented long before at the table, by Father. Wedges of pudding with ladles of meat and gravy were served, supplemented by sprouts and potatoes. There never were puddings to surpass Mamma's and it was no wonder we ran to school after mid-day meals, filled to the brim.

Visiting friends calling at meal times were welcomed in by Father as warmly as the stray dogs he fetched in for snacks. He quickly squashed us closer together around the table to make space for another chair. With the large amount of food which had to be prepared each day, another helping for the unexpected could always be found. Father did not believe in standing on ceremony, either they were hungry or they were not, and if the caller liked to be, he or she was a welcome guest. If two or three called at the same time, at Christmas for example, then a small bamboo table was set up near us all. There they were plied with fare until they declared they were 'full and had no more room'.

On any special occasion, when everyone had finished eating, Father brought out the port decanter and the cigars. He always kept both, but only if the visitors were sufficiently important did Father take them into the front room to join him in a drink and a cigar, whilst we were enjoined to "Stay where you are and help Mamma."

We all set to and helped clear the plates and table, passing everything, a large pile of cutlery, glasses and dishes, through the hatchway back into the kitchen. Then a conference ensued as to whose turn it was to wash and whose to dry the dishes. We usually knew whose turn it was and set to with little argument. As my turn came round in these young days I found it all very challenging. The knives and forks I saw as wounded soldiers who could live and survive their injuries, only if they were put with great haste back into the cutlery box. Sometimes this could be speeded up by giving them only seconds to live and I counted the time out under my breath.

As I grew older I took over the laying of the table which had to be done properly with the serving spoons in pairs across the corners and all the spoons, knives and forks facing in the right directions correctly about the set places. I enjoyed setting the glasses, and serviettes in their respective rings, for those who were important and old enough to use them, and took a pride in the table with cruets and water jugs before everybody sat down. But the best part about it was, that once I took over this job as mine, I was exempt from the washing and drying up.

There were some callers who must have had a terrible opinion of Father. These were the tradesmen. Woe betide any of them who called at meal times. Mamma was not allowed to answer the door. One of us was sent to 'see who it is'. Inevitably they asked for Mamma. As soon as we called to Mamma, it was like a red rag to a bull and Father shouted out as though he were still in Billingsgate,

"Tell them to go AWAY," adding in an even louder voice, if that were possible, "THIS IS OUR MEAL

TIME. Tell them to go away and come back at the proper time."

If Mamma got up from her place and went to the front door to deal with the greengrocer, insurance man, baker, or whoever it was, Father would shout out in a rage.

"CLARISS, come and sit down. They have no right to call at this time. Tell them to go away," and so on. Father had no intention of leaving the meal table for anybody and his temper and voice rose as the seconds passed by. Mamma never said a word in reply and dealt with the situation as though Father were not there. This was a demonstration of Mamma's 'if one is fire, the other has to be water', philosophy in action. It worked, for when she calmly resumed her place at the table, Father gradually subsided knowing that all his rantings had been in vain, and the same tradesman did exactly the same the following week. Father was noisier than any guard dog. Indeed Mamma always said, "Take no notice; his bark is worse than his bite."

If we had lived off the small packets of instant food, crisps and yoghurts that one sees filling shelves in the supermarkets today, I doubt if we would have been able to trudge about for miles all day long, as we did during the summer holidays, fishing, climbing and exploring. I think we young children would all have starved during the hours spent in our activities.

Returning from swimming or a day in Wanstead Park, or multiple ferry trips across the Thames at Woolwich to meander about in Abbey Woods, or a day with a sack dragging for 'tiddlers', we entered the house with cries of:

"Hello Mamma, we're starving!"

Mamma's answer was always:

"Eat then, there's plenty of food."

And if one of us on a school outing, had missed their dinner, it would be in the oven, kept warm and ready for our return, waiting to be devoured.

Twice weekly Mamma baked to restock the larder with supplies of tarts, cakes, sausage rolls, bread puddings, pies and equivalent dishes, enough to last until the next bake. Her pork pies with cold water pastry for the older ones to take to work for lunch, were better than any bought in shops. As she rolled the pastry on the large pastry board, we stood and watched, our eyes level with her elbows. At these times Mamma talked to us of her regret at not being able to visit her mother before she died soon after I was born, there being so many of us with me being the seventh and no money for fares to Lower Beeding. Reminiscing, Mamma was once more back there, helping her own mother in the cottage kitchen. There in the cottage in Plum Lane, she relived her meeting with the handsome Italian, when her brother Frank brought him home and Raggazone was invited to stay for the week-end. Cutting out the caps for the pies and sealing their edges with the floury fork, nostalgia gripped her as she extolled the many virtues of Emaly Brown. And as we waited to put the currant eyes, noses and mouths on our little gingerbread men, we watched and listened.

We heard all about the never seen by us, beloved Emaly. What a wonderful cook she was; how clever with her needle always doing everything perfectly; how the villagers loved her and relied upon her in their illnesses and to bring their babies into the world. Telling us how her mother was a true Christian in thought, word and deed, relieved Mamma's yearnings for loved ones lost. At baking times, standing at her elbow, we shared with her those days of love and joy with her family in Chapel House, the aptly named cottage, absorbing the gifts of the spirit that had been bestowed upon her by her mother.

Those halcyon days of meals together in the dining room, when steaming plates of home cooking were passed through the hatchway by Father, and circulated around; of battles under the table to 'leave the room'; of the excitement of trouping into the front room with special company and special food, only to be banished early to bed, flitted by as had Mamma's own childhood days. The days seemed long in the kitchen at Mamma's side as she peeled and prepared, cooked and baked and told us the every day stories of the country folk and of our unseen grandmother, Emaly Brown.

And so the rich pattern of Life was woven thread by thread. The unseen Potter's wheel spun and shaped us slowly and surely into the young men and women we were to become.

Chapter Six

Saturdays

Our parents were both extremely capable and well-organised, so the daily events and 'trivial round of common tasks' were an established order of things that we all complied with and were part of. Mamma was an excellent housewife and Father a good organiser and strict with it. He was the captain of the ship and gave all the commands, whilst Mamma was the figurehead who inspired us, leading us all in the right direction.

Almost everything that could be part of our daily routine, was planned by Father into a working system. In the early post-war years, when he was not in regular employment, his everlasting vitality was directed into the organisation of the household tasks. A system of 'jobs' for everyone of his children, except the baby, was worked out and we all had to get on with them, co-operatively and separately according to the task. There on the floor the small ones sat; a pile of newspaper oblongs in front of us to be folded into spills. Paper rectangles about seven inches long and four inches wide, had been cut by one of the boys. Then two or three of us had to fold them lengthwise, into spills.

I well remember my first efforts. I was given a large brass shell case to put the spills into. The shell case usually stood on the end of the mantle shelf with its partner at the other end. My folded spills soon unwrapped themselves but I pushed them into the shell case where they became a bundle of screwed up paper. Father tipped them all out on to the carpet where one of the boys had to refold them.

This small task was one that had to be continually done as we used lots of spills to save matches. A spill was lighted from the fire or kitchen stove and used to light the oil lamps, the gas mantles when we had gas, or Father's Woodbines.

Folding spills for Father, and collecting small twigs for the kitchen range with Mamma, early in the mornings, were the first tasks I remember doing.

We all had various jobs given to us every Saturday. Nothing was specific; Father decided who was going to do what. Sometimes two of us had to clean the silver which we hated as it made our hands black; others had to shine the knives with the powder from the bath brick, which had to be scraped first to collect a pile of brick dust. This was then picked up on a damp cloth and rubbed on the knife blades until all stains disappeared and the knives shone. Three or four of us scrubbed the inlaid linoleum which covered the dining room floor. We all enjoyed this. Kneeling on a mat beside a bowl of warm water we went about it in our various ways.

We each had a section to clean. Sitting back on our heels, a patch close by was chosen and warm water squeezed over it from the cloth in the bowl. A large bar of Sunlight soap was rubbed over the scrubbing brush which took both of our hands to hold. This was scrubbed vigorously round and round all over the wet patch until a rich soapy lather covered all the light and dark green and cream-coloured squares, swallowing the dirt. Now pictures and patterns could be made in the soap with the fingers until the lather began to disperse. Then it was time to squeeze out the cloth once more, and wipe off the soap and admire the intertwining pattern staring up, clean and gleaming. Even now a corner of the brush could trace a picture on the wet surface, but the grimy areas adjacent claimed attention and the only question was where to select the next patch. Meanwhile two or three others were doing likewise, and we sat back on our heels at intervals (much as the Romans must have done when laying one of those patterns of mosaic tiles,) to compare our progress and results. At last we all met up, the floor was totally cleaned and we tip-toed about placing down sheets of newspaper to preserve our efforts and help dry the floor.

In this way the dining room floor was given a good going over once a week with four of us scrubbing a quarter of it each, travelling around on our mats under the table, on which all the chairs had been stacked, and into all the corners and enjoying the fun of it all.

There were many jobs to be done on Saturday mornings, and whilst Father was home, unemployed, they became ordered and he had us all working in top gear. Most of these jobs were regular ones that had to be done every week. The front path had to be scrubbed. It was all white and black tiles about six inches square like a chequer board, and both the front door step and the step by the gate had to be scrubbed and whitened. The near-by coal lid would be black-leaded so that it came up shiny and smart. The pattern and the words of the maker standing out more clearly with each stroke of the black-lead brush.

We must have consumed a great deal of salt for, every week, it seemed, there was a block of salt to be shaved with a knife and crushed with a rolling pin, and put into jars. The block, the same size as the bath brick, was placed on a large sheet of paper, and the edge scraped and crumbled. This was an easy job which nobody disliked.

As none of us liked cleaning the brass which made our hands black as the silver did, it was shared out between us. There was the door knocker and the letter box to be blue-belled and polished. The large shell cases with the scallopped rims, which needed plenty of 'elbow grease' to bring out the fine engraving curling around the sides saying 'The Great War – 1914–1918'. The large brass fire irons in the front room and the heavy fender, were cleaned and polished weekly; but Mamma possessed very little brass as she said it took too much time to clean. The black-leading of the grates and the kitchen range, were done by Mamma, all shiny and fires lit, by the time the family were up in the morning.

The dusting in the front room was the most tedious chore. There were so many antiques there. So many things were perched on the tall, black chiffonier, that it took ages to move them all one by one, dust them and replace them carefully on their own spots. There were so many curved, carved shelves to be dusted; so many ornaments; Japanese vases, intricate porcelain candelabra; bronze cast horses with horsemen straining on their bridles; curling snake candlesticks and a thousand and one things, all perched in position. So together with Father's red, cut-glass decanters it took ages to lift them all, dust them and operate the Japanese trick boxes, which we always did as soon as we learned how.

When at last all ornaments and antiques had been lifted and dusted and replaced in position, there was the rest of the room; the piano, the chairs, the carved table legs and clawed feet; Father's Indian vases bigger than we were and Raggazone's Japanese vases, just as tall but not as wide. The mantelpiece held more ornaments which we could reach only standing on a chair. The Venetian blinds had to be dusted or wiped with a damp cloth, one slat at a time. All this was only part of what belonged in that room. Oil paintings looked down. Corner cabinets, thankfully locked, held carved Buddhas and ivory elephants together with an egg-shell thin Japanese tea service.

Whilst sitting on the floor dusting the pedals and ledges below the piano, we found we could play the piano from below by pushing up the keys. We were delighted as Father kept the piano locked before we started to learn.

All the jobs we were given to do by Father dwindled down to one or two regular things for each of us, when he was not there. But whilst he was at home without work to go to, the house became like a new pin. He had a natural urge to organise everything and everybody, including strangers and their affairs, so that it was no wonder that people came to him for advice about the law and their troubles. In the same way that they came to Mamma for advice about illness or their babies; for our parents, both, inspired confidence.

During Father's post war enforced stay at home the floors were polished like glass. He made a heavy floor polisher, a block of wood nearly two feet square, covered with felt. A long handle with a rachet was fixed on top. We called it 'the jumbo'. After the floors had been scrubbed and dried and the polish put on, the heavy 'jumbo' was pushed backwards and forwards all over the floors to make them shine. It was too heavy for the younger children to push, so we rode on it instead. With the older boys taking it in turns to push, two of us sat on the top of the 'jumbo', one on opposite sides, our knees high under our chins and our arms around the pole, hanging on to each other.

The 'jumbo' was unpredictable; it skidded and flew in circles around the floor as we hung on grimly leaning with the pole. Then suddenly it would change direction and throw us off on the opposite side. When we climbed back on again, it would suddenly spin around in circles without warning, quite uncontrollable giving us hair-raising frights. There was always someone else waiting to climb on for a ride, however short.

Father certainly knew how to keep his large family of children constructively occupied, whether it was making spills to save matches, picking up stones from his rose beds to put on the paths, polishing floors, knockers or coal lids or tracking down horse droppings with a shovel and bucket with the promise of 'tuppence' reward. Our reward for our Saturday jobs was our pocket money afterwards on Saturday mornings.

Everyone of us was given pocket money by Father, never by Mamma, until they went to work and earned their own. Father worked it out so that nobody had the same amount as anyone else. It was all according to age. First he consulted Mamma to make sure we had been helpful and had done whatever jobs we had been given to do, and then he lined us up with the eldest first. This was just before Saturday lunch and we stood in line for our halfpennies, pennies and twopences with Father thoroughly enjoying it all. He loved giving things away and would add a coin here and there for an extra job. He had a large-hearted generous way about him and made it all seem very important that we had earned the allocation of our weekly pennies, so that we felt both proud and grateful to get our 'wages'. Father could not help lecturing and we each received a short discourse with advice on improvement and had to wait and listen in line to everyone else's boring lecture from Father as well as one's own.

The polishing of the floors came to a dramatic end much to Mamma's relief. One morning, as Father came flying downstairs in his usual impatient way, he stepped on the mat at the foot of the stairs which promptly deposited him on his back as it took off to the front door, fortunately shut, where he skidded to a halt. Father was lucky. Although bruised and shaken in the collision with the door, he had no broken bones. Mamma received a long lecture about the danger of mats on polished floors but the ritual polishing with the 'jumbo' ceased. No longer was it seen in the 'mop' cupboard. Our rides up and down the hall, over the dining room floor and the passage, were over. It was banished to the cellar with the thousand and one other things relegated there. We missed the excitement of the 'jumbo' but Mamma breathed a sigh of relief.

On Saturday mornings some of us had to go to fetch the bread. We took the big bassinet pram with the large well in the centre with its removable cover for extra carrying space. We usually went for the bread in pairs. One Saturday morning Stanley and I went together.

The route was very familiar as most of it followed the well-trod path towards Wanstead Park where we all spent much of our young days when not at school. Pushing the pram between us, we walked along Altmore Avenue (where later barrage balloons flew, manned by the W.A.A.F. during the Second World War). Then on to the post office (where I took the five puppies for a walk and lost the important letter to Italy). Then left at the Off Licence (where a fire, thought to have been started at the back in a chicken run, had caused the Off Licence to be rebuilt) and along the wide Burges Road which had once been part of a large country manor. We passed the new Nurses Home which was two ordinary houses knocked into one, where mid-wives and home nurses could be found, until we reached East Ham Palace. This home of pantomimes and music-hall shows was where children went to see the Saturday morning pictures of Douglas Fairbanks, Buster Keaton, Harold Lloyd and Charlie Chaplin; There Gracie Fields was soon to appear and take Londoners by storm singing 'Sally'.

We were now halfway to the bakers. We passed the station where I took my first underground trip to Lavender Hill with Mamma when I was two. On we went towards Manor Park but the bakers we sought was nearer. This, our Mecca, was offering loaves at a halfpenny cheaper. With the pram outside the shop with the brake on, we both walked in to buy the loaves. In and out we went putting the large white crusty loaves into the well and then anywhere in the pram with room, until it was full.

Dawdling back home the new bread smelled delicious. There were long tins, square tins, split tins, seeded bloomers and unseeded bloomers, long sand-wich loaves and cottage loaves. We tried to resist the temptation to pull off a piece of the newly-baked crust, but the cottage loaves with their curved, floury, crispy crusts and mouth-watering smell, defeated us. By the time we had retraced our way all along the High Street, down Burges Road and along Altmore Avenue to home, either the top or the bottom of a crunchy, crusty cottage loaf had lost a strip from its outside and it was now inside us. The missing portion passed unnoticed as we threw the loaves into the big terracotta bread crock. Mamma checked the number against the list and counted the change, if any, for the thirteen loaves we had brought home. We never brought back brown bread in those early days as we could not afford it.

We children did a lot of shopping between us although Mamma and Father often went out together on a Saturday evening, fairly late, just before the shops were closing, to choose the best outs of meat at the lowest prices. Then Father bargained as though he were still in the fish market at Billingsgate, and argued about the goods being offered as if he knew more about it all than the shopkeeper, which was sometimes the case as with the fishmonger.

In spite of all the baskets of food we carried home, the kit-bags carried by the boys, frequent trips to Willie Wheatley's shop and Mamma's home-made preserves and pickles, there were times when we ran out of something that was needed for a meal. A case in point was Father's Worcester sauce. If no shop were open Father sent one of us to Annie Alcock's. Reluctantly, we ran the fifty yards to her door. Father's friend Jack Alcock was very easy going but Annie stood no nonsense. She answered the door and looked down at us.

"Please, Mrs. Alcock, Father says have you any sauce he can have and he only likes Worcester sauce?"

Mrs. Alcock did not mince her words.

"Tell him he has enough sauce of his own," she declared, "enough for twenty people," with which she disappeared inside into her kitchen, reappearing with Father's favourite sauce and a bag of dry brown bread for Mamma to make into bread pudding.

When we ran out of mustard pickle needed for a school day lunch, we were sent to Willie Wheatley's shop just around the corner. We called it Willie Wheatley's as he was always there, six feet tall, helping his mother or Father in the shop. Willie's mother sold everything but there were not many things we bought there. The vinegar ran out of a barrel and we bought two 'pennorth' if we took a bottle. The paraffin ran out, from a tap on the large drum and we usually bought half a gallon this being the twenties and very hard times. We took a basin for the pickled cabbage or mustard pickle which was to be had with a cold lunch, when all Mamma's large stone jars were empty of mustard pickle, pickled cabbage or chutney. We ran all the way there and back home where everyone looked into the basin to see how much we had been given for 'tuppence'. It was soon gone – "Down Bread Lane," said Mamma, along with the contents of all the large stone jars she was constantly filling.

Father did not believe in standing on ceremony. If he needed something and could not pay for it he acquired it somehow. As many of his friends were shop owners, he was able to help them with advertising and business promotion. All through the depression they helped each other over crises. Harry Manning had a tobacconist shop and from him Father obtained his cigars, the best that Harry had. The Hawkins lived over their draper's shop. Twice weekly Father and Jim Hawkins played billiards over the 'Black Lion'. Billy Cummings who was a traveller for a silver firm, partnered him at tennis. Harry Manning was a bowls champion and he and Father entered matches together and won trophies. He went fishing with Jack Alcock and other members of the Conservative Club. Mr. Barnes the secretary and resident caretaker played him at Rummy and Father also liked table tennis, darts and long walks. So it was not surprising that we were often sent, unwillingly, to deliver messages to any of the above. It was embarrassing delivering Father's words. They were invariably couched in terms that he might use to all of 'Us', very bossy and facetious. His friends always laughed as they listened to us repeating Father's words, and sent back good-natured replies, agreeing to his proposals, even when it was a request for a box of cigars.

Although I did not like Billy Cummings because of his remarks about my scabby knees when I was small, we liked going to his house to deliver messages and to get their replies. Maud Cummings, Billy's unfortunate wife, was ginger and freckled and kind. Billy treated her badly as we heard her tell Mamma on many occasions. He referred to her as 'Cummings' but she was always calm, unlike Billy who invariably looked about to explode. She made us welcome as though we were adults. She had no children and enjoyed entertaining us in her immaculate garden. Totally unlike our garden with its tall Indian corn, chicken run, pear trees, rose bushes and paths, the wash house and the poplar tree, her's was all smooth lawn and coloured deck chairs with neatly-edged flower beds. It locked as if nobody ever went there. We sat there in those gaily-coloured deck chairs and drank lemonade and ate biscuits handed to us by our kind hostess and felt as if we were in a picture book, so silent and spotless it all seemed. Meanwhile Maud awaited Billy's reply to Father's message and as Billy fancied himself as a great wit, we usually found his reply an unintelligible mystery.

The silver was kept high up on the kitchen dresser and Mamma complained that it was discoloured and blackened when gas light was installed in the district. Of course we had the gas put on but never liked it. It was trouble from the start. It hissed, flared and spluttered and kept us awake after being put to bed until Mamma came to put it out. So when electricity quickly followed, we had that installed in its stead. Away went the fragile gas mantles that caused so much trouble with their mysterious holes appearing nobody knew how, and in their place were uncomplicated light bulbs that needed no matches and were silent. Then Mamma decided to have an electric cooker, one of the first ever installed I should think. It was black iron and by now the kitchen range was unusable because of the furred-up pipes. The modern cooker took over all the baking, and life was a little easier for Mamma, with no fire to light each morning before the kettle and poringer could be boiled.

But when Father was still at home dishing out the Saturday jobs to his offspring, the electric had not yet appeared on the map, so that the words, "I want the silver cleaned today," gave us all a sudden desire to clean the knives, grind the salt, whiten the door step, scrub the floor, or any other job that freed us from cleaning the silver.

After the advent of the electric, the silver gradually disappeared somehow or other, probably due to hard times, so that eventually it was not there to be cleaned.

All the jobs were finished by lunch time on Saturdays and we were given our 'wages'. Some of us never had anything left but there were others of us who always had farthings tucked away, halfpennies and a penny or two, unless of course they were older and at work.

Roy always had wine gums tucked away among his books in his bedroom cupboard. Ralph always saved a halfpenny to buy and share a coconut bar with us, each week after our music lesson. Olive was very thrifty and industrious and ran errands for neighbours saving the money to help Mamma. Gilbert was clever and thoughtful, making money when he went to work and enjoying buying sweets for us and chocolate for Mamma. But when we all got our 'wages' from Father on Saturdays at lunch-time, we knew we were free to spend it that afternoon however we pleased.

Most of us went straight round to Willie Wheatley's shop straight after lunch. There, with our noses glued against his window, we stared at all the trays of sugar mice, liquorice dummies, sherbert dabs, aniseed balls, farthing strips, liquorice strips, coconut ice, locust bars, honey-comb, and nougat, and the jars of sugared almonds, pear drops, tiger nuts and so on. We knew we could not afford pea shooters, pencil sharpeners and balloons, and the many desirable objects we had gazed at so many times before.

Inside the shop, Mrs. Wheatley stood and stared out through the glass at us all, wondering whether we were going to spend our coppers in her shop or not. Long conversations amongst us went on trying to decide who was going to share what with whom so that we could all get full value for our money.

Farthing strips of toffee were favourite and liquorice strips came next as both of these could be peeled into four or five long thin strands, easy to share out among us. Post toasties were a delicious extravagance, and seldom bought as we got very few for our money, as were sugared almonds and pear drops. The farthing strip was voted best value especially as it was within everybody's price range. It was malty toffee, quite firm, yet soft enough to strip each section down the grooves and separate the flat strip into four or five strands, each about twelve or fourteen inches long. With our pieces hanging from our mouths, we dawdled along, letting it dissolve slowly so that it might last all the way to the park.

Our friends knew that we could not go out to play on Saturday mornings so they came for us on Saturday afternoons. A young school friend came to ask if I could go out to play. Father heard.

"Yes," he said firmly, never one to miss an opportunity of putting his foot down, "but first she must do all the washing up."

This was not fair but I knew better than to argue with Father if I wanted to go. As it was Saturday there was a great deal of washing up to be done with everybody home for lunch. I looked at it in despair.

"Never mind, Topsy," said my persistent friend Grace, "I will help you."

"We shall have to wait for the hot water," I said filling the electric kettle as we were in that era.

"Don't bother about that," said Grace, with a touch of Father in her voice, "use the tap."

All the piles of plates, dishes, fruit bowls and cutlery, were being snatched up by Grace before I had time to wash the food off and clean them properly, and it was the same with the saucepans and cooking things. A thick layer of grease was setting all around the sides of the bowl. I pointed it out to Grace, but she was becoming very impatient to go out and astonished at the never-ending pile of cutlery and crockery.

"Don't be so fussy," she said. "Do hurry up, Topsy, so that we can go out."

I was worried about the grease and I knew that both Mamma and Father would have everything washed over again if they saw how Grace was snatching up dirty dishes to wipe with the tea towel. The grease didn't worry her. I took a knife and fork and cut it off the bowl and wondered where it could go. Grace grabbed the knife and fork and the grease went somewhere and soon we were bowling Grace's iron hoop along the pavement, one of us on either side, hitting it with our sticks as we ran alongside trying to keep it from going off the kerb and into the gutter. It was nearly as tall as we were and rang and rumbled over the pavement, racing away from us so that it was all we could do to keep up with it.

The traffic was almost entirely horse-drawn vehicles and on Saturday there were plenty of greengrocers, bakers, milkmen, coalmen and rag and bone merchants. All going about the streets with their horses and carts, so that horse droppings were plentiful. When Father spotted some of us with apparently no job to do, he quickly found a bucket and shovel and tried to cajole one of us to seek and collect a pile of horse manure. Our faces told him how much we disliked the idea so that he resorted to bribery to make sure he had some of the steaming fertiliser for his rose trees. We tried to wriggle out of it, but finally, furnished with the shovel in the bucket, we set forth on the treasure hunt. How we longed for the cloak of invisibility as the sounds from clip-clopping horses urged Father to send us forth as quickly as possible. Before we knew where we were, one of us was trotting after the horses with our degrading equipment that destroyed our self-respect.

If we were lucky the valued find might be close by and swiftly transferred to the bucket with the predominating haste of self-preservation. Trotting home we eyed it askance as we debated whether Father would deem this small amount worth 'tupp-ence'.

Sometimes we were unlucky and were just in time to see a near-by sizeable heap being scooped up by someone else. We were indignant: it was unfair: our house was the nearest! We were forced to search further afield thereby increasing the chances of aggravation. Everyone knew what the bucket and shovel were for. Remarks were shouted and a boy or two followed along with the remarks, waiting for us to begin the operation. There was no escape. Should we run home and tell Father there was no manure this Saturday morning, or complete our task and satisfy our audience? We decided that the latter was the lesser of the two evils.

'Eureka'. At last there was something to put into the bucket. Ribald remarks were now flung at us.

"Hey! You getting the family dinner?"

"Didn't you get any breakfast to-day?"

Sometimes it was worse! We were recognised.

"Hey – old Nosey Parker – getting the breakfast?"

Other voices joined in, bawling after us, making the most of it before we could escape. Hands round mouths, copy-cats joined the tormentors as we made off with the bucket.

"Nosey Parker's got their dinner!" How we hated that name as it followed us along the street.

"Nosey Parker! Nosey Par – ar- ker! Nosey Par – ar – ar- ker."

At some time when we were very small, we went to the Saturday morning pictures. They were shown at the East Ham Palace. Silent films with Douglas Fairbanks Senior, Charlie Chaplin and Felix cartoons, kept us rivetted to our seats. We could not always afford to go. It was one penny to go in and as we went through the door with our ticket, a large square chewy sweet wrapped in paper, was handed to each child. These sweets being large, lasted a long time, and helped to keep the audience quiet whilst the auditorium was filling up.

All this time the great cinema organ was being played with popular tunes to which the ebulliant concourse whistled or sang in a heady crescendo of anticipation. Then slowly we saw the organ rising from the well in front of the stage, the organist seated with his back to us, his hands and feet moving rapidly up and down and sideways, over the keys, stops and pedals, as the children accompanied him with whistles, cat-calls and cheers. As soon as the organ had risen to the height of the stage, the organist rose from his seat and turned to bow and wave to the congregation – still flocking in. He was encouraged by hundreds of stamping feet, clapping hands, banging seats, screams and cheers, and all the other noises that children can make when they are out to enjoy themselves.

At last the lights dimmed. We all craned our necks round to look behind, over our shoulders, at the projectionist, to where he was positioned up above behind a small window of light at the projector. Then with a series of promising clicks, whirls and shapes, the film would start. The star, Felix, 'kept on walking', his hands clasped behind him above his powerful, tiger-like tail, and the organist kept us company as we shouted out the words of the 'pop' song that we all knew.

'Felix keeps on walking, keeps on walking still!

With his hands behind him,
You will always find him.
Blow him up with dynamite – but him you cannot
kill.
Miles into the air he flew,
He just murmured "Toodle ooh";
He came down in Timbuctoo,
But he keeps on walking still!'

The words came out with gusto from hundreds of throats. After the cartoon film of Felix, Buster Keaton or Harold Lloyd both looking like bank clerks, but amazing us all with their gymnastic skill and athletic feats of terrifying daring, kept us all hynotised by the improbable sagas wherein they performed all their own stunts. Craning forward on the edges of our seats, we showed our appreciation of their expertise and courage, with cheers, claps, stamps, 'oohs' and 'aahs,' backed up by the organist with dramatic cadences and stifling silences. All the while, bags of peanuts were being shelled in front of every seat, their husks smothering the floor.

By the time the main film with a well-known hero was on, most of the nuts and sweets were eaten and the serious business of enjoyment with terror, kept us all quiet, our attention totally captured. Douglas Fairbanks, sword in hand, leaped from balconies, fought his way up and down staircases, slid down curtains, swung on chandeliers and died horrible deaths in sudden and unexpected ways, for example, once at the touch of a leper. Never was so much enjoyed by so many for so little.

One Saturday morning, on leaving our seats together with all the other children, we crunched our way towards the exit over the shore of nut shells beached by the tide of retreating feet, to where the bright winter sunshine streamed in through the open exit door. We followed Stanley down the steps. What was the matter with Stanley's overcoat? Flapping apart at the back – held together by the collar – and the fact that he was inside with his arms in the sleeves, we saw that it appeared to be in halves. We were shocked and awed. How horrible for poor Stanley to have to walk home wearing it. Holding hands we ran home to Mamma.

"Somebody," she said, "has slit it down with a razor." Luckily Mamma was able to repair it.

The height of crime was to break a window. The cost of the glass or the service of a glazier was an extra expense that people could not afford. Many a time people knocked on our door to enquire the whereabouts of the boys, as their window had just been broken by a ball. We were chosen as everyone knew us and where we lived. But whatever the circumstances, responsibility was always denied by Mamma. She was adamant that her boys would never break a window.

"They would have more sense than to kick a ball near a window," she declared, and it was a fact that Father dared them to play football in the street so that they were sent to the parks. Even the garden was sacrosanct against balls because of Father's roses and tiger lilies.

There were many Saturdays when, money being scarce, Father waited until very late, past ten and nearly eleven at night, before he and Mamma went to look for a joint of meat. Many traders stayed open until these hours hoping for a late customer. With the public being on hard times and having little money to spend, the shopkeepers were badly off and hard hit and glad of an extra sale.

Late one Saturday I found myself trotting along beside Father as he held my hand and I ran to keep up with him and Mamma as we hastened along our road towards the High Street. It was dark and cold and damp, almost winter. I was still the youngest and Olive was 'on the way'. Breathless with running, I listened to Father conjecturing to Mamma on where to go and what he might buy. A long flank of beef was mentioned which Mamma would skin and roll and perhaps fill with stuffing, or an aitch-bone which was dearer and a luxury but had the rump of the beef and was a better proposition as it lasted longer.

We emerged from the dark road with the gas lamps in their pools of light here and there in the gloom, into the lighted High Street where we slowed down a little and I caught my breath with the frosty air hurting my throat. Tardy shopkeepers were putting up their shutters and turning off their lamps. We walked along the almost empty High Street towards Townsend's butchers. It was still open. The large gas lamps were flaring and hissing in the cold night air, high up outside the open-fronted shop. Their light glared over the joints of meat still impaled aloft on hooks, it seemed to me, in the cold dark sky. We dawdled past and back again, shivering. Very few people were about; the High Street almost deserted and silent, except for the hissing lamps. We dawdled back as Mr. Pike's voice reclaimed us.

"Buy! Buy! Buy!" he called, determined to make a last sale. Father looked over the prices of the meat. Mr. Pike, the butcher, who managed Townsend's shop, was impatient with weariness and cold, anxious to close up and leave after his long day. It was 'almost Sunday', as he told Father, urging him to hurry up and choose what he wanted.

Standing there, burly, balding and grey, his waxed moustaches stood out as though shouting out the word 'Pike'. His apron firmly tied around his ample stomach, reached right down to his boots. It impeded his progress so that all his steps were short and hasty and probably made him appear more impatient than he really was. He looked at Father knowing him well. Mr. Pike lived in one of the smaller houses in our street.

"Well, Mr. Parker, what can I do for you?"

By now Father had made up his mind what he wanted but he was not going to let Mr. Pike know. He was going to play him along like a fish. With his experience at Billingsgate Father knew how to go after a bargain.

"I don't suppose you have got what I want," observed Father gazing in an off-hand manner at the hooks which Mr. Pike was relieving of their burdens, hoping to accelerate Father's decision. Mr. Pike, knowing that Father had a small army of children to feed looked impatiently around.

"What about this nice leg of mutton?" he suggested, hooking it down with his pole from the metal bar outside the shop, and turning it over with his other hand.

"That's no use," scoffed Father, "I could eat that myself for breakfast." This was not far from the truth as he loved meat, especially steak.

After a few quips and market men's talk, whilst I held on to Mamma's coat, they arranged a deal between them for an enormous aitch-bone with enough of the rump on it to last for the family dinners for almost a week; roasts, cold slices, shepherd's pie and the chopped bone for the stock pot soup.

As Father had left home with an aitch-bone specifically in mind, a joint too large for most other families, he returned home pleased and happy. And Mr. Pike, knowing that no other customer would be along, removed the rest of the meat to the cold room, pulled down the shutters with the hooked pole and locked up the cold shop. Then putting on his cap and overcoat over his balding head and long apron respectively, followed us in the gloomy, cold night air, with his rapid, short, tired steps, towards his bed, down the long, dark road home.

The traders in the established shops knew us all and we all knew them. Right at the top of our road on the opposite side of the High Street, were the fishmongers, the Hackshall family. There were two or three men and one woman. Always quiet and polite they were very much alike with fresh complexions and pronounced noses. Efficient and unruffled, they looked like lawyers in spotless white coats, and only their name and their noses suggested fish. Father always sent us there for haddock which seemed suitable.

Near to the Palace was the sweet shop 'Larkins'. The window was crammed full of sweets but it was too high up so that you could not see what they had got. However it was very popular as it was on the Wanstead route and close to the East Ham Palace, and there for years and years.

The greengrocers Heard's had two shops, one near the Town Hall and one near the bakers which had the ha'penny off a loaf. The men at Heard's seemed to be great strong men like farmers and lifted the sacks of potatoes as if they were sacks of straw. The men at both shops looked identical as if they were twins, but as we couldn't be at both shops at once, they were probably the same men that we saw each time. When the Co-op opened, Mamma joined to get the dividend which was considerable owing to the large amount of food we bought, but Father was dead against it and didn't agree with co-ops as he was all for the small trader.

Going out for a pramful of shopping, we took a long list written out by Mamma after much thought and juggling with the figures and amounts. Written by everything was the exact amount required together with the price. If she wrote 'two ounces of cloves and one ounce of peppercorns and three sticks of cinnamon', that was the exact amount that she wanted. Each item was budgeted for and the list trimmed and altered to match the exact amount she could afford to spend, down to a farthing.

Inside the shops we read out the required item and the shopkeeper measured it exactly, ticking off the purchase from the list. Back at home the list was checked against the goods for correctness of price and size. If there were any difference in weight, or even a farthing out in any change, we were sent back to the shopkeeper to have it put right. Every halfpenny was of the utmost importance as it could affect the possibility of a meal for the following day. Discrepancies would start Mamma off on her usual lament, which was a dirge, which became a refrain.

'A farthing here, a farthing there,
And a ha'penny somewhere else;
A penny here, a penny there
And tuppence somewhere else.'

Before she could get on to, 'A sixpence here, a sixpence there', we were all chanting in unison, 'A farthing here, a farthing there,' which stopped Mamma in her tracks or I don't know where she would have stopped. The shopping list and change had to be exactly right as a missing ha'penny might mean not enough for next day's dinner.

Some Saturday nights, when Father was in work, he could afford to send us to buy fish and chips. With his fish market experience he recalled the trade names for the fish, names that seemed to be known only to him.

Much of the fish carried up the Thames and unloaded at Billingsgate, was caught by foreign fishermen, so that the names written on the sides of the boxes were foreign. The market traders and porters knew them by both their foreign names and the retail names for this country. Father remembering the foreign names decided that fishmongers should know these, and if Norwegian fisherman had marked boxes of Dog fish as Huss that is what they should be called.

Counting us and then the money for the fish and chips, Father began his usual lecture to those who were being sent to fetch it. First he checked to make sure that everyone could eat a piece of fish, and then made certain that it was plaice for Mamma, and then he recalled the various fish likely being fried until finally it was Huss for everyone except Mamma. Off we went, knowing full well that it was a 'tuppenny and a pennorth' that we were going to ask for, ours being rock eel, there being no mention of either Dog fish or Huss at the fish shop. However we made sure to mention Huss as if anything were wrong with the fish, Father would soon extract from us as to whether we had asked for Huss or not. He may have similarly renamed the plaice, cod, haddock herring and mackerel, but only the huss became impressed into my mind. The man frying the fish was hot and busy. Flouring the fish fillets; placing each carefully into the hot oil as he dripped it from batter; lifting the basket of chips to shake and pinch one to see if it were cooked; his every move followed by a queue of swivelling eyes. He diplomatically interspersed his actions with taking orders; setting kitchen paper squares over newspaper; draining the chips and extracting fried bubbles of batter. These he sold as 'ha'porths of cracklings'; until at last, all the fish was flung on to a rack. Then he speedily disposed of fish, chips and queue who departed warming their hands on hot newspaper packages. Through the doorway they hurried to be swallowed by the night, so swiftly, that the ringing till had scarcely swallowed their coins. With all this hustle and bustle, the fish fryer did not need the extra hassle of trying to guess the identity of the fish that Father wanted, so we diplomatically did our own translation.

Back at home we all tucked in, there were a good number of us on Saturdays, adding salt and vinegar to our own plate, hot from the oven and holding the long-awaited fish.

When all had finished, Father cast his eyes around and then delegated one of us to make the cocoa. Out in the kitchen, a long line of cups and saucers was lined up ready for the operation. Looking through the hatchway as Father did on Sundays, a call went through.

"Who wants cocoa?"

The call was followed by a medley of response from unseen areas of the dining room.

"Me." "I'll have one." "Mine with no Sugar." "Don't forget I like three sugars," etc.

The long heavy wooden table was between the cocoa maker and the hatchway which meant stretching across over the cups, whilst balancing on one toe on the saucepan shelf under the table, to look into and around the dining room and take account of the orders and who was saying what. In this precarious position, hovering over the crockery, we counted round the room.

"Who wants cocoa?"

Having made the circuit we went round again to make sure. A change of mind here and there was encountered about the exact condition of the cocoa required or not required.

"One, two, three, oh, you don't want one now; three, four five; yes, I know you don't want sugar; six, seven, yes, I know you always have her sugar; Mamma says you are not to have one as you feel sick. Was that six or seven? Seven, eight; she doesn't want one. I am going to start again," whereupon Father losing all patience shouted out "Why don't you make up your mind?", at some-one, and then bellowed, "Go with-out!"

Contradicting himself in the next breath he turned to Mamma with a loud command of,

"Make them drink it!"

And then the count was taken for the last time without any arguments and mean-time, the kettle had boiled.

The counting of the cups and saucers now began, placed in line all along the kitchen table, with the no sugars together, and one teaspoonful and two three and four lots for those like Father, for whom nothing was ever too sweet, the mixing began. Meanwhile questions and answers had resumed and were being flung back and forth through the hatchway to ensure all was being carried out as requested, the measure of sugar being the predominant factor. That interminable stirring of the ingredients in each cup seemed to go on for ever, and thirsty enquirers were told to "WAIT!" in a peremptory bark from Father.

With the family fussy about lumps and Father particular about cocoa being wasted in the bottoms of the cups, the smooth mixing was all important and time consuming. At last every cup was ready and filled and passed through to the thirsty, which was usually everyone after a salty supper of fish and chips.

"This is Mamma's, no sugar."

"Pass this to Father, four sugars."

"I hope you put plenty of sugar in it!" from Father.

"Yes. Four heaped teaspoons." And Father, sampling it immediately, pronounced his satisfaction.

"This is Ron's. No that was Joyce's. Better make sure. Change over then. Pass this to Olive – she wanted a small cup", and so on until all the cups had been passed through into the dining room with the last one clinched by, "And that's yours."

Occasionally on Saturday evenings, our parents went to the Alcock's to play whist or mahjong and we looked after ourselves with strict injunctions to "All go to bed at the right time". 'The right time' like the pocket money, varied according to our ages. There were those who went to bed early and those who went to bed at eight o'clock, like me.

With our parents out we were able to disregard these rules and arrange our own entertainments. Diversions such as the wrestling show for the children of our road and at another time, a magic lantern show, were surreptitiously 'fixed'.

Ralph's friend 'Scholar' brought his magic lantern and some slides. With Ralph's bedroom wall as a screen, the room he shared with Graham and Gilbert, we grouped together at a distance and sat down staring at the blank cream-coloured wall. We drew the blinds. A picture sprang onto the wall.

Magic was the word, the only word for it. How we all enjoyed it. Over and over again we wanted to see the slides. At last it was time for Scholar to pack up the magic lantern and take it home. He left. We were all too much awake and excited to think of going to bed so we thought up a game that we could not play when our parents were home.

Hide and Seek in the cellar was agreed to be a good idea. We used the house as well but the cellar, with coal dust and cobwebs over everything, was usually out of bounds for games. There, in the dark corners, the boys hid, and terrified us all and each other, suddenly switching on torches held in their mouths, trying to resemble ghostly ghouls, or pouncing out with ugly faces blackened with soot. Finally we went to bed tired out and Mamma came home to a quiet house.

"I hope you did not disturb the neighbours kicking up a shindy with your shinnanagins," Mamma would observe benignly at breakfast, in that cross-bred dialect she sometimes used as a result of her years with Father.

"Oh no," we innocently replied. "We played a few games and then went to bed."

Tea parties were usually held on Saturday afternoons and there were many of them as we all had birthdays to celebrate. Great excitement built up as we were got ready by Mamma. With new ribbons in our hair and party dresses made by Mamma, we got ready for the arrival of our friends.

The guests arrived about four pm and after gifts had been received and unwrapped, we sat down to the birthday tea. These were standard whether we were giving or going to parties. There was always the same fare: jelly and cakes; sandwiches of egg and cress, tomato and cheese, ham and tomato, and fish paste or meat paste. Sausage rolls, fancy cakes and trifle vied with the jelly to separate the plates of sandwiches and set off the birthday cake, in the centre, resplendent with decoration and the correct number of candles.

When all had eaten as much as they wanted, the tables was swept clear of all but small cake plates, and the birthday cake became the focus for all eyes. Candles were lit by an adult and then blown at by the 'party person', who often had help from all and sundry. They leaned over each other as they elbowed forward with puffing cheeks, until a few wisps of smokey ribbons signalled that the blowing was over and eyes were rivetted on the knife held by an adult. As it entered the cake, twenty, or thereabout, small plates were held aloft expectantly, with some elbow jostling, wrist pushing, scowls and growls, until all were commanded to put down their plates. Exhortations to wish were wasted on the fast eaters who rejoined in elbow jostling for further cake helpings.

The games began as soon as the table had been cleared and the chairs placed all around the walls. Blindfolds were found and 'Squeak piggy squeak', 'Blind Man's Bluff' and pinning the tail on the donkey were played. 'Pass the parcel', 'Up Jenkins', 'Please We've Come to Learn the Trade', 'Hunt the Thimble' 'Giants', heading balloons and any other games that didn't need a piano, as we were not allowed the front room for children's parties, kept us all happy, with Father giving out a sweet or two as prizes, until it was time for the visitors to leave.

The boys never seemed to be going to parties as we girls were. We and our friends were constantly in and out of each other's houses. Instead, the boys went off to football or cricket in the parks or for fishing and adventures further afield. With all our birthdays and all our friends, it was a continuous round of giving and going to parties.

One Saturday, in bed with a chesty cold, I was thoroughly enjoying special attention: a nice warm room, the oil stove alight, books to look at and the feeling of being special, of everyone attending to my slightest wish. Suddenly all was spoilt. As I lay there snug and cosy, on this bleak wintry afternoon with the early darkness closing in, I propped my book up against my knees where they made a hillock under the bedclothes and idly wondered whether I would get bread and milk, Mamma's staple diet for the sick, or if I would be allowed a lightly-boiled egg, which would mean that I would soon be downstairs. The doorbell rang. The caller soon left and Mamma came up to see me.

"That was one of your friends," she said. "She wanted you to go to her party this afternoon."

The words electrified me. I sprang out of bed as though a lion were after me. Galvanised into action by the word 'party' I started to undo my nightie buttons even before I landed on the floor, saying as I did so, "Yes, of course I want to go."

"Nonsense," said Mamma firmly, steering me back into the warm nest so precipitately abandoned; the cosy cocoon a source of enjoyment seconds ago, now swiftly becoming repugnant, an abhorred prison.

"I would not dream of letting you out from this warm room," continued Mamma, tucking me up firmly in bed.

Eagerly I explained that I would wrap up well.

"Certainly not," said Mamma. "You have been in bed all day and you are not going out to a party on this bitterly cold afternoon."

Tears were of no avail and I suddenly felt so well, that the thought of a nice boiled egg in bed, lost all its attraction. Staying in bed with the certainty of missing a party now seemed like a punishment and I didn't enjoy the tea, whatever it was, as all the while I thought of what would be happening at the party without me.

One Saturday, near to Christmas, when we were very small, Ralph, Stanley, Phyllis and I, were invited to a party at the Town Hall. The party was for needy families as a special treat, and there were many such families in the wake of the war. Many had lost their men and many men were disabled, reduced to begging in the streets, singing in groups as they walked the roads, or selling matches in shallow boxes hanging on a string around their necks.

I am not sure who chose us to go to the party, but it was probably some of Father's Conservative Club friends. Whoever was responsible for organising it, they made it an excellent affair. Everything was first class.

The Great Hall was used for the occasion. At one end, tables had been arranged, their snowy-white table cloths sweeping almost to the floor. Each table top was a feast for the eyes with food beautifully arranged. Christmas trappings intertwined and linked the wheels of sandwiches, pyramids of cakes, jellies in myriad moulds and trifles of perfection. Each place was guarded by a serviette rosette sprinkled along the length of the table like snowbuds. It looked like a long Christmas card, the artist trailing its length with scarlet and gold, silver and green, the decorations linking and separating the rich sprinkle of shapes and colours on the white backcloth.

The scene was mesmerising. At the other end of the big hall was a huge Christmas tree reaching up towards the lofty ceiling. After we had eaten all we could manage, games were organised. Phyllis didn't want to join in so we sat beneath the tree on the shiny floor, gazing up at the tiers of presents rising far above us into the branches. There we stayed whilst the children skipped and sang and played about the hall.

Streamers and balloons suspended from the ceiling, vied with the decorations to welcome us, but the tree surpassed everything, even the beautiful tables. It stood there, in all its nobility, bearing the gifts for every child, large toys, unwrapped for us all to wonder at. Opposite the tree stood a grand piano, open wide and being played for the children's 'Oranges and Lemons' and 'Good King Wenceslaus'.

The time flew by. Soon everyone was gathered under the tree to be handed a gift by Father Christmas. A grand piano exactly like the one at the end of the hall, was handed to me, but mine was all white. Never had I been given anything so wonderful. It was the best thing about the party and cemented the scene in my mind forever. Although only about fourteen inches long, to me at three years old it seemed huge. It made lovely tinkling sounds. Stanley had a nice little concertina which was ideal for him, being so musical but he never got a chance to play it. When he returned home with it, Graham and Ralph took it away from him to play it, "and," he complained. "They fought over it until it was broken."

Saturday evenings usually found us contented enough playing in the dining room. In summer time we would be in the garden or conservatory until bedtime, but the conservatory gradually went into disrepair as we grew bigger.

On winter evenings there in the easy, wicker chair, dozed Father, whilst six or seven of us ran around him playing 'He'; did hand-stands up against the wall; skated cigarette cards up against the skirting board; blew up balloons and then let out the air with excruciating squawks; went under the table and swung on the long bar beneath, which ran its length hidden by the long table cloth; knocked on the brass book-case handles; played charades wearing Mrs. Alcock's old shoes; ran in and out of the room playing 'hide and seek' or 'mothers and Fathers'; knocked each other's knuckles with conkers on strings; crawled about after elusive 'five stones', and generally went through a range of activities to suit the time available.

All the while Father snoozed through it until we began to argue or knock too loudly on the brass knockers. Then he brought us all to heel with the sound of his voice like a lion tamer cracking a whip. Then we were all given something to do like playing 'schools', or a game like 'Spillikins' which was silent, almost.

No doubt about it, Father held the reins whatever we were up to.

Chapter Seven

Sundays

Sunday mornings nearly always followed the same pattern. Mamma was up first and made the breakfast for us all, but first she settled Father. The last thing that any of us wanted was Father with us at breakfast.

One of us was sent up to Father's bedroom with a strong, hot cup of tea. If it were too hot he poured it into the saucer as he dictated his orders to us.

"Wait there," he commanded as he disposed of it quickly. Father never left anything in his cup but a few tea leaves glued to the bottom. The cup and saucer was then thrust into our hands with advice on carrying it carefully and we took them down to the kitchen where Mamma was preparing Father's breakfast on a tray.

First the tray cloth went on and then everything that he could possibly require was put on the traycloth. Worcester sauce was always there no matter whether he was having smoked haddock, eggs and bacon, sausage, mushroom and tomatoes or steak. Whatever it was, he put his favourite sauce over it. Somewhere on the tray a space was found for the marmalade, butter and bread, or a little toast. He ate little bread which served to clean his plate, continental fashion.

After delivering the tray, which Father eyed keenly to see if there were anything he could reject to leave more room for manoeuvre, the bearer was allowed to leave with instructions about the timing of his second cup of tea.

Before Mamma had all our breakfasts ready a great knocking on the bedroom floor above would be heard.

"Oh dear!" sighed Mamma, "what does he want now? One of you run up and see."

An argument would follow between us.

"You go."

"No, I've just been up there."

The knocking grew louder.

"Be quick," urged Mamma, "or he will be down here and then I'll get nothing done."

At the thought of Father coming downstairs early on Sunday morning, we were galvanised into action.

"Don't all go," wailed Mamma, "you go", singling out one of us. "Run upstairs, do, and see what he wants and be quick."

Invariably it was for one of us to go and fetch the newspapers; take the tray down at the same time and tell someone to bring his second cup of tea.

Pleased we had all conspired in keeping Father out of the way in bed, propped up with the Sunday papers and busy with a toothpick, we were free to go about our Sunday morning's activities without Father's dominating influence.

Depending on the time of the year and the weather we could be either in or out. It was football, cricket or scouts, for the boys; for us girls, mothers and Fathers indoors or in the garden something similar, which took for as long as we played. Sometimes, in bad weather, we would all be indoors, swapping cigarette cards, playing with marbles or conkers, or playing five stones or draughts or some other game.

Mamma meanwhile, sat with her sewing basket, putting on a button here, a stitch in there and darning a pile of socks-stretched tightly over a wooden mushroom, ensuring everyone was clean and tidy for the day. The rest of her morning was spent in the kitchen preparing the food; roasting and baking whilst chatting to any of us there. We begged for pieces of pastry, dough or gingerbread, or whatever was being prepared, to make our own little shapes to go into the oven with Mamma's. She also gave us a few currants to make faces on the dough, or to eat. We were eventually told, "Be off now, or we shall never get any dinner today."

Mamma always fed Father like a prize fighter. "The way to a man's heart is through his stomach," she told us over and over again as we grumbled about the heavy trays that we carried upstairs on Sundays.

Father would know when dinner was almost ready by the smells drifting upstairs and because of the time. But as dinner time approached, Father's walking stick could be heard on the ceiling above, summoning attention.

"Run upstairs and see if he wants his shaving water yet," said Mamma. Up we would go.

"Ask Mamma what time the dinner will be ready," ordered Father. This meant another trip upstairs.

"Can't someone else go," we grumbled down in the kitchen.

Complaints from first one and then another of us about going up and down stairs when we wanted to continue with our games prompted Mamma to say, "Never mind. He doesn't mean to be thoughtless; he doesn't think to save your legs." But the truth was that

Father believed that children should be kept busy and needed constant exercise. Running up and down stairs to wait on him was an excellent way to ensure both. In this way, his patriarchal domination over us all continued with the aid of the heavy, knob-headed, cherry walking stick.

When Father shaved, everyone kept clear of the bathroom. He used cut-throat razors, one for each day. They were slotted in a special razor box with the days of the week by each slot. Each razor had the day of the week engraved on it. Woe betide anyone who happened to be near when he cut himself.

Phyllis and I were fascinated by the ritual of it all. Peeping round the open door of the bathroom we watched him. With feet astride he glared into the mirror. Elbows high, the lower two thirds of his face covered with lather, his black eyebrows beetling out aggressively above his deep-set rivetting dark eyes, he resembled a bandit about to blast off his carbine. Close by, the strop hung from a hook below the bathroom window where Father shaved at the mirror. Pressing his jaw-line firmly with three fingers of his left hand, he scraped off a tentative strip of lather down his right cheek bone. Dissatisfied, he wiped his soapy fingers on the razor towel hanging by the strop which he now lifted horizontally towards himself with his left hand. Then lovingly stroking the keen edge back and forth the length of the strop; holding the razor delicately where the blade met the handle; gripping it by his thumb and first two fingers, with his little finger raised, he deftly rolled the blade over at each reverse of direction. Then once again he took up his stance at the mirror. All set, with feet astride, he cut a second swathe in the lather with care and exactitude.

If the shave was not going well and he spotted us watching in the mirror, his voice blared out and sent us scampering. This made Mamma cross with us.

"Oh dear!" she sighed, "I hope you have not put him in a bad temper. You know what he's like when he's shaving."

At other times we peeped round just as he'd finished and was starting to hum. Then, if he saw us he would laugh and dab a brushful of shaving soap in our faces so that we ran away and complained to Mamma.

Phyllis put an end to all this interest in Father's razors. One day she went up to the bathroom and decided to have a shave. Down she came with a deep cut on her cheekbone. That was the end of shaving as far as we children were concerned.

In summer, Father did not always have his breakfast in bed. It depended upon whether he had been up late the night before playing billiards or Rummy with his Conservative Club friends or whether he and Mamma had been entertaining for Mahjong or Whist. Early one Sunday morning, he took Phyllis and me on the tram to Wanstead where we took a long walk across the Flats to Leyton to visit some of Mamma's relations. The lady, named Edith, opened the door. She was very impressed by the way we were dressed in some of Mamma's finest needlework. Inside we were given beef sandwiches with mustard in them. What a struggle went on to eat the sandwiches and to hide our distaste of the burning mustard. How our eyes watered and our noses smarted. It was more than we dared do to voice our dislike as Father would have thought it ill-mannered. We were thankful when Father decided to return home for dinner, in spite of the long, tiring walk back across the Flats for two young children of three and five, to the tram terminus for the ride back home.

On Sundays mornings at about eleven o'clock, a little old woman appeared from around the corner of the street, walking along in the middle of the road. The road was empty of traffic, there being no traders or horses and carts on Sunday and cars few and far between. Before her she pushed a pram; just a shell of a pram, a small deep body with two curved handles and four small wheels. She was small, rosy-cheeked, and smiling. Her long clothes reached to just above her boots. Always bare-headed, her grey-brown hair straggled partly loose to her collar and was caught up in an untidy bun behind. Wheeling the pram before her, she drew slowly nearer until we could see the rows of toffee apples fixed on wooden sticks standing neatly in boxes, fitted inside the pram. If we were lucky enough to have a penny we ran towards her holding it up so that she stopped and waited for us. Casting our expert eyes over the regimented toffee apples, shining green through their coats of brown, we searched for the thickest stick with the largest apple. Pointing at it, fast in it's place, we looked on anxiously as it was wrenched free, hoping that not too much of its delicious, brittle overcoat had been left behind.

Against Father's wishes we went to Sunday school. He poured scorn on our being in Sunday school when we could be out in the fresh air on a sunny day. We had to run all the way to get there in time because of our late Sunday dinners. We went from one church to another to try them all out, changing after a few weeks. Sometimes we were given a beautiful little celluloid cross with a Bible text on it and a floral motif. These served not only as book markers, but as recruitment incentives among our friends. We went from Methodist to Wesleyan; from Anglo-Catholic to Congregational and any others we could find within an area of four or five square miles. We couldn't understand why they had differing names. The hymns were the same; the talks were alike; the congregations varied but the only really distinguishing feature was the venue.

One special treat was the visit of those friendly, comic sisters of Jack Warner, remembered by millions as Dixon of Dock Green. The sisters whose stage names were Elsie and Doris Waters were clever comediennes. The Congregational Church in the Barking Road was crowded with children and adults when the sisters appeared on the platform of the Central Hall. They made us all laugh with their comical stories but from that time on I never felt that it was a real church. The vast hall with the platform stage seemed more like a concert hall and the peace and magic of the holy church seemed to be missing.

And so I continued to attend first this Sunday school and then another, usually on my own to see what they were like. I didn't tell Father where I was going and this must have been a further incentive. Finally they gave me a prize for regular attendance. It was Mark Twain's *New Pilgrim's Progress*. The print was tiny and it put me off reading it. I was now nine and had read John Bunyan's *Pilgrim's Progress* more than once avidly, by candlelight, in bed. Thrilled by Christian, I took all his adventures literally. Mark Twain's story failed completely to capture my imagination.

Summer and winter, our Sundays were brimful of things to do. If we were not in the garden, or indoors because of the weather, we were in the parks or in the kitchen with Mamma. If we went to Wanstead it was quite a long way for small children for just half a day and we developed huge appetites before we returned home for our dinner.

One Sunday Phyllis and I wandered off to Wanstead under instructions as to when to return. The going back home became long and exhausting and we were thirsty and hungry. As we neared home we passed close to where our parent's friends, Billy and Maud Cummings lived.

"Let's call and ask them to call to play Mahjong with Father and Mamma," said Phyllis. "I'll tell them Father sent me to ask them."

We found the house where they lived in Shakespeare Crescent and knocked at the door. Phyllis spoke up delivering the fictitious message.

"Please come in," said kind Maud. "You must be very thirsty, it is so hot," leading us through the house into their picturesque garden. There was the velvetty green lawn with deck chairs awaiting our arrival it seemed. How gratefully we sat down to rest our tired legs and hot, aching feet. How delicious was the lemonade and the biscuits. Thoughts of what Father would say were pushed aside. Only the present moments of refreshment mattered. Soon it was time to return home where we ate our dinner without a word to Father about our call on his behalf. All was revealed later that evening when Mr. and Mrs. Cummings arrived unexpectedly, to play Mahjong.

These late midday Sunday meals, well into the afternoon, ensured that our appetites were sufficient to unfailingly clear our plates. Anyone who didn't was quizzed. "I hope you haven't been eating beforehand!"

With the meal over, the table cleared, the dishes washed and put away, the chairs were tidied under the tables or against the walls and we were free to do what we wished. Nobody was allowed to worry Mamma. At the request, "Where is my doll, jumper, book or ball?" Father would bellow "Look for it. Don't expect your Mamma to find everything for you!"

The afternoons were long and peaceful in spite of our numbers. Settled down in an easy chair with his feet up, Father looked around.

"Now who wants coconut toffee?" he asked. Everybody did.

"Who is going to buy it?" he asked next.

It would be decided that we all should go to be out of Mamma's way for a little while after her morning of cooking. So off we went with our instructions to buy so much palm toffee for Mamma and Father and so much coconut toffee for us children. We were soon back unless we took a diversion to the Old Iron Bridge to watch a steam train pass beneath. Then Father broke the coconut toffee with a hammer whilst it was still in the bag as it was so hard. It was distributed among us at staggered intervals and lasted a very long time, especially if it were allowed to dissolve slowly until the coconut only was left.

One Sunday when Ron was a baby our parents decided to take a rest. Before long a crowd of us were on the roof of the wash house and the boys were daring each other to jump off. When they told me that I couldn't jump off as I was too small that did it. I pushed my way to the edge and took off, inspite of all they did to prevent me. I plunged head first on to one of the curly tiles that bordered the rose beds. The tile gashed my brow just above my right eye. Poor Father came rushing downstairs to the back door. He picked me up and laid me on the long wooden kitchen table. Blood filled my eyes. Father placed a large folded clean handkerchief over the wound but it was soon soaked with blood. I was astonished to hear Father say with a sob in his voice as he looked down at me, "My favourite child". This was nonsense as we all knew that Joyce was his favourite child. He picked me up and carried me all the way to Doctor Collins. Once more Doctor Collins stitched my head repeating almost the same words as before, "that it was lucky it wasn't my eye" and adding that I was lucky that it wasn't my brain. Bandages were wound around my head and another went over the top and under the chin like a knight. I enjoyed wearing those bandages. I was seven and felt like a warrior from Finn's band.

For some time I was kept home from school and spent my time doing all the things I always did which included climbing and chasing about. Outside in the front garden, I stood on the railings which was quite easy as they were fixed on top of a small wall. We usually climbed on to the wall and stood on the bottom rail and held on to the top rail where we could see everyone passing. Miss Hough and her mother floated by. Her mother in her long black gown and her little black bonnet like a Dresden doll, and Miss Hough with her fixed smile and poor unfortunate fixed head, trying hard 'To take the dairy off' as Mamma would say.

Old Mr. Rowe approached, distinguished and slightly lame, leaning heavily on his rubber-ferruled walking stick, but walking briskly. Reaching me where I stood perched up on the railings, he looked at me with concern. This retired chemist was of striking appearance. His blue eyes twinkled down as they roved over the crossed bandages about my head.

"What have you been doing to get yourself into the wars?" he enquired kindly. I told him about the tile. His hand came out of his pocket with two bright pennies in it, just as GrandFather Brown had when I was two. I was quite sorry when the bandages were taken off for good.

There were many cosy familiar things associated with Sundays apart from coconut toffee, ginger-bread men, the toffee-apple lady and Sunday school. There were, for instance, chestnuts to be roasted over the dining room fire or the front room fire, in winter, as the evening was drawing in. There on the carpet by the fire we sat, gazing at the red-hot coals. Perhaps the lamps were not yet lit and the room was bright with the firelight. A bag of chestnuts were to be roasted.

There was quite an art in roasting them which we learned from Father and from those older than us. First the fire had to be good and a place selected for the shovel to be placed. With the aid of the poker and the fire tongs a level spot was made for the shovel. Meanwhile a layer of chestnuts had been arranged on the shovel, as many as possible without undue overlapping as there had to be room to turn them all over. Before each one was put in position it was cut on the rounded top with a sharp knife, for about three quarters of an inch. This done, they were pushed closely together, flat side down. The shovel load was now put on the red-hot, previously poked and flattened part of the fire. The handle soon became too hot to hold and a kettle holder had to be used to protect one's hands. If left to itself the shovel might slip or turn so that the chestnuts fell into the red-hot embers and burned unless we could rescue them quickly. As someone held the shovel we all watched as their brown husks gradually turned black and a delicious smell of roasting chestnuts, which is quite different from any other smell, filled the room. The interest of all of us was concentrated on the chestnuts.

Now it was time to remove the shovel on to the hearth and turn over the enticing nuts. Some were pounced upon, declared 'done', their jackets curling back from the splits revealing the soft edible seed, gently steaming. These were pushed off into the hearth whilst the others were shuffled over, with Ohs, Oohs and Ahs from those sucking a burnt finger. Those pushed into the hearth were helped out of their blackened husks by pinches from eager volunteers, and who's ever turn it was to have the 'next one', juggled the steaming morsel between their palms until sufficiently cooled to eat. We sat on the hearthrug around the front of the fire with a sheet of newspaper on our laps to collect the mess as we picked up and dropped the red-hot chestnuts, tentatively pinching their brittle cases which fell away if 'done'. When all had been cooked and eaten and the mess tipped into the fire, Father, dependent upon the state of the fire, delegated one of us to toast him a piece of bread.

Father loved a piece of toast made over the fire. He carefully fixed the bread on the long toasting fork, and when he judged it to be firmly speared, he cast his eye around for someone to hand the fork to.

"Here you are," he would tell the chosen victim, "hold that over there." 'There' was where Father already held the toast in place away from smoke and flames. Soon we were calling, "Shall we turn it over?" or, "I think it is done".

Father took it from the toasted operator and inspected it with "It isn't done yet"; adding as he saw the disappointment on the over-heated face, "just a few more seconds." And the fork was thrust back at whoever was toasting the bread, to finish it. Sometimes the piece of bread fell into the fire and Father rescued it with, "I told you to toast it not burn it.

You're no good, I'll give it to somebody else to do." Which always brought forth excuses instantly rejected by Father. We all toasted crumpets in this way hoping they would not fall into the fire which they often did as they were difficult to keep on the fork which was too wide for them.

In those long, long winter afternoons whilst we digested our enormous Sunday dinner with the aid of heading balloons, hand-stands, rowing each other about the floor and trips to get the coconut toffee, we played and romped by the firelight as the darkness gradually stole in. Soon the flickering shadows projected on the walls, set Father debating whether to light the lamp. Then, in the twilight, the sound of a bell could be heard, faintly at first and then coming closer. With the curtains not yet drawn we ran to the window to see the muffin man. Soon he was nearly here, a flat tray carrying the muffins, balanced on his head, his peaked cap partially hiding his face. In his left hand he held the wooden-handled bell whilst his right, raised above his head, held the tray level as he swung along. He didn't call out 'Muffins', the bell did it for him and it told us that he was close by the gate, as we clustered around Father who was counting out the muffin money. Then we all ran out with money for muffins for everyone. Seeing the door open and children running out, the bell was still and only our chatter could be heard. And as we ran back indoors, the bell resumed it's refrain, 'Ting-a-ling'; 'Ting-a-ling'; 'Ting-a-ling' and then a pause as the muffin man stopped and slowly turned his head round to look behind him for tardy customers. Then on again, past the silent, darkening, curtained houses, down the deserted street, the bell marking his itinerant progress, long after he was swallowed in the darkness. The sound too receded into the distance. All was still, and we knew that no muffins would appear again until twilight of the following Sunday.

Now it was dark and with the lamp lit, it's warm light cosy and golden about the room, the curtains cuddling us in and shutting out the night, the tea table was laid with salads, tinned fish, jam tarts and Mamma's cakes. Rivalry, egged on by Father, might now begin, as to who could make the best toast over the fire. There was always a great demand for it with the beef dripping from the Sunday joint, usually the great 'Aitch Bone' which provided a basin full with the rich jelly beneath. With plenty of people wanting toast there was chance to practise, but the fire could not be let too low and speed was essential.

It was quite late by the time our very late 'tea' was over and little time for games. Perhaps a game or two of dominoes and building with cards, or a quiet half hour with 'Spillikins'. Then it was, "Good night and God bless", from Father with a kiss and a hug, and upstairs to prepare for bed and prayers with Mamma. And then, clean and contented, safe and sound, we sang our songs until we fell asleep.

The Street

In the twilight preceding darkness – the lamplighter came. We saw him dimly through the gloom, and ran to watch him raise the long pole to light the lamp high on its metal standard. The gas sparked and died, and sparked again to splutter into life. Now the street was lit and shapes sprang into view. Vanished was the murky pool. Our shadows appeared – looped to lamps. They loitered behind or raced ahead as we ran about, miming our every move. Night descended – dropping magic! It changed the very air we breathed filling our veins with vital force – renewing our energies. Time now was everything. Soon there would be calls for us to "Come in!", but we had marathons to run and wings on our heels.

In the great hush that came with darkness, our imaginations ran riot. We were enchanted, caught up in the unknown that spells adventure to the young. There were prisoners to be taken, captives to free, giants to kill. The unfathomed well of night was all about breathing its excitement we did daring deeds. Strength surged through us as we raced the streets and mists stole up to scarve the lights. We ran like hares as swift as the wind until, suddenly, sadly, all too soon, doors banged open, light splashed on pavement – names were called and farewells sounded. Backward looks were guillotined as doors slammed shut. In ones and twos we were called to roost. Like wild birds, soon all were caged. Tucked in our beds our thoughts soared on, winging like arrows, until the Sandman came gently. Then with eyelids heavy with the magic dust, sleep came and we sped away in dreams. And out in the lamp-lit street, suddenly, for another night, all was still.

During the week-days life was always busy about the streets. Horses and carts travelled the roads. Summer brought the ice-carts; huge blocks dripping water at the back. There, on hot days, small boys and big ones, ran beneath, knees bent, faces upturned with mouths agape to let the cool water in. Then backing off as the cart stopped, to watch the leather-aproned men grappling the ice off the tail-board, with huge hooks held with a leather gauntlet. Then on to trolleys to be trundled as, puffing and blowing, carters disappeared with the ice, into the butcher's and fishmonger's shops.

Any cart with a cleared space at the back, left by unloaded goods, invited the attention of young lads. Running behind, they followed closely, until a pause in the cart's progress allowed them to heave themselves partly over the tailboard. There they clung, feet off the ground, and were carried along unbeknown to the driver. Until a cry from passing 'likely lads', with hands cupped around their mouths, directed the driver's attention to any bird of passage with the hoarse instruction, "Whip behind yer, Guvner!" This set the carter lashing around and behind from overhead, with his whip, his attention being needed in front by his horse and the traffic. People crossed the roads willy nilly; cyclists knew nothing about safety or the Highway Code which had not yet been thought about.

On mornings when Father tapped the barometer and said it was going to be hot and Mamma knew he was right, he told her we must all go to the park for the day. It was seldom we were allowed in the street. In spite of this we knew all the children there, and played with most of them at intervals.

Death, hitherto unthought about, came suddenly. Little Annie Streeter's mother died. As the grown-ups talked, Annie and I looked at each other. Her brown eyes were wells of sorrow. We did not speak. It seemed impossible that death could be anything to do with rosy-cheeked Annie with her dark curly hair. We were both three. We were both bewildered, beyond speech.

Other sad things happened at times. There was Lennie Nicholson, a nice tall lad, who caught the flu. After a few weeks in bed ill, he reappeared, but now he was much shorter and his back had developed a large hump. We were told that the virus had affected his muscles which no longer supported his spine properly. It now curved over by his shoulder making him a hunch-back for the rest of his life. Leslie's character didn't change and it was sad to see him striding past, still patient, quiet and reserved, carrying his unde-served burden.

There were other sad happenings. Mrs. Bull next door, whose Airedale I had struggled to carry home when I had thought it lost, believed she was about to become a mother after many years of married life. Happy and excited at the thought of a first child, she told Mamma all about it. The doctor confirmed it. But then suddenly, she went into hospital, and instead of a baby, a nine and a half pound tumour was removed and within months she was dead.

Mrs. Bull's neighbour was her sister-in-law. She called the doctor to see her husband who was acting strangely. He was sent away and we were told he had 'gone off his head'. This was about the time that little Lesley on the other side of us, died of diphtheria. Mama told us we were lucky to all be fit and well, which was exactly what other people were constantly telling Mamma.

This was the world depression of the 1920s. We were all shocked to learn of suicides of Fathers, overwhelmed by financial worry. It seemed to be the nicest people who gave up.

Mamma might well say she was waiting for her ship to come home when there were things we wanted and could not afford. But our ship was there safe and sound in the capable care of our parents, and we were all safely aboard, surviving outbreaks of measles, mumps, whooping cough, flu and scarlet fever; the scarlet fever which which we never got. But we had all the others in turn; sometimes one or two of us, and sometimes several together. We had them all except for scarlet fever and diphtheria.

Mamma said we had all been immunised by her blood as a result of her many illnesses at one stage of her younger days. We heard how she lay in bed all one summer with first one illness and then another, her mother nursing her through chronic sickness. In this way she acquired an immunity that had lasted her ever since.

Many years later, when we girls were all teenagers, we contracted gastroenteritis. How glad we were to have Mamma; ministering to us all. One after another we took to our beds, sick and feeling very ill. It was high summer outside, but we all lay shivering, racked with pain. Thankfully we all counted ourselves blessed to have Mamma filling hot water bottles and seeing to all our needs.

Next door to Eddie Almond's house opposite, lived two small girls, Connie and her young sister. Connie Howard's garden was all lawn. We had no lawn. Father and the older boys, had concreted it over, burying at the same time swords and pistols from the war together with a couple of old bikes. We were left with the patch of Indian corn, flower beds full of Tiger lilies, roses, herbs, lupins, red hot pokers and any that took Father fancy, and the poplar and pear trees. All these surrounding a large wooden garden seat, sturdy and strong, on a concrete playground, both made by Father, to survive the energetic games of his sturdy children.

How thrilled we were to go into Connie's garden pushing over the lawn, Connie's large dog on wheels (almost as tall as me) with its curved over handles. But it was for only a short while as they moved away after a very little time.

One very hot summer's day, I staggered home from school feeling wretchedly sick. Barely able to reach front door of our house for nausea, I rattled the letter box, but nobody came. I leant against the door and bending, looked through the letter box. All was still, there was no-one at home. Sometimes if Mamma had to 'pop out' she fixed a piece of string across the inside of the letter box and around the latch, so that we could pull the string and open the door ... I could find no string. Feeling very poorly I walked across to Connie's house, but there was no-one there either. Almost unable to stand, I went back to our door step and lay down across the whitened step. Eddie Almond's house was directly opposite to ours; Eddie whose water wings had set me up as a swimmer. Suddenly a voice from a long way off, out of the hot day, said "Come with me, I will give you a nice cool drink."

It was Mrs. Almond, solid, quiet, reassuring. She took me into her cool parlour darkened with the curtains drawn.

"Lie down here on the sofa," she said, "and I will fetch a nice cold lemon barley."

I felt too sick to drink the lemon barley but felt obliged to do as she so kindly suggested. No sooner had I drunk it than I was sick all over the floor. My head ached I wanted to lie on the floor. I was ashamed and scarlet with germs and embarassment. Mrs. Almond was very kind and understanding. "Never mind," she said, and cleaned it up without any fuss.

That evening old Doctor Collins came and said I had nettlerash as he looked at the large red blains which had now appeared all over my body, and ordered the usual pink medicine which we had for everything. Father came home and came to see me after he had had his tea,

"I know what is wrong with you," he said, poking me in the chest to make me laugh, "you've got the Wiffle Woffles." But Mamma suspected the shell fish that we all ate frequently, supplied generously by Father's friend Jack Alcock.

Two doors from Eddie Almond's lived Reggie and Frankie Wyatt. They seemed to be going off to play cricket with their Father, (whom I only ever saw in long white trousers,) most of their spare time when not at school. Frankie was boisterous but Reggie was reserved like his dad.

Further down the road, just before Mrs. Alcock's, lived Dennis. He was kept closely at his mother's side and having a slight lisp, was regarded as a 'softie'. One day as I bounced a ball on the pavement, I saw Dennis emerge through his gate with a two-wheeled 'fairy bike'. It drew me like a magnet. I flew off to play with him. But his mother kept a rigid eye on us and the bike. I inveigled him past our house and around the corner where I rode the bike joyfully back and forth as Dennis sat patiently on somebody's railings. Suddenly his mother appeared and grabbing the bike with one hand and Dennis with the other, dragged them both back into her house. I gave up, realising the struggle was unequal.

Esther with black shiny hair, rosy cheeks and a perpetual mischievous smile, called one day to look at our tortoises. We had three. Like the three bears they were: large, middle-sized, and small. Esther wanted to pick one up, but was giggling yet afraid.

"They won't hurt you and they can't bite," I told her and handed her the middle-sized one. Just as she took it, the tortoise stretched its neck and put its head out to look around. With a scream, Esther let go and dropped the poor thing on to the floor. Its beautiful shell was split right across its back and the tortoise died. We all felt very sad as we hadn't realised that anyone could be afraid of a tortoise.

When we returned from school and Mamma was out, we sometimes found she had put a string across the latch for us to get in. If the string wasn't on the latch, we knew that she wouldn't be long. However, we knew how to get in when tired of waiting. The heavy cast-iron lid from the coal-hole was lifted and placed against the wall beneath the bay window. Then one of us volunteered to go down the coal hole. It was quite easy to do. We lowered ourselves feet first down through the hole feeling the shute with our toes. We held on to the rim of the coal hole as long as possible as we aligned ourselves with the shute, and then let go, sliding the rest of the way down and landing on top of the coal. Then climbing off the coal on to the cellar floor, we dusted ourselves as best we could and stamped our feet, and walked up the cellar staircase. The door at the top which led into the hall, had a door-latch. This was easy to lift as there was a gap where a screw-driver or chisel could be inserted to lift the latch. All this took less than a minute before we had run to open the front door and let everybody in.

One day a crowd of us congregated around the coal hole gazing down into the blackness and toying with the idea of either sliding down over the coal or waiting for Mamma to return. No-one was keen on the trip over the black, dusty coal as it was a very hot, sticky day. But we were all very thirsty. The coal lid stood ready against the wall as we argued as to whose turn it was to go down. Then one of us noticed that Marjorie Adams had joined us and was standing there, watching and listening. She lived about fifty yards along the road but seldom came out to play. She was plump and usually with her mother. We all agreed that Marjorie should try the coal hole but she was not interested. We all tried to persuade her and finally she was cajoled into it. Poor Marjorie Adams was plump. Her legs were twice as round as ours. In spite of our combined assistance we could not get her down the coal hole. Even worse, we could not get her out again! Tugging and pulling, we tried hard to free her. She began to cry. Finally she was freed and ran home with long scratches all down her thighs. I can't remember the sequel, but she probably kept well away from us.

The streets, full of horses and large carts, barrows and hand carts with an occasional motor car, were cartoons of action of which we were all part. The actors in the daily drama seemed more closely woven with the onlookers than today. Carters were seen and heard, grinding their wheels over the ruts shouting their wares; horses hooves rang out on the cobbles; whips were cracked over horses' heads by drivers. They often stood as if in a chariot race, as though their lives depended upon arriving somewhere in record time; and heavy loads defeated the best efforts of both men and beasts.

The streets were never still on weekdays. Everyone was busily and noisily doing whatever it was that they were engaged to do, and among and alongside all this, the young carried on their activities. Hoops were bowled – wooden ones along the pavements by the girls, and iron ones in the road, by the boys. Tops were spun and whipped into the road where there was more space to send them flying, or spun themselves off the path by accident until pocketed for a moment as a horse and cart took priority. Large coloured humming tops as big as our heads soon became scratched and dented on the stony roads. Pulled into action by a string, they led an independent dance of their own until they hit the tiniest obstacle; then their musical hum became a grumbling tipsy wobble which quickly toppled them over.

Along the street the lucky ones had bicycles, skates or doll's prams. Bikes had a step at the back on which a friend could balance and be carried along, whilst holding on to the cyclist's shoulders. After a while they would change places so that the passenger now took his turn to pedal the former cyclist along.

Some summer days were stiflingly hot and then the water carts came around the roads to lay the dust. The back of the horse-drawn cart had a pipe running right across with lots of holes in it. Water contained in a tank on the cart, ran into the pipe and streamed out on to the road. On those sweltering days, we loved to see the ice cart crawling by, the horses taking the great blocks to their destinations. Then the boys would be after it, the carter flicking his whip to keep the boys off the back. Several boys hanging over the tail board, would increase the horse's load considerably.

Milk was brought round each day, early, in a large churn standing on a cart which was usually pulled by the milkman. He ladled it out into the customer's can or jugs. Our cans hung on a nail in the porch. There were pint, half pint and quart cans with hinged lids on top. The milkman's measure was a small can on a long handle which he dipped into his large churn and filled, then emptied into the customer's jug or can lifted from the hook.

Early in the morning the milkman could be heard calling,

"Milk – Oh, Milk – Oh!" and most people would hear him well before he was near as there were few wireless sets and people were listening for his call and I don't suppose there was anything being broadcast from wireless stations early in the morning. Later in the day the coalman followed the same route around the roads, calling mournfully,

"Co-Al! Co-all!" each word becoming two. Even without looking we knew if he had a heavy load or not. When the horse had a full cart he went slowly; a weary rhythm of hoof beats on the grit and the carter calling loudly and slowly, to catch attention, and if you looked you could see him up there, standing on the cart behind his horse as he held the reins; turning his head in all directions so as not to miss a customer, for it was difficult for him to manoeuvre the horse and a heavy load to turn, once past a house. A large board with 'One and eleven a hundredweight' was fixed at the front and back where it could be seen clearly. It was in figures – 1/11d cwt. Now that would be a little less than ten pence, and a hundredweight now costs £6.50 or whatever it may be by the time you read this.

Empty churns were left together on the street corners to be picked up later by a milk cart. And then we heard them being rolled along on their sides, the heavy metal rumbling and clanking over the paving before being hoisted up on to the carts to be pulled away by horses. The sound of the heavy churns was unmistakable, as was the sound of the empty coal cart later in the day. It rumbled over the cobbles at a fast pace, the horse clip-clopping back to the yard, shaggy hooves flying, beating out a rhythm of freedom for the end of the day, with nothing but a pile of empty sacks behind.

It always seemed to be in hot, dry weather that the tinkers arrived. Pushing a contraption on wheels which appeared to be a conglomeration of articles, endless things suspended from hooks and bars: bundles of cane, pots and pans, saws and shears, straw mats and broken chairs, all lodged somewhere about the ramshackle affair. It was neither a cart nor a wheelbarrow, but rather like a pile of Spillikins hung about and caught in a cobweb, but all for use and a purpose rather like the parts in a Heath Robinson cartoon. Somewhere at the back was the grindstone with handles with which to guide this miniature workshop along the roads.

The tinkers, invariably Irish, offered to mend – "anything, atall – atall."

Mamma found a cane seat to be repaired. Weaving the cane strips deftly back and forth, the long, thin strands flying swiftly under and up, round and through, the old untidy, broken seat was repaired faster than we could follow. Then the useless remnants strewn on the ground by the step, where the tinker sat with a holding peg or two between his teeth were swept. In the meantime, Mamma had found scissors or knives to be sharpened. A crowd of us watched fascinated as he sat at the grindstone to pedal the strap which turned the wheels. And as he spun the wheel the high hum of the blade edge being honed rose and fell with the action of his dapper feet. He accompanied it with snatches of song or whistled a bar or two so that he and the wheel together, became a tiny orchestra.

But these tinkers were men of very few words. They worked with speed and gathering up their bundles of cane and restowing any pots and pans, mats or knick knackery, about their one-man workshop, they were off with their money in their pocket, and vanished like leprechauns.

Sent to find the tinker to sharpen a pair of scissors that had been forgotten, they were nowhere to be found; disappeared into thin air. When we ran back home to tell Mamma she observed mysteriously,

"I expect he has gone to Tom Tiddler's ground," wherever that was.

Itinerant onion sellers from Brittany, appeared at the door once a year. Dark-jowled like Father, they stood on the door-step dressed in baggy, navy-blue jackets and trousers, their faces weather-beaten and brown, matching the onions dangling from the pole held balanced on one shoulder. These men from Brittany across the Channel, travelled around on bicycles. At the end of summer we saw them, cycling slowly in the baggy uniform clothes of the French peasants, black berets close on their heads, doing their balancing act. One hand held the heavy stick loaded with onions balanced over one shoulder, the other hand gripped the handlebar to keep the bike steady. All about the machine, other onion strings were craftily suspended so as not to upset the balance as that they pedalled slowly and steadily like Doctor Collins did on his bike. With their handsome, golden, shining onions and their swarthy, healthy, tanned faces, they were a picturesque sight – moving portraits in blue denims and golden brown. A string of these beautiful onions was always welcomed to hang in the larder.

Plenty of buskers travelled the streets. They were not truly beggars, they were people on hard times in the dreary aftermath of the war. Some were injured and all were without work, trying to earn something to keep themselves and their families in food. Wet, cold days were hard on the buskers.

One old organ grinder came regularly to grind away at his organ outside our house. In his tattered coat he stood, turning the handle with desperate haste. Always bare-headed, he swung the handle violently as he observed all about him apprehensively. We children stood and watched him from a distance, fascinated as he muttered aloud to himself, incessantly. Every now and then he swore loudly at nobody in particular, like an old and hungry lion giving voice to his misery and hunger. Even when a copper rang down on the road from a window suddenly opened and shut, he went on jangling out the raucous music and voicing his feelings until, suddenly, he picked up the coin and, muttering still, moved off. The organ was trundled fifty paces off and dragged to a halt. Every sound registered in the still of the Saturday afternoon, and once more, he and the organ together, wrestled out their plaintive cacophany until he rattled the iron-wheeled mechanism away, to jangle and curse on another spot selected for this dual treat.

War veterans worked in small groups, singing together, moving along the streets slowly, some disabled with a missing leg or arm or both, and some in wheel-chairs. With patches over eyes or moving on crutches, they stayed close to one another in song, body and spirit; sad relics from the war now over. With the great depression affecting everyone, very little was given away to these heroes. In doorways, sheltering from cold, blind match sellers stood on winter days, waiting for a coin to drop into the tray where the matches lay. Buskers travelling alone, worked the roads when the traffic was gone, keeping to the centre playing an instrument. Small groups of miners from Wales lifted their voices in unison. Standing shoulder to shoulder, moving along in a slow shuffle. They proclaimed their nationality with sad sweet harmonies, driven by starvation to tread the streets of London and sing for coppers, there being no work in the mining valleys.

These were hard days. The world-wide slump left its mark and hit doubly hard at those already suffering from loss of health or limbs; it was hard on the widows with children whose men had been killed in France or Belgium or Germany, and the families decimated by the flu epidemics which raged both during and after the war.

There were plenty of gypsies about then, independent characters who sold their own hand-made wares; pegs cut from ash, hazel, chestnut and birch or any other wood handy. Fashioned from one piece like a wooden-top doll or from two pieces of wood fastened together with a metal band, shaped to grip the clothes line. Attractive flowers constructed from wood shavings dyed in bright colours were arranged, along with dyed grasses and coloured scarves, in baskets made from osiers of willow or reeds, and brought to people's doors by buxom gypsy women. In the baskets also there was lace they had made, but their stock in trade was telling fortunes with the plea,

"Cross my hand with silver, lady, for luck."

Their homes were usually brightly painted small wooden caravans on large wheels and they travelled in families and were proud of their independent way of life. Mamma never had her fortune told but often bought their pegs and gave them clothes that might be of use to them.

Many people wandered the streets seeking a living. As I followed Mamma about whilst she was dusting her bedroom one morning, we heard the strains of a violin coming through the window from the street below. A thin-legged, pied piper-like figure was travelling slowly along in the road, as beggars always did, playing a fiddle. With a little jig and an occasional turn around, he jogged slowly past our house. Mamma gave me a penny and opened the window for me to throw it out. It fell with a ring on the road and rolled away. The fiddler stopped and raising his eyes looked all around until he saw us. He touched his forehead in an expression of gratitude before looking all around for the coin. There were no women vagrants in those days, only the gypsy women selling their baskets of lace and pegs and the toffee apple lady with her pram of toffee apples.

We were usually well aware of all that went on around our home. Staying close to Mamma when we were not out in the parks with the boys, we watched her at her work. We watched as she scrubbed the black and white chequered path from the front door to the gate making the tiles so clean it was a shame to walk on them. We watched as the steps were whitened making the tiles even more distinctive, and the coal lid blackened and polished so that the house front was smart and respectable for another week.

One bright frosty morning I ran to and fro in front of the gate as Mamma carried out this ritual chore, clutching a small plaster doll in my arms. It was really a small plaster ornament which one of the boys had won at the fair. I ran back and forth trying to get warm as Mamma finished cleaning the front, the bitter winds made my hands ache but I felt proud of the doll and proud to be out with it. It suddenly began to sleet. Mamma was finished and about to go inside. She called me to come in.

"Come along, Doll, you will be frozen." But the excitement of running with my own doll held me outside the gate.

"The North wind doth blow and we shall have snow," chanted Mamma. Just then a figure walked around the corner into our road. It was a man carrying an enormous brass cornet. He walked along the middle of the road as all street performers did. The sleet fell faster – the man hastened his steps – looking for shelter. Mamma stood on the door step watching him. Our house being second from the corner, he was soon near. Then she called him to shelter under our iron, latticed porch. I ran and stood by Mamma. The glass roof kept the sleet off but the open front and sides were no protection from the freezing winds. The man stood there, a sorry sight; wet and shivering, the cold heavy cornet freezing his hands as the plaster doll had frozen mine in the icy wind. There was little to give him in 1920. Mamma gave him bread and dripping and a mug of cocoa. We stood and watched him shivering as he warmed his hands on the metal army mug and looked out at the weather. I was surprised at his expressions of deep gratitude for the food and drink.

When the road was being mended, a watchman sat by a fire all through the night, whether it was summer or winter. There he sat by a glowing brazier, wide awake – ever alert to guard the workmen's materials. The lighted fire was just in front of a small hut and he sat just inside the doorway if it were raining. The lighted coke with it's gaseous smell, showed red-hot in the darkness, even in summer, crimson fire in a black basket. The watchman, wrapped up well in all weathers, would perhaps be smoking an old pipe, usually of clay, and in his thick, dark, heavy coat and woolly hat, he could scarcely be seen. He seldom moved, and if you didn't know he was there, you'd think there was no-one. The occasional sound of a cough in the still night, or the crunch of his boots on the gravel as he moved a few yards to inspect and refill a lamp, were the only signs of his presence. There he sat all the night long, like an owl, so still, gazing at the glowing fire and listening in the silence. His only company the soft clink of a few cinders now and then, settling further down, until it was time for the bucket of coke standing ready, to bethrown into the brazier. There snapping and cracking it spat at the heat, became red-hot – and took over the fire.

The favourite street people were the Punch and Judy men. When we saw them putting up their tent, the children came from all directions and crowded around whilst the men disappeared inside. We stood enthralled by the antics of Punch, the sufferings of Judy and all the assortment of characters in the unique cast, familiar and loved by all both young and old. The crowd were mesmerised by the unexpected events: the knocking out of Judy, the Doctor taking her pulse with a large pocket watch held against his ear; the policeman catching up with Punch only to be soundly knocked about with his own truncheon; the crocodile who swallowed the alarm clock, ticking loudly as it caught Punch by the arm and leg; the string of sausages which flew about between the puppets finally disappearing nobody knew where; the dog Toby, head on one side – evading the killing punishment that was meted out to everyone by his master, and finally, the hangman caught by the villain Punch and dangled for all to see, in his own noose. How we all laughed and cheered and joined in with the, "Oh no you wonts," each time Punch declared, "Oh, yes I will."

The Salvation Army always came around the streets at Christmas and sometimes on Sunday evenings. They set up their music stands in a circle in the middle of the road near a corner or around a lamp-post in the winter. There they played their excellent music; if it were dark, by the light of their lanterns. But in summer it became quite a party treat and people stood around listening and joining in the singing. Then the collecting boxes were taken and shaken among the crowd and around the doors, and the band moved away to another spot to cheer up the evening with their sounds.

Once a month, on Sunday mornings, the sound of the scouts from a nearby street, could be heard approaching, marching to the lively sound of their trumpets and bugles in time with the beating of their drums. We all ran to the corner close to our house, where we knew the procession would pass, just in time to see Ralph leading the band. Up in the air he threw the mace with rhythmic precision, keeping the pace for the bugles and trumpets. Just behind him were the drummers. How smart they looked in their rows, their coloured scarves cleverly knotted about their necks and laced around with the white cords supporting their instruments. Rows of badges decorated their shirt or jersey sleeves. And the whole band with healthy, youthful faces beneath their wide-brimmed bushmen's hats, intent on their sounds, looking neither to left nor right, passed close to us as we stood on steps and railings the better to see them all.

Turned out as neatly as new pins, they made a colourful sight as they passed, stepping out in unison with their drums and bugles, showing off their sturdy legs in their short trousers and knee high socks with garter tabs flashing green against the navy. Sometimes Stanley was blowing the bugle or beating the drum together with Ralph, side by side. How proud we small girls felt to see our brothers marching with the scouts. All too soon the procession was past and we stood holding hands as the sound of the band receded from us as they marched away and disappeared around another corner and soon was heard no more.

There were other street processions like the mob that appeared at voting time. When it came to polling, Father and Mamma were poles apart. Mamma ever practical, voted Labour, thinking prices would be fairer and the needy cared for. Father believed in private enterprise and self help. Voting officials coming to the door to persuade our parents to accompany them in their cars to the polling booths, were treated to a long lecture from Father whatever their politics. From Mamma, likewise, in the other camp, a long account of the needs of families, and questions from Mamma, on why they only bothered about the electorate at election time. It was strange that Mamma, who had been brought up in security with plenty, was all for the deprived, and Father who had experienced a childhood full of hardship after the early death of his Father, was all for making people help themselves.

Out in the streets the goings on at election time were amazing. Organised by the various parties, crowds of children that Father called kids and other names, gangs collected by supporters of the candidates, went about in ragged mobs armed with sticks and paper banners, shouting out verses in an unmusical refrain.

Early in the 1920s they chanted:

"Vote vote vote for good old ... ie.,
Punch old ... .. ey in the eye.
If he comes to the door,
We will knock him on the floor
And he won't go voting any more."

Bawling out the words in a loud hoarse jingle they rushed by, up and down the streets, filling the road, banging cans and drums as they tore past, waving poles and sticks whilst tattered and torn like themselves, the paper flags and ragged banners, streamed along above.

These were not show-biz personalities, these mobs, but they certainly caught the public eye – and ear. For President Nixon, James Stewart spoke up before the election and Sammy Davis Junior spoke up afterwards, but it was the same Hip Hooray and Bally-hoo that went on, just the same as all the Razz-a-matazz for Eisenhower and Ronald Reagan. In 1984 election jingles for candidates for election in the United States were based on the best in popular music and even

Metropolitan Opera. Not so in Britain, in the 1920s, the children made up their own.

Voting night with people worrying about who was voting and who was not going to, was frenetic and tempers grew hot. Sitting up all night awaiting the counting of votes was just as much a compulsion, perhaps more so, than today. It was more spontaneous and not spoonfed into the people by the media. News travelled fast by word of mouth and the early morning papers were eagerly bought and read, confirming or confounding opinions, bringing about arguments.

The boat race engendered nearly as much feeling, but instead of red and blue, light and dark blue rosettes and matching ribbon flashes were sold in the streets. Just as they were opposed in politics, so were our parents opposed in their support of the Oxford and Cambridge crews on the Thames. Now all the boys in our family supported Oxford and wore the dark blue ribbons like Father, whilst we girls supported Cambridge and wore the light blue ribbons like Mamma. We felt sorry for the losers whichever team it was and the race was followed with great excitement by the public on the wireless and seen the following week at the cinema, on the newsreel.

The streets were a kaleidoscope of life, ever changing. The continual struggle for existence that could be seen going on made everyone aware of the results of the war. Buskers and beggars were the flotsam and jetsam around us. People intermingled in a freer way, sharing thoughts and problems. There was not the anonymity that exists today. People gave what they could to street sellers, so many of them blind or crippled in the war; or shell-shocked (their shaking limbs telling their story) and a copper or two was dropped into their tray of paper flags or boxes of matches.

Strange figures abounded in the streets. One late afternoon just as it was getting dark, a tall thin figure appeared in our road. Dressed all in black with bent back, he was playing a flute, and as he went along, now and then did a little jig. Was he a wizard or a spy? I knew I must follow and discover what I could. Around one or two corners he went but no-one came out to throw him a penny. The gloom of the winter afternoon began to swallow him until finally he and his black clothes merged into the dark and I was lost. I ran along the streets swiftly darkening, looking desperately for the corner I knew so well. Then with a great feeling of relief, I saw Willie Wheatley's sweet shop and thankfully ran home.

One day, seeing Ralph, dressed very smartly for scouts, disappearing through the front door, I ran after him. He was some distance along the road, walking very fast. Feeling there was an adventure in store, I followed. Along the streets we went, turning corners as I ran after him keyed up with anticipation. Suddenly he crossed the road and entered a large church. I was just in time to see him disappear inside and the door closed. I ran across and tried the door. It was large and heavy and I was small and thin. A great feeling of aloneness swept over me. I stood by the shut door and looked along the street. It was all strange and I felt far from home. I ran off, wandering along one street after another knowing the feeling of being totally lost. Suddenly once again like finding the missing piece in a puzzle, I saw suddenly, Willie Wheatley's shop, and found my way home. The frightful feeling of being totally lost, cured me of ever following anyone else.

Gilbert was given the job of painting the front railings. I stood and watched him. It was fascinating. It was all so easy to do, just dipping the brush in the can and stroking it over the iron railings. How clean and bright they looked after each stroke. I pestered him to let me have a go.

"Alright, Doll, I'll give you tuppence to paint the railings," he said giving me the brush. I was excited. I began on the next rail. The paint didn't seem to go on properly. Gilbert watched. I dipped the brush in the can. Still the paint didn't stick on, it ran down the sides. I left that one and began on the next. It was worse. It was bumpy. I suddenly realised that the railings each had four sides. I looked along at all the others. They now looked dreadful. It would take hours, I could never paint them all; there were so many of them. Gilbert watched as I struggled to hide my feelings. It was not worth tuppence, it was much too hard. What had seemed so wonderful so shortly before, was now very depressing. As I had worried so much for the job I felt obliged to paint them, especially as Gilbert had offered me tuppence; I felt miserable and disappointed. But he knew exactly how I felt. He took the brush away and gave me the tuppence.

Some of my older brothers had bikes and although small and thin, I climbed up and sat on the saddle when I saw one leaning against the wash house. Finally the day arrived when I could actually reach the pedals with the tips of my toes. One day, Seeing Ralph's bike, leaning against the kerb in the road outside, I put my leg over the cross bar and found I could just reach the pedal. I was too small to sit on the saddle so I stood on the pedals and started off. Soon I was at the corner and had to keep going. The bike had a fixed wheel! Round the corner I went and round the next corner. Soon I was passing our house and feeling terrified. Round the corner we went and round again and once more the house was left behind. I took my feet off the pedals but they still went up and down and round and round and the cross bar was impossible to sit on. I put my feet back on the pedals the bike going faster and faster. I put my weight back on the cross bar but it was now worse with the pedals out of control. See-sawing from side to side I tried to keep my toes on the flying treadmill, as I passed the house once more and headed for the first corner. After a few terrifying circuits I once more approached our house. Ralph stood at the gate looking up and down the road for his bike.

"Ralph! Ralph!" I screamed. "Stop me! Stop me!"

Whereas I had thought myself lucky that he was not there when I started off, I now saw him as my saviour. Running into the road he caught the bike as we drew alongside and the diabolical torture came to a halt. The brakes were too far from the handle bars for me to reach and I never borrowed Ralph's bike again.

Graham's bike took my attention next. It was bigger and heavier like Graham, but it had a free wheel. I soon discovered that I could put my leg through beneath the cross bar and scoot along and even pedal with one leg under the bar. As the bike was as tall as I was I had to be careful to balance it against me. I often had a 'go' on it in the garden when it had been left by the wash house. One day I decided to take it out for a ride. It was in the wash house but I manipulated it out, through the garden and quietly along the hall and through into the street. How enjoyable it was. I went up and down with the large pedals, one leg under the bar, as I toured the nearby streets. Suddenly I saw a small crowd; there had been a minor accident.

Curious, I stopped to stare. Engrossed in the drama I was rudely awakened by a sharp slap. The bike was taken away from me and there stood irate Graham. I never borrowed it again as he needed it for his work.

On fine days when Father had not sent us off to the park, probably because he wasn't there, we whipped our tops on the pavements; bowled and skipped with our light wooden hoops; rolled marbles along in the gutters to try to win some 'glarnies' those multi-coloured glass ones; bounced our balls endlessly to the accompaniment of jingles; skipped and raced, hid and mimed, well into the long light evenings. On cold wintry days, we made slides, and often snowmen with coal eyes, carrot noses and twiggy arms. Then pelted them with snowballs whilst the boys pelted each other and their friends, being able to throw much harder than we girls could.

There were so many things to do in the street that we never did in the parks. An odd wheel from a perambulator was a lot of fun. With a short stick through its centre and a longer one held beneath to guide it we sent it spinning, running after it, turning it skilfully this way and that until it hit against a bump or a crack and going haywire, went off on its own until recaptured. Then we were off once more as it sped away, controlling its meanderings with the skill acquired with practice.

We discovered the fun to be had with sticks. What tunes we played on the railings as we ran by, one after another, dragging our sticks against the iron bars with joyful abandon. We used them to drive our hoops, tapping them skilfully to keep them on course. Sticks became swords, kites, cricket bats, rounders batons, bows and arrows. They marked out trails and hop scotch squares when there was no chalk to be had.

They made whips for our tops and hockey sticks for stones. They cost nothing and exercised our skills and imagination. Lucky owners of penknives whittled away for hours. There was nothing quite like it; just whittling with somebody's knife. First the bark was peeled and then a fine point made for a cricket stump or a sword and our initials carved, cutting our fingers in the process.

The kites we made were extraordinarily unsuccessful. We never seemed to be able to get them going. We ran our legs off to get them airborne, but they dragged themselves along the ground, tangled in trees after split second flights, and were fragmented, it seemed, in inverse ratio to the time spent creating them. We changed the design, the shapes and the materials, but it was all to no avail. We didn't know in those young days that the secret of the kite lies in the length of the tail.

Our tops were far more successful. We made whips for them tying string onto a stick. The string had to be fine and strong and was wound round and round the top which was stood carefully on its pointed end and held steady by the stick and one finger. A sudden sharp pull with the stick sent the string rotating the top and then it had to be whipped to keep it going. Some were much better spinners than others and travelled steadily across the pavement and off into the road where they continued to spin. We followed, whipping them as we admired the whirl of colour we had chalked on top. The whip could be passed to someone else to have a 'go' and then you could have it back, the top still spinning.

When we found a good stick we carried it around with us all day and guarded it jealously like a new friend. It helped us cross streams in our pole vaults;

steadied us on pipes crossing ditches; showed us the depth of the water; knocked apples and conkers off trees; was the post in 'Release' and carried our socks and jumpers tied around in knots as we grew too hot. They were invaluable and when we saw a 'good' one lying abandoned in a hedge or bush, we all rushed to claim it.

Street skipping was very popular as the smooth pavement didn't catch the rope. Skipping ropes were a girl's best friend. If you had a good longrope or several short ones to tie together, everyone wanted to play with you. There were plenty of volunteers to stand at each end and turn the rope continuously. Everyone joined in especially for 'Higher and Higher'. As the long lines of children waited in turn to jump, they knew that if a friend were at one end, or if you were liked, the rope would be lowered a teenie 'bit' so that they would not be 'out'.

All skipping was accompanied with chants from the onlookers. Running through the rope turning slowly with only four skips, the voices sang in unison:

'Slow skip,
What you like –
A dolly
Or a pepper,'

repeated without pause as the next skipper ran into the rope before it descended and picked up the next sequence.

The best skippers were revealed in the fast skipping with 'bumps'. The favourite jingle was and maybe still is –

Misses ....   D .... I .... FF I
C .... U .... LT .... Y

A .... R .... It .... H
M .... E .... TI C

The Misses was the preliminary skip to get started and the first eight bumps followed. It lived up to its name and most were caught 'out' long before they got to the Arithmetic.

Ropes were snaked along the ground and looked deceptively easy, but many were caught in the snakes as they ran over. Phyllis was good at 'bumps' but I wasn't as I was always chasing about and playing 'Release' instead of staying with the skippers.

The streets were favourite for bouncing balls for the same reason as they were for skipping. Children spent a great part of their time developing skills with balls in ways peculiar to the young. Reciting jingles and rhymes, they were passed from hand to hand, up and down walls, under and over legs and behind backs, with quick twists and turns, hops and jumps sandwiched between, integrated into the rhythm. Patting the bouncing balls to walls and ground a thousand times a week, children learnt co-ordination of hand and eye that could not be improved upon in any other way or with any other device. Chanting almost meaningless jingles, the rhymes kept up the rhythms:

The complications were introduced on the end words of each line and when this had been completed successfully, it was all repeated with inventive variations with double tricks and left-handed tricks and so on. There was no end to the diversities to challenge the best performers, and all who took part were judged impartially by the onlookers, the criterion being, you were either 'still in', or 'out'.

We followed each other along the streets, running with one foot in the gutter and one on the kerb which wise-heads now term 'mimesis' but we called it 'follow the leader'. We were well conscious of what we did, especially when we had to stop as our leader came to a halt to examine the condition of the aniseed ball she was sucking. As we gathered together to contrast the state of our own aniseed ball with all the others, holding it between a sticky finger and thumb, we ascertained the size and colour relative to those being likewise displayed, comparing the scarlets and browns of our tongues, attracted attention from youngsters without aniseed balls. A jeering remark from boys across the street sent tongues and sweets back out of sight. This prompted,

"Made you look,
Made you stare,
Made the barber cut your hair.
Cut it long,
Cut it short,
Cut it with a knife and fork!"

A few other such taunts sent us girls running off on our lop-sided progress down the street, followed by cat-calls and cries of,

"Cowardy cowardy custard –
Eat your mother's mustard!"

I don't suppose the boys ran off as we girls did. They enjoyed a fight.

When the long hot day was over and the evening cooled, we were faced with the weary trek home. On these long walks a game of 'Knock down Ginger' gave us something to run for and took us home quicker.

People became very irate when they opened their doors to see us running away. They came out into the streets and shook their fists at us which was what we enjoyed, there being, by then, some distance between them and us. At home, after tea, the boys having enjoyed this, suggested tying some door knockers together with black cotton. Adjacent houses were soon cottoned on to each other and a sharp knock before we hid started them off, knocking on each other's doors as they pulled them open. This was never kept going for long as people soon found the cotton, whilst we kept hidden.

Life in the streets was a daily newsreel. All was hustle and bustle where time was of the essence. Everyone went about their business earnestly, whether it was the brewer's dray, spick and span – proud with shires, visiting the publicans, or the wheeled milk barrow with the churn of raw milk which had to be scalded. Beggars or tradesmen, they all moved daily on their way in the battle for existence.

As in Hogarth's day, when people paid to look through a telescope at the heads of the Jacobite rebels stuck on spikes on Parliament Hill, so now the streets revealed the daily drama. It was all there to be seen; the war survivors, the hungry victims of the depression, and the general population, all swept along with business as usual, as Life must go on.

And behind these busy streets, in quiet back gardens, Buff Orpingtons, Rhode Island Reds, Light Sussex and Black and White Leghorns, scratched about busily in the grit and laid their fresh, warm eggs in sweet-smelling straw; pecked corn and ate their evening mash, happily unacquainted with the technology of battery farming. Children ran across roads as yet uninvaded by cars, as parents gossipped at gates swapping ideas and tit-bits.

The sea of Life was in the streets awash with the world about us. Like the swimming pool, the daily struggle could be seen and heard, opening and closing with the daylight and the darkness. And in this ocean of work and worry, play and laughter, we children darted about like the diatoms in the pond, thriving among the weed. Ever busy we were; learning through play, playing at Life and our days were long. The streets and parks encompassed our horizons providing a perspective which became part of ourselves.

Chapter Nine

Outdoors

We spent a large part of our childhood in Wanstead Park.

In Roman times a sizeable settlement was there but in 1086 the recorded population was only eight and by 1670 there were only forty homes in Wanstead. Until the nineteenth century Wanstead was very wooded and part of Epping Forest. Wanstead Flats, the lower forest, was part of an ancient heath until it was linked to the outside world by turnpike along the Woodford, Chigwell and Leytonstone roads. Sometime in the seventeenth century, the owner of Wanstead House diverted two streams from the River Roding, to construct artificial lakes and water courses which exist today. This was our summer playground where we spent the long summer holidays complete with the day's sandwiches and whatever else we chose to take with us. Wherever we went, Wanstead Park was the zenith of our childhood wanderings.

The Manor of Wanstead belonged to Queen Elizabeth's favourite, the Earl of Leicester, and then to his son, the Earl of Essex, and was visited by the wealthy from Elizabeth's court. Wanstead House was of the finest and held paintings by Holbein, Raphael,

Rembrandt and Van Dyck. Hogarth painted the Assembly at Wanstead House in 1729. In recent years it was used for art exhibitions and demonstrations by well-known artists and for other creative activities.

The keeper's cottages were still standing in the centre of the park, housing the forest keepers at the time we played there and may be there still. We often saw them wearing their brown jackets, knee-breeches, gaiters and large-brimmed hats, going about their duties in the park. Quiet men, tall and imposing, they instilled respect in the hordes of children who invaded the park in summer. In November they paraded in the same uniform in the Lord Mayor's Show.

Of all places we went to on our outings all through the long summer holidays away from school, Wanstead Park and Wanstead Flats were favourite. Father instructed Mamma that we were to go to the park for the day and we were given our fares for the 'tram'. It was quite a long way but we often walked both ways so that we could spend our fares on sweets.

Furnished with packets of sandwiches we dawdled the three miles or so to the park. Arriving at the Flats, first we made for the ponds and sat on the grass by the water's edge to eat our sandwiches. This freed us from carrying them about with us. The next move was to take off our shoes and socks and paddle. After about an hour or so of walking about in the water looking for fish, and sitting on the bank skimming pebbles, counting the bounces on the water of the aquaplaning stones, we ran on to the sand hills. There were three or four of these sandstone hills. We could run up and down them or all along the tops chasing each other: playing 'He' or 'Release' or trying to fly a kite. By now it would be early afternoon and time to make the long trek down Wanstead Park Avenue to the big park, the Mecca for us in summer, Wanstead Park.

A long way it was and we looked with envy at gardens we passed where children played on swings. The houses were large and fine belonging to well-to-do middle class families. It was a long dawdle and many a stop before the park gates came into view. As we saw the huge open gates, fixed back among the trees, our pace quickened. Once through the gates all was changed. The hot, tiring street was left behind and we felt the tall gloom of great sycamore trees above encompass us as we entered the leafy green world of the park – cool and quiet about us.

We now had to choose which way to take. Every path in this oasis from the hot summer streets was well known to us, so that whichever way we chose we knew exactly all about it. To the right were the tall groves of trees alongside a stream which seldom attracted us first unless we were seeking conkers or fishing. Besides, it was longer that way to the Glade which we always made for. It was here on the right, under the tall trees that Miss Hopkinson had brought our class of seven years old for our nature ramble.

By unanimous consent once through the park gates, we usually walked straight ahead along the tree-lined gravel path, passing the boating lake on our left, where Father and the boys hired skiffs, following the path towards the woods until it ended as we reached the cricket green with the large padlocked chests on the boundary, now we were adjacent to the first woods. After a rest on top of the chests, we climbed down and entered the woods. At the fringe we passed the tea house where sweets and snacks could be bought and found ourselves in a sparse part of the forest, extending quite a distance to left and right, but with very little depth. In the middle of this wood was a low hill up which we ran, jumping over huge tree roots exposed on the slopes by erosion. There on the top we held a short council as to whether to stop for a game of 'Release' which we usually played on the hills. Then on towards the Glade, the long wide strip of green, the cleared space between the two woods.

We were always delighted to reach the Glade. Now back in the sunlight we threw ourselves down for a rest, our shoes and socks thrown off, resting our feet in the lushy growth by the forest edge, spreading our toes to catch the cool grass between. There we luxuriated, planning our next moves.

It was afternoon time and we lay on our backs, the sun dazzling through our eyelashes. The sunny Glade stretched far to left and right cutting the forest in two and was itself a forest of a multitude of different grasses: Rye and Meadow, Oat and Cat's-tail and many others, where hosts of insects lived their busy lives. Down among it's thorough fares, Bloody-nose and Sun beetles, earwigs and spiders, ants and ladybirds, went about their business, intent and single-minded like all the other creatures there; over the scene, wild flowers splashed colour and every-where among it all, the crickets sang.

Lying there in the Glade, this was our half-way house. After the morning spent on the Flats, racing over sand-hills, paddling in the ponds or sitting in our arm-chair trees, we were glad of the Glade for a rest. The afternoon would now be spent in the great park with its dark, mysterious woods, still lakes and pools, but now we lay here to recoup our energies.

The crickets claimed our attention, scraping con-tinuous melodies they dared us to catch them. At our approach they fell silent; invisible – they struck up again elsewhere. Rare captives escaped from cupped hands until we gave up the chase.

Long they sang as we lay content regathering our energies, gazing up into the blue ocean of sky, fascinated by clouds of sailing camels, elephants and giraffes, pushing each other along and changing shape in seconds. Finally rested, we gathered our impedimenta and wandered off across the Glade into the other half of the forest, towards the lily pools and Grotto, where, following the water-course, we knew we could find the stepping stones once more.

Once out of the Glade and back among the trees, it was dark and gloomy. All seemed dank and still: there were few birds and fewer children: others of our ages seemed to play near to the park gates, the boating lake, or along the right-hand path leading to the conker trees and the stream beneath with sticklebacks to be caught. But by far the majority of children preferred the Flats where they had the ponds, the sand-hills and the 'tram' terminus by the sweet shops. The long, tedious walk down Wanstead Park Avenue must have deterred many from visiting the park.

These woods were part of an ancient forest and forest still. This second half of the woods was denser and the hill here much steeper. The tall trees were close together, the undergrowth matted: paths rambled about often to disappear into a tangle of thorny brambles. We quite easily became lost and quickly out of sight and hearing from each other if we were not careful. After a few hair-raising runs down the sides of the hill, catching each other at the bottom, we moved on through the forest to where it bordered the path by the lonely lily stream, always deserted and still, gloomy and quiet, where Father went to fish, where only carp and perch moved silently beneath the lily leaves.

These ornamental waters constructed for the rich, centuries before, were not meant to be paddled in. They were oozy, full of weed, covered by large round lily leaves making the water dark sheltering the fish, and there was thick mud at the bottom. The edges were deep unlike the ponds, bounded by wood-slimy and slippery with algae; and the sunlight came down only fitfully between the branches of the trees high above.

Here by the lily stream we gazed at the waxy white and pink lilies, hoping for a glimpse of a perch or carp beneath but we never saw any; no fish moved, only the weed stretched between the spreading lilies wavering slightly with the slow moving stream. Along the path grew stitchwort, bluebells, hemlock and meadowsweet, speedwell and buttercups, all the year round, except for the bluebells.

The lily pools were just a stop, on our way to the Grotto; the Grotto always mysterious and menacing, beckoning us on. Turning right along the path, we walked on until there it was – the Grotto, no doubt constructed along with the artificial lakes and water-falls in the seventeenth century. Suddenly revealed through the trees, the ruined walls rose, ominous above a stagnant lake, which disappeared under a gloomy archway where the punt was moored. This sinister spot fascinated us. The punt was always there but never any sign of a person. Only a fleeting movement of a bird might be seen out of the corner of an eye. The sun, obscured high above the canopy of broad leaves, shone through a green filter that darkened the Grotto and the scum-covered pool. Those who were big enough to reach them, scrambled on the ruined walls and looked at the still punt, out of reach, half obscured under the arch, apparently unmoved since our last visit. Tall, tangled Meadow flowers and nettles grew in that damp place. We moved away – afraid of the swamp underfoot.

The Grotto and swampy pool in Wanstead Park was chosen as the place concealing the body of the murdered missing man in the film *The Big Sleep*. In the book, Raymond Chandler wrote ... "The place was as lonely as a churchyard ... a branch broken off by the wind had fallen over the edge of the sump and the flat leathery leaves dangled in the water." The sinister atmosphere of the Grotto gripped my imagination whenever we saw it as children. Many years later in the film, Robert Mitchum stood on the very spot, gazing at the scene, bringing it all back to me. It was seemingly unchanged, as sinister as ever, as he stood gazing at the stagnant pool by the ruined Grotto.

Leaving that dank spot where chill winds always seemed to come down through the green overhead canopy, moving the massing pond-scum imperceptably towards the tunnel. Under the archway, it disappeared from sight among the ruined walls. We found our way back to the gravel path alongside the lily stream, and travelled on to our next chosen port of call.

We knew exactly where we wanted to go and had our favourite places to visit wherever we went. We were now heading for the stepping stones, but first we had to find them and our pace quickened.

Running along by the stream, on and on we went until we were approaching the back of the park. Now the water was fast flowing. From time to time we stopped, thinking we could see the stones covered by the water, it was nearly always a false hope and on we went again, almost giving up, telling each other that we had missed them; that rain must have raised the water level and hidden them. Perhaps we had passed our beloved stones and had not seen them, there being bushes, nettles and undergrowth covering the stream edge here at the back of the park. What agonies we went through at each false sighting; the stones we saw in the water that were not the stepping stones, that treacherously led us to slip and fill our shoes. Walking and searching, never really sure where they would be found, four or five pairs of eyes and legs were looking and running until suddenly we all saw them, almost hidden by tall meadow sweet and Canterbury bells, bushes and nettles; at last there were the stepping stones!

Sometimes the water was deep and to cross over the stones we had to take off our shoes and socks. These stones were usually wet and slimy and we had to take care not to fall over in the stream. But in times of drought they could be dry and then we ran over and jumped back and forth to make the most of them as the shallow stream gurgled and ran swiftly past. It was always fast-moving as it neared the back of the park and could be menacing when the water rose above the stones after heavy rain.

We sprang back and forth from stone to stone until at last we stayed on one side or other of the stream. On the far side out of the park, we lay in a large field which was a meadow of buttercups, daisies and dandelions; and sitting about we threaded them together with clover, making chains for necklaces. This side of the stream was open and quite different from inside the park on the other side of the stepping stones. Here, wide, open and sunny, the tall meadow flowers hid us completely as we sat making our daisy chains, whereas across the stones in the park, it was overgrown with bushes, blackberries and nettles. Hidden hordes of midges waited to bite us, where they lurked with voracious appetites in the grass under the tall trees.

We had to go back over the stepping stones to go home through the park. Our return route back to the park gate was now quite different from the one we had taken to find the stones. Now following the path on, away from the Grotto, we reluctantly left the stepping stones and keeping by the stream, made for the weir. Weary now after our long day of play, we walked half-heartedly, but, just as the stones had, now the sound of rushing water revived our flagging steps. Then we saw it; the stream widening out into a lake which became huge and overflowed into a narrower lake over a shallow weir. We walked on and on, and now we were on the path that followed along by the park fence, under tall trees, and the narrow lake narrowed further and became a stream. The stream became stagnant flanked by tall chestnut and sycamore trees and here and there reeds and shrubs and tree roots kept us from the water's edge, where swans preened and rested. We were back in Miss Hopkinson country, where she had brought our class of seven year olds to collect autumn fruits.

Leaning tree stumps grew far out over the water and we clambered over them, carefully avoiding the swans. We remembered Mamma told how the keeper on Lady Loder's estate at Lennards Lee in Sussex was crossing a small bridge when he was attacked by a nesting swan and had his leg broken. So, in this way, picking up a feather here and there, a conker or an acorn, with an occasional short scramble over roots or through a bush, or a hop over a branch, or jumping from stone to stone at the water's edge, we were gradually nearing the park gates. There, feeling absolutely exhausted, we forced ourselves to walk that long weary avenue back to Wanstead Flats and the tram stop. We never did have any money for the tram back and we began our trek from the tram terminus of three miles or so to home. Past the ponds we walked where only that very morning, but now so long ago, we had sat to eat our sandwiches; towards Manor Park where the Earl of Essex public house reminded folks that the Manor of Wanstead had hosted the élite of Queen Elizabeth's court; on towards home, dragging our tired feet, until, close to home, the thought of food accelerated us and then we were there. Washed and fed and tired out, we were all soon safely tucked up in our beds.

Another day would be quite different. Reaching the Flats as we called the ancient heath known now as Wanstead Flats, we came to the trees by the ponds. There were about six or seven of these – twisted, short, stunted, bushy trees. We knew the topography of that spot and the topiary of each tree. Each had its own character, with wonderful natural seats and armchairs formed from twisted and gnarled branches, especially fitted for small children. We could see at a glance if anyone was in them for their heads poked out of the top. If not, we dashed for our favourite seats and were soon installed, like koalas ensconced, loathe to move, remarkably comfortable. In our positions we could see anyone passing near, and providing we kept still and kept our heads low, we were passed, virtually unnoticed. Leaning back in our pseudo armchairs, like nesting birds, we surveyed all about us.

There we stayed for some time, perhaps eating our sandwiches, relishing our positions; jealous lest some other newcomers took our places. Sometimes on arrival we found other heads poking out above the knotted and gnarled branches that showed us we were not alone in knowing the secret seats that we found so attractive. Nearby there were other consolations. Cool, clean water to paddle in, boats to sail, sand hills to race on, kites to fly.

Summer days could be relentlessly hot. Moisture was at a premium. The bottle of water or lemonade we had brought for a hot day had long since been swallowed. Crowds of thirsty youngsters lined up at the water tap, but in very hot weather the tap ceased to flow – it became dried up. August, one year, had such a day. High summer found us on a picnic with a kind mother of two sisters Nellie and Renie Collings. There we were, several little girls on the Flats for the day. How hot we were; our bottle of drink long since finished and the water tap dry. I ran once more to the water tap hoping to fill the bottle, but the tap remained dry. The air was stifling and the dry tap made us thirstier than ever. I decided to go home and fill the water bottle. I ran all the way home and then all the way back along the High Street to Manor Park and on to Wanstead. Mrs. Collings was astonished when I gave her the bottle of water. She could not believe that I had run all the way home to get it, about three miles each way. Her eyes began to shine and I thought she was going to cry, but all she said was, "I think you are a brick."

Right over the far side of the Flats near Leyton-stone, not far from the ponds where Father and the boys went for Sunday morning swims in their birthday suits, and where they skated in winter on the Hollow Pond if the ice were thick enough, in that area the Fair would be set up. Blaring out its arrival at Easter, Whitsun and August Bank Holidays, it attracted crowds of people from all around, Leytonstone being the nearest. We were all attracted to it, but I never really liked the fair. The din and heat and dust, or mud and pouring rain were the drawbacks. The long walk across the Flats which was necessary to reach the fair was an added aggravation, dreary and uninviting. There was absolutely nothing of interest on that bee-line we made towards the far-off fairground. The feet of the crowds travelling in the same direction wore the grass away. No wild flowers survived on the stony gritty expanse which covered this wide area during fair time. No buttercups, daisies or clover invited us to sit and have a rest. If we sat by a dandelion, shepherd's purse or yarrow, it was among the grit where these plants struggled against all odds – and what was normally a heath was mostly now like the far-off fairground itself, muddy and stony.

In the distance the fair was just a faint twinkle of lights and the noise came to us faintly on the wind. But as we stumbled and ran to keep up with the older members of the family, the noise grew louder and louder. We saw the Helter Skelter getting bigger and bigger and the Great Wheel grew larger and larger, until suddenly the Big Dipper and the Scenic Railway burst into view. There they were, studded with lights, magnificent, towering above all the rest! We had arrived. We stopped running and stood on the fringe, dazzled by lights, confused by din. Noise exploded about us like fire crackers. On the outskirts, trying to collect our wits together we stood, alongside a noisy, belching steam engine. We were bewildered after the long, anxious, tiring scramble across the arid heath. We stood, wondering what to do first and where to go.

The din and bustle from machines and people confused us. We had the money perhaps for one ride each or one 'Go' at the coconuts. We wandered around, loathe to spend our coppers until the very last minute. The boys wanted a 'Go' at winning a prize. We watched the Rifle Shooting and the men bringing down the mallet with all their might to make the bell ring; the Chair o' planes swinging out against the sky, full of couples suspended on fragile, slender chains; the Big Wheel suspended in mid-air, whilst those at the bottom bemused, climbed out, from their seats. All around were stalls where people rolled pennies, hooked tin fish on magnets and threw rings to try to cover pound notes, half crowns and six pences. At tent openings and on platforms, strangely garbed men and women shouted out attractions that awaited out of sight, which you saw if you paid to enter; and on the Wall of Death round and round the motor cycles raced, climbing higher and higher up the wall, until they almost shot over the top; then down they went again and stopped until the next spin.

We wandered about in the fairground, trying to keep together and decide where to spend our precious coins. We fancied the Dodgems as three could squeeze in the front of the car, but the men only allowed this if you were very small. The coconut shy was voted a good idea and in no time at all we had won a coconut and had drunk the milk and were wrestling to get the coconut out from its shell which we had broken with a brick.

After a few hours, our teeth clogged with coconut, we reluctantly decided to go home. All about us, sounds and scenes dragged at our heels like magnets. From the Big Dipper intermittent screams rose in crescendo as the cars fell like arrows, silenced abruptly as they crawled slowly upwards again like caterpillars towards the next terrifying plunge. Ear-blasting cacophanies ground out as the machines rotated the roundabouts, swirling, twisting, rocking and vibrating, competing with screams and yells from the riders on the contraptions, who had paid to have a 'go' on them in order to have their insides terrified as they were flung this way and that. But above all, climbing the sky like a toy and plummetting so suddenly that only the screams of the people on it made it real, rose the Big Dipper, overpowering us all and our stomachs churned in sympathy as we watched from the ground, seeing it fall like a meteor whilst we walked slowly backwards, away from the inferno of light and din until we turned our feet away to the long, weary traipse home. The power engines and laughter, the honky tonks and cries gradually melted into a confused sound fading into the distance, until, looking back we saw once more the fair as a silent glimmer in the distance.

For a change we went off to the Woolwich Ferry sometimes. We walked to the Town Hall, where we took the tram or the 101 bus. We always went upstairs, where there was a good view over everything. Up at the front we pressed against the window. Leaving the Town Hall behind, it took us past the Central Park on the right, where the district sports were held, past the Conservative Club that Father belonged to and where his friends Mr. and Mrs. Barnes lived as resident caretakers, on towards the sewer bank which ran like a hill, close to the Beckton Gas Works. There men far below, always busy as though working on an anthill, could be seen moving in all directions.

Looking down, we saw trucks on rails coming and going like boxes threaded on string, and from the high tram car or bus, the small figures appeared bending and working like midgets in a puppet show. Once past the Gas Works, we looked for the swing bridge. If a large ship were about to enter or leave the Royal Albert Dock the bridge was high in the air and the road with it. All the traffic was halted and it could be a long wait whilst the ship was manoeuvred through, in or out of the dock – a miracle of navigation, with only inches to spare on either side, and the men running along the wharf to see that it was clear amidst a lot of shouting in foreign tongues and noise from the ship's sirens. If we thought it was going to take too long, we clambered down the stairs and jumped off the tram or bus and ran along the footway close by and up the stairs to cross over the metal bridge, but the metal bridge had enclosed sides so that all we saw we had to see from the bottom at the wharfside before we went onto the bridge, where we could see nothing.

We heard the Lascars from the crew running and shouting as the large vessel was being squeezed carefully under the bridge, so close that on the wharf we could stretch out and touch it as it scraped the sides and went on up or down the river.

All around huge ships were docked, with painted funnels and strange flags from all over the world. Mighty cranes for loading and unloading ranged along the wharves in droves and in all directions. Lascars leaving the ships, coming and going, moved silently, dark and slight with their rocking gait peculiar to seamen, with straight backs, leaning and rolling on their haunches. If the delay was long, we went off to walk the few remaining streets that led to the river itself where the ferry came and went.

There by the river we had a conference. There were choices as to our next course of action.

"Let's go under the tunnel," someone said.

"No. I want to go on the ferry first."

"What about Abbey Woods?"

Mostly we made a bee-line for the ferry, where we ran up the ramp and watched the approaching ferry boat swinging in circles across the river.

These boats were quite frequent and even if we had just missed one, another would soon be there to pick up all the waiting cars, lorries and passengers. Anxiously we studied them, watching how soon we would be aboard. There were three ferry boats; one coming, one going across and one stationary either here on our side, or over on the other side. When we were lucky, we saw one just coming in with lorries and cars ranked skilfully together on the upper deck. The paddles flailed furiously through the water, churning it into foam with a great rushing sound. Down below, the engines noisily changed gear and brought the ferry clanking to a halt by the quay. There it bumped itself against the great creosoted sleepers of the wharf, with the throbbing and grinding of engines and metal. Then the gangway was unchained and clattered down with a great ringing shudder as it reached terra firma.

Meanwhile, a rope had been thrown from the deck to an onshoreman who had skilfully caught and secured it to a bollard as the passengers were released across the gangplank and the first cars came slowly, lining up for the off. As soon as they were on the move, the waiting cars and lorries on the wooden approach road began to move on board, skilfully directed into position so as not to waste an inch of space or a second of time.

The passengers speedily disembarked, their footsteps echoing over the wooden boarding; the traffic controllers waved cars this way and that; everything was soon off and the ferry reloaded; the rope thrown back to be coiled neatly, secure in its rightful place on deck, all passengers were on board and we children were running to see the throbbing, hot engine rooms below. The smell of the river was all about us; the hot oily machinery, the creosote on the piles, the dank odour that can only belong to a great industrial river, the smell of the Thames.

There below, we watched the men in the engine room. In steamy heat men were busy, working as if their lives depended on it. They took no notice of us as we clambered alongside their engine room, peering through every opening, as they shouted at each other above the din. Men were busy shovelling coal, oiling parts with oily containers with long spouts and using greasy rags to keep everything clean and free from slippery spills. They were nearly all totally absorbed and we might as well have been invisible.

After a brief look at the engine room, which we had seen so many times before, and noting that it was all just as we had expected, we ran off upstairs, about the ferry, through the covered passenger way on to the open deck, where we turned all the vacant seats the other way about so that they were now facing each other and then flipped them over to all face the same way again. Then it was up the iron staircase to see the lorries and cars, but we were not allowed on the deck. Then down again to watch the river craft as by now we were in mid-stream and there was a good view up and down river.

A police patrol boat might swing into view and we speculated on what the police inside were about and bound for. Old sailing barges, fully loaded, with huge brown sails spread, moved lethargically along, as swifter flat-bottomed counterparts, loaded with coal or covered with tarpaulins, roped together in fours, fives and sixes, sped by, either motorised or in tow behind a tug. Now and then we sat briefly watching the river craft, the passengers, and seagulls wheeling and calling. Larger vessels were going steadily up river towards London or down towards the estuary past Canvey Island where the river was five miles across. Like quicksilver we darted about, seldom still, down to the engine rooms again, up to the top of the staircase to look at the car deck, down again to watch the paddles churn the water furiously, propelling the huge mass of the ferry along. We noted how smoothly the other ferry in the river was swinging round, to haul itself across the river in the opposite direction and alongside the opposite bank. The water boiled furiously in the paddles; the passengers seemed wrapped in their thoughts. Everyone on the vessel was remote, concentrated in themselves. Only we were free, darting about like swallows, unable to settle for more than a few minutes. We knew that as soon as we got off the ferry on the other side we would quite likely get the other ferry back again and explore that in the same manner.

When we did just that, we were not to be cheated out of our trip to Abbey Woods so we would race back once more to the Woolwich side in order to go to the woods. We scorned a third trip across, so ran down the metal staircase that spiralled down and led to the tunnel that went under the river. What a long way down it was. At the bottom we saw the tunnel at last. Into it we went, shouting and calling to hear our voices echoing from the curved walls. The walk was a three quarters of a mile and seemed interminable. Then at last, once more we climbed the spiral staircase, on the Kent side this time, and ran up towards the open air, until out of breath, we were once again where the first ferry had taken us, at Woolwich.

Then began our walk to Abbey Woods. Up the long steep boring road we went; past Woolwich Barracks and the Arsenal, where Father had worked, for some months during the war of 1914 to 1918, as an inspector in the making of munitions. We walked on and on, until we reached the woods where there was not half the fun to be had at Wanstead. Among the gorse bushes we hunted for birds' nests and played at hide and seek until we began the long tedious trek back again through Woolwich to the ferry on which we longed to be.

Too tired to chase about, we had to content ourselves with one trip to the engine room, a few manoevres on the moveable seats which were like the tram seats. Once back on the north side of the river we endured the walk through the mean dockland streets, which always seemed menacing to us; past the swing bridge and the forest of now silent, still, cranes, until all the river smells and sounds were far behind together with the sewer bank. Then we longed to see dear friendly East Ham Town Hall with its clock like Big Ben which told us we would soon be home to quench our thirst and eat, and the long day with all its familiar adventures was almost over.

The same river smells of oil and tar, creosoted timbers and ropes, barges and tarpaulins, washes and wakes, also hung around Barking Creek. Nearby was the ruin of Barking Abbey, once one of the most powerful of Benedictine Monasteries until Henry VIII used his rapacious power to have it demolished in 1540. There, Matilda Queen of King Henry I was Abbess in her time.

The lovely old church nearby, All Hallows-by-the-Tower, its early name Berkynchirche, was where Captain Cook was married. Later he was murdered in Hawaii but his widow lived on at Barking for more than fifty years, dying at the age of ninety three. Her gravestone can be seen at Benfleet further down the river.

We often went to the small park by the Abbey ruins to play on the swings. Nearby factories told us the exact time, when all their sirens and hooters signalled at midday for lunch. Then all the workers from Bryant and May's match factory and from the Metal Box Factory, streamed out for lunch and we knew it was time to go home ourselves. It was by here that I fell in the river and where the one-legged boy, possibly a gypsy, had walked the tiled balustrade of the bridge on a wet, slippery day.

Some distance up the River Thames was the Tower of London. Father took us there once but, as he had train fares to pay as well as the entrance fees for all of us, it was the only occasion. First of all, he showed us where lions had once been kept by the moat and pointed out the ravens which had their wings clipped so that they fluttered about awkwardly on the grassy slopes by the ramparts. They were clipped as it is said that if they ever fly away, the Tower will fall in ruins. He showed us Traitors' Gate, where unfortunate prisoners were brought in by boat when the river was at the right height to flow under the spiked gate. Then we saw the weapons in the White Tower; the halberds and pikes, the cross-bows and swords and suits of armour. We saw the square where the block had been, where poor Ann Boleyn and Lady Jane Grey were each beheaded and so many others also.

Mamma and Father rested on a seat whilst we ran about to see as much as possible until Father declared it was time to leave. Once outside, we children sat on the heavy cannons lined up outside alongside the river; we looked at Tower Bridge and saw the busy tugs pulling barges roped together, their cargo covered over and roped securely. Thames river police moved about in their launches and noisy sightseers on pleasure steamers passed by. All craft up and down the river, sent their wash in their wakes to come lapping at the shore in fretful surges, long after they were past.

At last, Father would wait no longer; everyone had sat on the cannons; Mamma said it was past our bedtime and in a tightly knitted bunch, holding each other's hands, we crossed the wide road to the tube station and home.

Not being able to afford holidays we had days out instead. Great treats were the days with Father and Mamma when all the family went out for the day. Father loved London and took us all to London Zoo when he could afford it. But this was rare and we went only twice when I was very small. Wandering from animal to animal and enclosure to enclosure, we became very tired. Father would not let us miss anything and it seemed a shame that the only place where we could sit down and still see the animals, as the benches were raised, was in the lion house. We preferred to stand close to the cages and watch the keeper feed them with great pieces of another animal's carcase. As Father made sure we were in the lion house at feeding time, it was crowded and we had to keep together or be lost.

The polar bears seemed to float so lightly; they moved – rocking over the edge of their platform and gliding about, never still, with Father holding me up against the wire to see them better.

It was very hot inside the monkey house and very smelly, so we were all glad to move on to see the camels, who looked rather moth-eaten with their tufts of woolly coat and bare skin here and there. The elephants passed us, giving people rides on their backs, but Father could not afford any for us. The great pythons awed us; A dead mouse or two in their pens accentuating their great sizes like tree trunks.

The giant tortoise, over four hundred years old, seemed undisturbed by the crowds, or the attention he attracted. Seldom moving and exciting comment as he slowly took a step towards a cabbage remnant, only to remain frozen on the spot for an age, not even moving his head. No doubt, thousands of events took place all over the world before he finally lowered his head to the cabbage. The humans, impatient, unable to wait for the next move, went off to stare at baboons or the gorilla. Notices everywhere told people not to feed the animals, but everywhere people were busy feeding them as though the notices said 'Feed the Animals'.

We loved the giraffes, sailing with their quaint heads in the sky, peacefully chewing a wisp of hay and gazing in an aristocratic way at us under their long lashes. The hippos were delightful, upheaving through their pools to twitch tiny ears and open huge mouths with their yellow fangs barring the edges to catch the buns and apples people threw into them. Apples and buns were the elephants' favourites and they soon neatly tweeked them away from outstretched hands and cupped them in their sensitive trunks, then deftly into their mouths. They also were dainty steppers and their huge weight was transferred from one spot to another with an indefinably delicate equilibrium. These silent giants viewed the crowds with an air of all-knowing tolerance and a wisdom as old as time. So many animals to see, we were tired out and frequently sat down whenever there was an empty seat to be had. Father spent a lot of time picking me up to see the animals better and we all became very thirsty and grubby clutching at the wire around the cages.

Parrots squawked, baboons shrieked and hooted, orang-utangs bellowed calls in terrifying sounds, monkeys howled and we all chattered and scraped ourselves over the concrete paths, determined to see everything.

At last, it was time for the Zoo to close and the crowds streamed out through the park, on a long walk towards the tube station. We raced to the water tap on the way, for Father would not let us stop, and so on to the train, where we all found seats and some fell asleep to be woken at the end of our journey, and trot along, dead tired, to home and into bed.

I can't remember Father taking us to the British Museum, but we went there. It was an exhausting business. The great flight of steps at the front entrance was a challenge when one's legs were small. At the top we wanted to sit down, but were propelled inside by the crowds going in. There on the left were the steps down into the Egyptian rooms. Father impressed upon us that we must see the Rosetta Stone which gave the key to the ancient Egyptian civilisation. There it was, in the Egyptian room, a slab of stone with strange engravings.

Great marble statues lined the sides of the chamber. No doubt it is all changed now and what we saw then is now a blur in my memory. Galleries of show cases filled with artefacts from ancient times. Staircases with priceless things at every turn: Mummies partly bandaged in their coffins which fascinated and repelled us. We went into the library. Beautiful books decorated by monks centuries earlier amazed us by their beauty and finesse; superb decoration and complete scenes encompassed within a single letter! Exquisite colours were safeguarded within the show cases locked in the library in the museum.

All these, and hundreds of other priceless treasures kept for everyone to see at no cost at all, drew us back on other occasions and we found ourselves again going up the great marble staircases on hands and feet to rest ourselves. At the end of another long day out in the holidays, we returned home knowing how lucky we were to be so near London and yet so near the forests and open spaces of Essex.

The Victoria and Albert Museum never seemed as interesting as the British Museum. Perhaps it was because we went on our own and had several things at home like the things in the Victoria and Albert. Things like Father's vases and Raggazone's vases. It seemed that we could easily become locked in this museum. It was very quiet and often seemed deserted. We lost our way and sometimes came to a dead end. When the galleries were being changed around and we found ourselves confronted by scaffold and planks, this made it seem lonely and menacing, so we seldom went there.

The Science Museum at South Kensington was the exact opposite. First, there were always crowds of children there from many different places. Some were with their parents and some with schools. Never was it deserted and crowds of children watched each other try out everything there was to try, like making a large clock wind itself up. The large pendulum was the first thing we saw on entering. Moving back and forth with the movement of the earth, it never stopped.

The great Blue Whale in the Natural History Museum staggered us with its length, as did the diplodiccus. Triceratops and tyrannosaurus, the sabre toothed tiger and the mammoth elephants, all fascinated us no matter how often we went there. We knew exactly which things we wanted to see and each viewing was thrilling; the stegosaurus and the other fossils, such as pterodactyls, proving their existence long ago by surviving as rock fossils.

We imagined the rain, day and night for years, as the earth cooled and then the seas being formed and giant ferns growing by the swamps. There the dinosaurs roamed until they vanished, leaving their bones and a few giant footprints here and there for us to know they once existed. Some think they vanished as a result of a comet hitting the earth. All these things at the Natural History Museum were a never ending source of fascination and no matter how often we went there, there was always lots we hadn't seen before.

A day on the tram would take us to the Monument, where we paid three pence to walk up the 345 black marble steps to the top. The column of Portland stone with the flaming urn on top was a favourite climb for us as we could see all over the city from the top. The Monument, now dwarfed by the towering post war buildings, is 202 feet high – the exact distance of the Monument from the house at 25 Pudding Lane where the fire started in 1666, devouring 436 acres of houses and streets and 89 churches.

We made several visits to the Monument by Old London Bridge. This bridge which now stands in America, having been taken down piece by piece and reassembled after its journey across the Atlantic.

In the spring, we sometimes took the train to Laindon to see the bluebells at Laindon or Langdon Hills. From the station, for us, it was a long, steep tiring road to the woods. There we roamed about; climbed a few trees; lay about in the grass threading clover chains; looked for drinks or ice cream to buy and picked the bluebells. They stood in their thousands looking totally desirable but we knew that as soon as they were parted from the earth, they no longer kept their magic. Only in woods are they so enchanting, yet we wanted to take them home to Mamma. It was always a hot day when we went to the bluebell woods and we lay about among the bluebells in the shade of the trees cooling ourselves on the carpet of bells. When the heat and thirst became unbearable, we took to the hot pavement to track down ices or drinks. Then back into the woods to lie among the blue and green. As the afternoon wore on we became tired and, collecting armsfull of the bells of every shade of blue, from almost white to deepest azure, we trekked downhill to the station and back on the train home.

In the summer, we took the train to Hainault Forest. Hainault, part of the Royal Forest, was kept for Kings to hunt there. Like the trips to the bluebell woods, we chose a hot day when we were wanting to be in a cool place. The walk from the station to the forest was quite a long way and we found it exhausting. Buying a bottle of R. White's Lemonade helped us along but the strong clip on a spring holding the stopper firmly in place, needed strong fingers and only the boys could manipulate this.

By the time we reached the forest we were tired from walking and very thirsty, the lemonade being long since gone. At last, there was the entrance gate by the keepers' cottages and the long, long walk along the entrance drive to reach the forest. Luckily some genius had set the water tap half way along the drive and there we filled the empty bottle. Only that bottle of water made a hot day in the forest bearable. Children seem to become much more thirsty than adults. Once again, the road was uphill, until at last we were among the gorse bushes at the forest fringe. We lay among the hillocky rabbit warrens peppered with small black droppings and rested awhile. Sometimes a young rabbit would appear, nibbling nervously, and we kept very still, but the slightest movement sent it flying. As our energy returned, we started travelling down the slopes, rolling over and over, our arms pressed to our sides trying to resemble logs, racing each other, hoping to avoid rolling into the gorse bushes: frightening the rabbits there.

Then we played cricket, rounders or French cricket with a suitable piece of wood and our ball. There was plenty to do and no wonder we became thirsty. With so much clear space there were many ball games and plenty of sticks about for hockey, cricket stumps, rounders bases, tracking markers, Hot Rice and so on. When we were finally too hot to run about, we went down to the lake where children were fishing for sticklebacks. There in the cool water we refreshed our aching feet and legs and then back into the forest for a game of Release or tracking. The forest went a long way; down to Chigwell Church and on to Lambourne. It was easy to lose the way and we took care to keep near the paths or by the fence, where the keepers told us there were badger setts and foxes dens. In between all our games, we went to and fro to the water tap, where there was always a crowd of children pushing and arguing, queueing up until they reached the tap.

Then they kept their mouths glued underneath and had to be dragged off, when they promptly rejoined the unruly queue.

The keepers were dressed in the same manner as the keepers at Wanstead Park and all the children treated them with awe and respect, on the rare occasions that we saw them; for they were seldom seen.

The old iron bridge was close to our home and one of our favourite spots for a short visit. We were there inside ten minutes and it crossed over the railway lines which carried both electric and steam trains from various places in south-east England to London. We ran up the flights of steps on to the bridge, which had strong upright meshed fences through which we could see the trains coming and going. With our faces pressed close against the metal mesh, we saw a steam train approach. We closed our eyes waiting for the clouds of steam to envelope us. Suddenly everything about us was swallowed in a white cloud; the train was beneath us; the bridge shook uncontrollably; the noise and excitement were tremendous. We rushed to the opposite side of the narrow bridge before the engine could get away but it was blanketted in its own steam and so were we, When we saw it again and the bridge was clear, the engine was some distance away and the rest of the train was just finishing rocketting past beneath us, and the bridge, as it thundered along. Then the last carriage was gone, a speck in the distance and, with our fingers hooked in the iron mesh, we stared and waited for the next steam train to come along.

We saw the electric trains running smoothly beneath us as they travelled with a high-pitched whine in both directions. We stared down at the yard; coal hills, empty trucks – awaiting the wrecking of Sunday quiet by the steam train. An occasional dog sometimes trotted up on to the bridge to wag its tail and be made a fuss of and then it ran off on a trail of its own, knowing just where it was going.

Not many people used the bridge whilst we were there, which was usually on our way to fetch the coconut toffee on a Sunday. It wasn't really on our way but we included it when it came into our heads to do so.

As we stood on the iron bar at the bottom of the mesh fence, gripping the holes in the metal with our fingers, which became blacker and blacker, a puff of steam from a funnel on another approaching engine induced a fever pitch of excitement among us and in seconds the furious cloud was all about us as we swiftly unhooked our fingers and raced to the opposite fence. But we were cheated by the swirling mist from seeing the engine below, once more it was revealed to us only as the nauseous cloud of steam and coal gas was billowing away, swirling after its progenitor. We were never able to see the engine emerging from beneath the old iron bridge, no matter how we tried to win the race of three or four feet between the fencing meshes. But, oh, the excitement as we repeated the blind dash in the blanket of noisy steam in innumerable endeavours.

Not far from the Old Iron Bridge were the Arches. Now the positions were reversed. We walked beneath the Arches in profound gloom, dank and earthy-smelling only to be found in tunnels, whilst now overhead the engines and trains passed out of sight, with only the muffled rumbling along the tracks above, making us aware of their journeys. We used the Arches rarely and only as a short cut to Valentines

Park to save a mile or so of walking. All was silent as we passed beneath these dark gloomy metal arches, except for a train perhaps, overhead. So we whooped and called to send the echoes flying and startled a pigeon or two.

Valentines Park was not really the sort of park for children. Although there were lakes and beautiful gardens with azaleas and rhododendrons, it did not offer adventures or tree climbing or any of the things we enjoyed so much at Wanstead. There were no sandhills to race over, no paddling for hours to catch sticklebacks, no woods to track in and explore, no stepping stones to discover and no mysterious Grotto to lure and scare us. It was a grown-up's park, unless you were big enough to go on the boating lake.

Inside the park was the old house, now known as the Mansion, built in 1690 by James Chadwick. The house was famous for the great vine that was planted there in 1758 by the head gardener. It was of the Black Hamburg variety and flourished and spread 200 feet along the south wall and was reputed to produce an annual crop of several hundredweight of grapes. In 1769 a cutting from it was struck to produce the famous vine at Hampton Court. Unluckily the Valentines Park vine was destroyed by a new head gardener from Sandringham. He tidied up the garden, removing the vine and putting it on a bonfire. The estate steward was just in time to see it burning and so the great vine of Valentines was destroyed.

The Recreation Ground near our home had a play area, locked in winter.

There were lots of different things to do there when it was open in the summer. A long queue of children drew up outside, waiting for the lady in charge to arrive and unlock the gates. As soon as she was inside the small wooden gate she leaned over and harangued the boisterous elements who always fought their way to the front of the queue. Then, when she deemed them to be duly quelled, she opened the gate just wide enough for two small children to wriggle through. In no time at all, the swings were all taken and those still outside the small barrier looked with envy, never resigned, and argued as to who should be turned out of the play area to make room for others. Some in the queue wanted to go on the flying maypole and declaimed loudly that those presently flying round in the air, supported by one elbow, had been there long enough. Others, boys with hoarse voices like street traders, croaked out that the Jazz (The Jazz – a horizontal plank which moved back and forth rising high each time. Boys stood at the ends – holding on to the poles which sent it higher. Those seated in the middle held onto a small handle – a precarious position.) was really for boys and girls should be turned out. A scuffle here and there following some argument or other kept the queue occupied; and the lady attendant, who was equally as fierce as the rowdy boys, kept up a barrage of threats as to who would not get in "Unless they behaved theirselves". As we stood listening to all this 'argy-bargy' as she classified it, we were almost struck dumb. Father had trimmed our behaviour to such an extent that short of a life and death issue, we kept clear of trouble and the boys only fought back when attacked, but otherwise avoided any bother.

At last some of the children were ordered out from the play area and those likely lads and lasses holding well-fought-for places at the front, elbowed and pushed and shoved to be first through the gate. But the lady in charge was a match for us all. Reaching over our heads, she selected this one to be pulled in and that one to be pushed back, the majority of children happy to oblige with a shove or two, and in this way we all finally had a turn in the play area.

Inside, we made for the maypole with wire ropes flying round it fixed at the top. They had strong metal loops at the ends, through which we put our elbows, gripping the rope above with the same arm. With the other hand we grasped the rope above, higher up. So, in this way, with the body weight partly on the doubled up elbow and partly carried by the two gripping hands, we ran round the pole, the rope spinning round with us hanging on the ends, and as it was getting up speed, we let fly, flinging our legs and feet out sideways to fly with the spinning pole for a few seconds and then run and fly again until our elbows ached so that we ran off for a rest on whatever was vacant for a few seconds. Then it was up and down on the see-saw with great jerky thuds as we landed, unless the weight at the other end was balancing well, then instead it was hard work to keep it going and a good spring as we landed was needed at either end to keep momentum. The Jazz seldom had a space on it as it attracted the rougher boys who stood up in ruffian pairs at each end, each gripping a metal supporting bar, to make it go as high as possible, whilst those in the middle clung on for dear life and were often reduced to tears in order to be able to get off.

The swings were not as good as those in the small park by the ruins of Barking Abbey, where the swing chains were long and light so that you could go as high as the side supports even with your eyes closed, which brought on a great sinking feeling.

There was little else to do in the Rec. except play cricket or ball, or hide in the hedge which was almost worn away by the number of children who played there, and we were lucky to find a piece of hedge which concealed us. Looking through the railings behind the hedge, we would see horses at the drinking trough and across the road were the Bonny Downs.

There were other parks in the area that we went to occasionally, but these, although much nearer than Wanstead Park, were not half as interesting as that great park.

The only holiday that we ever had, that is, a going-away holiday, was thanks to Gilbert. He was always thoughtful and kind, and became a generous, intelligent young man. He paid for a holiday for three of us. He loved giving us things and once organised a knitting competition between some of us girls when we were little – we each tried to knit a scarf as we were just learning to knit, I stretched mine as far as I could. This showed the great holes in it where stitches should have been. The edge of it went in and out where stitches were lost and then joined on again. At one stage, it became very narrow indeed.

Of course, it was just an excuse for Gilbert to give us some pocket money, which he did when our efforts were beginning to become very tedious and when arguments arose as to who was doing the best.

Gilbert was also a tease, as were the other boys. One day, when I was quite small, two or three years old before I started school, Gilbert took me to buy some sweets. We left the shop and began the long walk back home. "Can I have one of your sweets?" asked Gilbert. I offered him the bag. His blue eyes smiled down at me as he took one. Very soon he asked for another and another. I felt upset, but as they were his gift to me I tried not to show it as I took the bag out from my pocket where I was trying to save a few, but very soon, before we were half-way home, they were all gone. I felt choked. My fingers clutched the empty bag in my pocket, but I kept it hidden, embarrassed that Gilbert might see how I felt. I was hot and bothered and Gilbert was full of merriment. We walked on together as he laughed down at me. I understood why he was happy – he had eaten all the sweets. I became very quiet and felt miserable and ashamed of being ungrateful. Suddenly, Gilbert put his hand in his pocket and held out all the sweets. I felt even more ashamed of myself when I took them all back and understood that he had saved them all for me. I remember the joy in his eyes as he saw how happy I was. He was eight years older than I.

When Phyllis, myself and Olive were thirteen, eleven and nine respectively, Gilbert paid for us to go on holiday. This was through the 'Country Holiday Fund,' which enabled children in certain circumstances to go away cheaply for a holiday in the country. We were eligible as members of a large family, unable to afford holidays. I don't know whose idea it was, as Father was dead against anything that smacked of charity, but no doubt it was Gilbert's as he was always quick and alert about everything.

Off we went on the long train journey with lots of other children to Gloucestershire, but I remember nothing about that journey until we stopped at our destination. We three sisters climbed out at a small station where we were met by a man in railway uniform and his wife and two small children. Mr. Rowbotham was the signalman. They lived in a small cottage by the signal box and that is where we stayed. I cannot remember the name of the village, but it was close to the River Severn.

Mr. Rowbotham, our host, was the only signalman and he had an artificial leg from just below his left knee. As soon as I knew about his leg, I continually urged him to take it off. It fascinated me to see the springs attached and to see him fix it back on again and strap it around and walk on it. Patiently, two or three times a day at first, he sat down and undid the leg whilst I crouched down the better to see the whole operation from start to finish. Mrs. Rowbotham seemed just as fascinated by my interest in her husband's leg.

There were several boys in that small village and it was not long before I was roaming around with them everywhere they went. Nearby were the railway trucks; empty, high-sided containers with a few knobs of coal and plenty of coal dust at the bottoms. We played in them, scrambling somehow up the sides and dropping down inside. Some of the boys were big enough to give the smaller of us a leg-up to get out. I nick-named them all, but now only remember 'Curly Brown'. I suppose I named him that because of his black curly hair. He is the one I remember. He was well built, chubby in his knee length short trousers. He had very rosy cheeks and spoke in a soft country voice when he spoke at all. He was a sturdy friend and the other boys tagged along with 'Curly Brown' and me.

Nearby, was the fast flowing river, part of the River Severn. We went to the sheep dip and watched them being forced into the narrow ditch. It took all the strength of the men putting them into the dip as the sheep fought and struggled to escape. Once through, they soon raced off to join the flock.

Out in the river a raft was moored, but none of the boys could swim to it. I decided to try and show them that I could. They all thought I could, but I was afraid that I might have to give up and swim back. In I went struggling to do the impossible and managed to reach the raft. I scrambled on to it, exhausted, and lay there. A chill wind was blowing and soon I was cold. I looked at the expanse between the raft and the bank. All the boys thought I had found it easy, but I was afraid I would not be able to get back. With everyone watching, I dived in and began the struggle to reach the bank. Gasping for strength, I finally made it. Exhausted, I climbed out but nobody seemed to notice that I had found it a great struggle. The next day and every day after, sometimes more than once, I swam to the raft but had to lie there alone as no-one else could make it.

After that first time, I knew I could do it and was not so terrified of being swept away by the current. As I lay on the raft getting my breath back, it was sometimes warm and sunny and I lay watching the weed flowing parallel with the current until I felt strong enough to make the return journey. Back on the bank, I received envious looks and admiring remarks from the boys, but I never told them that I was scared in the powerful river.

In the railway cutting there was plenty to do and it never occurred to me that I was a girl, I was quite happy to be one of the boys. Phyllis didn't seem to be having much fun because she was growing up and didn't fancy getting covered with coal, climbing in the coal trucks and looking for grass snakes. When we found one of these harmless creatures, the boys waited for a train to approach and then laid the snake along the rail just as the train arrived, so that it was flattened completely. Although I would not have done this myself, the village boys had their own code of conduct and it never occurred to me to interfere with it. When we couldn't find a grass snake, we put each other's hats under the trains and enjoyed squashing them flat.

The Rowbothams had two children – Edith and Brenda. Brenda was about my age, about ten. She was quiet and I don't remember her playing with the village boys and me. Her small sister, Edith, was about three and followed me everywhere I went and cried unless I took her with me now and then. At the back of the house was a wall beside a deep drop. The boys and I ran along the top and dared each other to jump down, but it was too far. Below the wall Edith trotted, trying to follow me with the boys. I had to pick her up and take her into her mother as I was afraid that she might get hurt. She cried bitterly as I ran off to rejoin the boys.

I spent half the holiday carrying her about, as she wouldn't leave me.

A girl from the village appeared one day. The boys drove her away with cruel remarks and rude words. She wanted to climb the wall but they jeered at her. I was shocked at their unkindness and to hear her addressed as 'Bitchie'; but to my protests they laughed and said, "That's her name." She was never allowed to join us whenever she appeared and then I saw her no more.

A young man named Don came to see Mr. and Mrs. Rowbotham. He made a great fuss of Brenda and offered to take her for a ride on a horse. I found myself feeling very jealous. I thought and thought about the horse, although he never came back whilst we were there.

In the village there was a man I had christened 'Bill Sykes'. He had a horse. Every time I saw him with his huge cart horse, I pestered him to let me ride on it. He was always busy, but promised that one day he would take me to the next village for a ride. One day he appeared at the door with the horse. I was lifted up onto the back of the horse and, being very small and wiry, had to sit with my legs splayed out across its wide back. It seemed an interminable journey to that next village. 'Bill Sykes' walked beside as we clopped along. He had no idea that I was being tortured. I felt as though I were on the 'rack'.

At the village, I said little or nothing, but stayed on the horse longing to be at the end of the return journey. At last, 'Bill Sykes' was ready to walk the horse back. When the torture came to an end and we were once more back at Mr. Rowbotham's cottage, I was lifted down. I could hardly walk and had to tell everyone how I had enjoyed it. I didn't ask to go on the cart horse again. I consoled myself on the trip by trying to be like the Greek stoics and thinking all the time that it would not last for ever. Besides, I had pestered 'Bill Sykes' so much for the ride, that I had to be grateful and tell him how much I had enjoyed it.

Meal times were a marathon. Mrs. Rowbotham enjoyed having us all to cook for and made plenty of meat puddings and sweet puddings to follow. She placed enormous helpings in front of us. After clearing my plate, she gave me extra helpings. I felt fit to burst. I undid all my clothes in order the better to help Mrs. Rowbotham enjoy watching me eat. Each lunch time I had to undo even my liberty bodice, which had lots of buttons all down the front. I felt I had to eat as much as possible as my two sisters were so fussy. Phyllis, always finicky at home and no better here, disappointed Mrs. Rowbotham, who thought she was giving these children good food (little knowing that Mamma did exactly the same), liking nothing better than to see all of us eating a good meal. Olive wouldn't eat. She was fretting and home-sick and had a poisoned hand, so that she cried and was quite off her food. I felt it was up to me to show Mrs. Rowbotham that I was thoroughly enjoying the holiday and her cooking.

For some inexplicable reason, Mrs. Rowbotham, who was not very old, much younger than Mamma, seemed fascinated by me, rather like her little daughter, Edith. Each night she came and kissed us all good night and then spent about ten minutes tickling me. She made me explode with laughter. I could never understand why she went through this ritual every night, which she seemed to enjoy.

The holiday soon passed, what with Edith trotting round me; the boys to chase about with, climbing trees and coal trucks; swimming to the raft; Mr. Rowbotham's leg; rocks and walls to climb and nicknames for all the new friends we had in the village.

At last the day came for us to leave and the forgotten journey home took place, but one event whilst away I'll never forget. A letter came from Father, who was out of work, this being the depression. In it he expressed his delight that I had passed the scholarship to the Grammar School. Enclosed in this letter was a screw of paper with a silver threepenny-bit inside. This was my reward. It meant a great deal both to Father and to me.

Dear Gilbert. He never knew how I had wrung every scrap of enjoyment out of that holiday that he paid for. How I had enjoyed everything about that village and all the characters I had re-named. How Curly Brown and I had led the legions in the railway trucks. Neither did he ever know about Mr. Rowbotham's leg or my battle with the River Severn, nor the sheep dip, nor little Edith or Bill Sykes. And I was never able to tell him, as all too soon he died in a motor cycle accident.

Chapter Ten

Mother

Father and Mamma had been very comfortably off when first they were married. Father had a wholesale fish business at Billingsgate and Mamma (was recently) a well-to-do widow with her locally connected couture work. They were able to afford a nurse-maid to help with the children, and the maids lived in as the children increased, and they were able to live well.

We who were born later, when the war had taken its toll of jobs and incomes, heard all about these nurse-maids. In the pre-war affluent times, they were hired as living-in helps with the five boys, Roy, Gilbert, Graham, Ralph and Stanley, all born within seven years or so.

Mamma said, "The nurse maids were never satisfactory." If they were good with the children they were perhaps dirty and never cleaned themselves. Some were lazy and read novels all day, when they should have been looking after the children. If they were clean and worked well, they were untrustworthy and stole. They were all girls who were sent out to service because they were a problem at home. They stole the soap or linen, helped themselves to money or let the children cry and neglected them, as they sat with their heads in paper backs. "I tried to train them but they were so unsuitable that we had to get rid of them," she sighed.

She illustrated this with the account of Ralph who had been taken out in the big bassinet. He was nearly three and walking and talking like any other toddler. The girl took him to the park and after an hour or so returned with him. He would not stop screaming. The doctor was sent for. It took hours to pacify the baby and the doctor said he had a terrific shock. The girl would not admit that anything had happened. The doctor threatened to prosecute her but she would tell him nothing. Ralph stopped walking and talking and had to learn again. He came out in a severe rash which reoccured each year.

"As for the girl," said Mamma, "I told her to pack her bags and go. We were never able to find out what had happened on that walk that day."

"Only one girl," Mamma told us, "was excellent in every way and she left to get married." Violet Pinder was the nurse-maid par excellence.

"I never had to tell her to do anything," Mamma told us, as she put the feather duster around and we trailed behind her through the house. "She could be relied upon to do everything herself, properly, and as well as I could do it myself. She was as clean as a new pin. I could trust her absolutely with the children and she was as honest as the day. When she left to get married, I missed her terribly and there was never anyone like her."

All the first five boys had a nurse-maid who lived in and helped Mamma, but by the time we girls began to arrive, the war had taken Father away and there was no money coming in from the market. Soon Mamma found that all her own money and the little from

Raggazone, as Father had refused her claiming anything from Italy, was gone, and she was having a struggle indeed. She grew potatoes and vegetables in the garden and earned a little from sewing, but people were hard up with all their men away at the Front. Her letters from France suddenly ceased and the allowance from the War Office stopped. Father had been classed as a deserter!

Mamma was at her wit's end. What could she do against the power of the war machine that had taken Father and now callously punished her and the children? After repeated, fruitless visits to the Town Hall, she sat down and wrote in desperation to Lloyd George, the Prime Minister, telling him of her plight.

"I wrote," Mamma told us all, "that I had five small boys to feed and was expecting another child. I told him, 'One day there will be another war and you will take my five sons to fight for their country as now you have taken their Father and we must starve because he is lost.'"

Lloyd George wrote back.

"Take this letter," he wrote, "to your Town Hall, and they will instantly pay you the money owing to you."

Mamma did this and was given the money owing to her and her allowance resumed. Father was found to be in hospital in France and had lost touch with his regiment which had been decimated in battle.

Mamma was a true countrywoman, observing the weather each day she forecast what we should wear. Seeing the poplar and the pear trees, half obscured in the garden, on foggy mornings, she told us how, early in the mornings, from her bedroom window in Lower Beeding, she could see Chanctonbury Ring appearing through the mist which stole over the Downs. And hearing the blackbird's cry, she wistfully recalled her sister Aggie mimicking its notes as she sat high in the apple tree.

Setting about the day's chores or the cooking on the long wooden kitchen table, she told us of her mother's beautiful pastries and roast pheasant, whilst she stoked the kitchen range and put bread to prove. We stood and watched and listened as she squeezed water from the bread for bread pudding and told how she had always been kept at her mother's side, chaperoned at every turn; going to Chapel three times each Sunday with her mother; in large lacy hats and long lace gloves up to their elbows in summer, and warm bonnets and fur muffs in winter. Always with her mother on the visits to the cottagers, she helped to carry the medicines, broths, cakes and pies to the less fortunate.

In that community, living closely with the estate, the Brown children mixed with the children of the 'gentry'. Mamma recounted how Robin, Lady Loder's son, had been gentle and quiet whilst Pat, his sister, was a tom-boy and loved to ride to hounds. The village came to life in our kitchen on baking days, as she recalled helping her own mother with the baking for the villagers. Once more she was skating on the pond and told how Kitty, 'the flower of the flock' in one of the village families, went under the ice and was brought out drowned, whilst her sister who had to be wheeled around in a bath-chair, paralysed, lived on, a prisoner of her disability to the end of her life.

We heard how, at school, a girl had pushed a pansy strig (a thin stalk – like a twig) into Mamma's ear where it broke, causing severe pain so that she screamed. Whereupon the teacher called Mamma out to be caned. She took the cane from the teacher and broke it in halves. And with it all she told how she loved the country and wished she were there still; riding her bicycle into Horsham seven miles each way daily, after she had left school and was apprenticed in an *haute couture* business.

Because of her ever-growing family Mamma was unable to visit her mother. Apart from all the children, there was the war and the cost which she could no longer afford. Her mother wrote to her frequently, the following letter less than three weeks before I was born.

Chapel House,
(Lower Beeding Sussex.)
Crab Tree
June 28th '18

My own dear Clarrie,

I was thankful to get your letter this morning. I think I must have answered your letter, I know I am very forgetful, but not enough to forget you dear child, for we are always talking about you and many folk have asked me after you this week, and I pray that you may have a good time and a good getting up and be able to come to us for a few days and hope there will not be anyone else here, so that we may have all the talking. I am glad that Geo gets home we were afraid that he had been called away, for the head folk seem to have no sense, somehow. I know it is selfish of me, but I have wanted you so very much sometimes, & I am so helpless to help you. We were spared through the winter & then came the load of work in the garden, & there is still, & Charlie is not able to do as much as he used to do. He has to work hard and the rations are poor, & he has had all his teeth out. I shall be glad if he ever gets a good sct, for I know well what it is to be without teeth. I have only three old ones & am getting quite old. Mr. & Mrs. T. Day came here at

Whitsun, from Sat. to Wednesday, and Lennie came here for two weeks holiday, and Frank & Edie were here with him for the second week, & they all went back together last Monday morning. It was well for me that Edie was here for I was poorly last week. Am glad to say I am alright now. You will be sorry to hear that altho. there was such a splendid show for fruit, nearly all the crop are a failure, because of the Blighting Pest of Caterpillar. We have a few raspberries & I have made a bit of mixed Rhubarb, Gooseberry and Raspberry Jam. Now dear child, you say you do not hear from Aggie, I seldom do myself, but the girls write. Aggie is always very busy and very very bitter against the war. I told you that poor Dudley had been gassed, & really ought to have been sent home, but he was sent back to his unit again. So poor Aggie is always in a worry but I do hope they wont take Wallace, or she will go off her head. What can we do. I only keep praying that the war may end soon. All the men are going from here, it is awful. Charlie Gilbert has three fingers blown off, so he is not fighting just at present. There are a lot of young widows about here. Georgie hopes to come down August Bank Holiday for a week and Geo. P., Dollie and children about the same time. But I do not know yet when any of them are really coming, or how, & everybody has to bring their own rations, it is worse than horrid. I wish your home was nearer to us, but it is no use wishing. All the house here needs cleaning up & I have not the strength to do what I should like to. I told you that Frank Goachen & wife are next door, so she helps me with a big wash. They are quiet and beautifully clean.

Georgie Sharp's wife has got her 5th child, a week old now. We are having nice weather & I wish your baby was a week old, so that you could get your few days here before anyone else came to interrupt us. I should dearly like to see all the dear children but must wait till I can run up after the war. We hear the guns every day from the Front. Dad is working at the Hop Gardens & will be glad to know you have written, & we shall be very thankful to hear that all is well with you. God bless you all & keep you all from harm. Heaps of love and kisses for Everyone of you from your loving old dad and Mum

Geo. & E. Brown

We shall be looking for news.

This was Emaly Brown's last letter to Mamma before I was born nineteen days later on July 17th that year. There is one other surviving letter from her to Mamma which was written early in the new year when I was five months old. It was to be her last letter as she was to die of the flu two months later, so that she was never to see Mamma again.

Chapel House,
Crab Tree
Jan 7th '19.

My own dear Clarrie,

I know you are thinking you are forgotten, but indeed you are in my thoughts by day and night, & I just wish that I could run in and see how you and the dear chicks are getting on. If you had not so much to do, you would feel lonely, but I am often with you, in fancy, and I do ask God to help you and give you strength to do all you have to do. Thanks dear child, for your card with all good wishes. God bless you and grant you all a very happy New Year. I had a very nice long letter from your Geo, but have not had time to answer it. Will, as soon as possible. I do want to send something to you. How do you do for veg? Drop me a line and say, & I will try to send you a bit. I do hope you are all keeping well. Just had Willie Pronger from last Wed, till Friday. He goes again tomorrow morn. We shall all be thankful when all the boys are in good work again, but as your Geo. says, "We must just be patient for a time." Charlie sends a special message of love and good wishes. Kiss all the dear children for granny and grand dad. With heaps of love for all. Ever your loving old dad and mum,

G & E Brown.

Mamma fretted and pined to see her mother again, but it was never to be. The war ended, but the hardship of the great Depression was only just beginning and then the great influenza epidemic struck. It was world-wide and it travelled to Lower Beeding as to everywhere else.

Grannie, Emaly Brown, became ill and went to bed. Then grand-dad Brown became ill too and joined her. Emaly got up to care for him but being far more ill than he was, it was too much for her. All of her family hearing that she was very ill went to visit her in their childhood home, Chapel House. They told Mamma that she lay in bed with her eyes fixed on the door, looking and looking for someone, but too ill to speak. Mamma knew that it was she that her mother looked for in vain. Father was still in France, I was a baby of seven months and there were six other small children.

"She must have been longing and hoping I would go to her," Mamma told us sadly, "but I could get no-one to take care of the children."

Emaly died on March 8th 1919 and is buried in the churchyard at Plummer's Plain. Mamma never overcame the great feeling of despair she felt at not being able to be with her mother when she needed her, and for the last time.

Mamma's relations were all in Sussex and Kent and several were publicans. On rare occasions when a teenager she was allowed to stay with her Aunt Bertha who kept an inn at the Pantiles in Tunbridge Wells. Mamma said she enjoyed these short stays as she was allowed to help her aunt in the bar where she polished the glasses. Another uncle kept The White Horse Inn in Horsham. We heard little about him.

Mamma's cousin Jennie, had been the village post-woman in Lower Beeding, when Mamma was cycling daily to Horsham to learn how to fashion gowns. Jennie not only worked the electric telegraph, but walked miles to deliver the mail with the post-bag slung across her body, up hill and down dale, in all weathers, even in deep snow. Jennie married and went to live in Ditchling which nestles on the Downs just behind Brighton. There, married to Jack Evans, they kept The Sandrock Inn as publicans, and raised their family of two sons, Cecil and Brian. They grew up to take over the management of the bars with their mother, when their Father died when Cecil was only twenty four. For years, Jennie and Mamma lost touch but the Second World War brought them together again. Then Mamma and three of my sisters went to stay at the Sandrock for some time, whilst Father, still working in London, was busy with warden and Civil Defence duties near our home.

In an out-house at the Sandrock there stood an ancient fire engine tender. Brightly painted, in pristine condition it stood as though ready for action. It looked to be horse-drawn with the two shafts in front. The buckets were hanging on the sides and on the wall beside were polished brass helmets. It later went to Lewes museum but Cecil still has a helmet.

Uncle William lived in Lewes, and for many years when we were small, made all our boots and shoes and gaiters. These were all hand-made and it was a pair of Uncle William's pink leather shoes, that I wore the day I fell into the River Roding, which the gypsy cleaned for me when she cleaned all my clothes.

I remember sitting on a small stool in our kitchen, being shown how to button up my boots. All the way down the outside of the boot were small round brown buttons. I was given a button hook. How difficult it was. The hook was pushed through the button hole and then round the button. With the hook now through the hole and round the button, the button was pulled through the hole and the hook slipped off. With luck that button was now secured in the button hole. Then the next button was fished through its matching button hole in the same way. This was made difficult as the boot top fitted the leg and the hook had to be pulled firmly through whilst it gripped the button. This had to be done over and over again, as there were ten or more buttons very close together, and two rows – one down the outside of each boot.

We had our gaiters to button up as well but we didn't use the button hook for these as they were not such a tight fit and the buttons slipped through more easily, so we used our fingers. Those brown leather gaiters, fleecy-lined, were cosy and warm. Reaching down from our knees to over our insteps; we loved wearing them in the cold winter.

Warm in our muffs, made by Mamma, we trotted along, wearing our boots and gaiters, beside the pram, vying with each other to get close to Mamma and hold on to the pram. When we all went shopping, there would be two rows of us, one on each side of the pram.

For some years all our boots and shoes were made by Uncle William, unseen, far away in Sussex, but then it stopped and I suppose that he became too old and then we heard no more.

Great Aunt Jennie, born at the Crab Tree Inn with grandfather Brown, went to live at Southwater. Whenever we wanted something that we could not afford, Mamma said,

"You'll have to wait until my ship comes home."

"When will that be?" we pestered.

"Oh," said Mamma sadly, "ONE day the ship WILL come home as surely as eggs are eggs."

Then we went to look at the picture of the ship, high on the wall, that Father liked so much. At these times Mamma said sorrowfully:

"There's your great aunt Jennie at Southwater living all alone in a great big house, and I have so many children I cannot visit her. Yet she has so much money she doesn't know what to do with it and has no-one to leave it to."

We felt sad for great aunt Jennie, unknown to us, all alone in a great big house with only money for company. She lived to be a few days short of a hundred.

Mamma's sister Dolly lived near Lavender Hill with Jack her son, who teased me on my visit there when I was two. Nearby on Lavender Hill lived her other son, Will with his wife Lizzie. They had no children and begged Mamma to let one of us stay with them for a little while. I was sent.

I must have been three. There was no-one to play with, but 'Aunt' Lizzie, who in fact was married to my grown-up cousin, seemed terribly amused by everything I did. She was continuously laughing at me. She was plump. Great chuckles of laughter emanated from within her and rippled out all over her as wobbling with weakness, she sank onto a chair. There, wiping her eyes she recovered and we discussed what we should do. It was amazing that there seemed nothing to do. Whereas at home we were busy from morning 'til night, with so many things to play at, yet at Aunt Lizzie's the days stretched endlessly before us. 'Uncle' Will was out on the buses taking the fares and we sat there in the flat debating whether to take a walk up the steep hill. There was no garden to explore and no baking being done for me to make my own piece of dough into a shape or figure. I worried to be allowed to peel the potatoes.

Standing on a chair I stood over a small round bowl holding a small knife. The potatoes were a great disappointment like painting the railings had been, and far more difficult than I had supposed. I tried hard to hold the small new potatoes with one hand and the knife with the other, but the straight knife would not connect with the round potato. I stood upon the chair looking down at the bowl of small potatoes wondering how people managed to peel them and leave them white and clean. Aunt Lizzie stood beside me to make sure I did not fall off the chair. I felt hot with shame at being unable to complete the task that I had worried to do. I persevered, with Aunt Lizzie shaking with laughter. She was as bad as Will's brother Jack had been, when mother took me to Aunt Dolly's, when I was two. Then I was on a pile of cushions wrestling with a spoon and egg, now I was standing on a chair struggling with a knife and difficult potatoes. Like cousin Jack, Lizzie was convulsed with laughter. Finally, when I had tackled all the potatoes, they were whisked away and climbing down I was given some coppers as a reward. I was impressed by the fact that I had been allowed to do this job standing on a chair. At home this would not have even been considered.

Will was a London bus conductor and wore a leather money satchel that went across his shoulder and hung in front of his body alongside his ticket and bell machine. Like Mr. Rowbotham's leg later on, the money satchel fascinated me; it looked important like a piece of uniform. I worried him to put it on; it was heavy and finally he hung it on a hook in the hall. One morning, as he was shaving, I climbed up onto a chair and lifted the bag off the hook. I climbed down and put the bag across my shoulder. It was a lovely feeling to be wearing the satchel; it reached down to my ankles. I sat on the chair to drive the bus and then climbed down to see to the passengers. Looking up I saw Will watching me in the mirror. The hall of the flat led straight to the bathroom where he stood shaving with the door open. Seeing that he had suspended his shaving to watch me, I suddenly felt very guilty, overcome with confusion, worried that he might think I was taking the money. Whether there was any I do not know. I climbed up on the chair and hung the satchel back on the hook.

Mamma had lent me to Lizzie to keep her company during her lonely days whilst Will was at work. But all I can recall about my stay there are the potatoes, the bus conductor's bag, Lizzie alternately laughing at or hugging me, and the long tedious walk up the steep Lavender Hill.

Separated from her folks and unable to visit them through lack of money, the shortness of life impressed itself upon Mamma. She had lost her first husband, the beloved Raggazone, very suddenly, whilst she was making plans to go to live with him in Italy, taking their baby son Roy, with her. Learning Italian at the time she occasionally referred to what might have been; the Italian she had learnt-now almost totally forgotten; lamenting that coltello, forchetta and cucchiaio, (knife, fork and spoon) were all the Italian she could remember.

"In the twinkling of an eye he was gone," she sadly reflected. "It is but a short journey from the cradle to the grave."

At these times we listened, dimly understanding, whilst she imparted her reflections on life as she baked and sewed, scrubbed and polished, regaling us all with an account of her better days, when she had bags of sovereigns, a good bank account, and could afford somebody in to do the heavier chores.

She had met Raggazone through her brother Frank who lived in London and had met the handsome Italian at a club. He took him to meet his family at Lower Beeding where Emaly Brown was never happier than when entertaining. A beautiful cook and well educated, she could converse with anyone. The rich Italian fell in love with the shy country girl watched over so carefully by her mother. They married and moved to London near her brother where they had a son, Alfonso, called Roy by Father. It was there in the London flat that Mamma received the fateful news of Raggazone's death and burial, at Port Said.

Taken ill suddenly on board ship where he was chief chef, Raggazone was treated for appendicitus. The treatment was purging but in reality he had typhoid fever. He soon died and, in that climate, was quickly taken ashore for burial. Then cables were sent to his next of kin informing them of his death and burial, at the port.

To help her recover from the shock and with Roy only a year old, Mamma began to fashion clothes once more, in the small flat, although she had no need of money. In this way, a client introduced her to Father.

Although of Mediterranean appearance, Father was a true Londoner. Captivated by the great blue eyes and beautiful country girl complexion, he soon proposed. Mamma said,

"He took my hand in his saying, 'You need someone to look after you', and removing my ring, replaced it with his own and said, 'from now on, you are mine'." Soon they were married. Father bought large Victorian furniture and they began to hunt for a house large enough to take the furniture. And then the family began to arrive until there was all of 'us'.

The newly built house with four bedrooms, was soon furnished and carpeted tastefully. In Mamma's bedroom, the dining room and the front room, there were bells fitted by the fireplaces, with pulls for summoning the servants. By the time I was old enough to play and pull them, only the front room one was working and before long, that too was out of order and eventually Father removed all the connections. The windows were all fitted with venetian blinds which we all hated dusting and cleaning with a damp cloth, and these too gradually became broken. They were replaced with roller blinds but we gradually broke the springs in these. Father hated anything over the windows and was always glad when blinds or curtains were missing for any reason. To Mamma's, "Go and lower the blinds", or "Draw the curtains," to one of us, Father would countermand with, "Leave them where they are; nobody is going to look to see what we are doing." And they were left with the windows uncovered until Father went out of the room, when Mamma immediately drew the curtains, or lowered the blinds, herself.

There in the lamplit room, sat Mamma at her sewing; Father tinkered with his latest project; designing a poster or magazine; an invention which he hoped to patent, or the cat's whisker wireless set he had constructed when it suddenly became all the rage. As we all sat around doing whatever was interesting and occupying each of us according to our ages; we all listened through the head-phones one after another. Roy finished off a piece of fretwork with intricate design, which he sometimes sold. Gilbert chattered excitedly about the latest silent film, a book he was reading or his latest idea which he thought Graham should know about. Gilbert, like Father, was always interested in everything, and as he and Graham were always together, he shared all his thoughts with quiet Graham. Ralph and Stan might be sorting out their cigarette cards, drawing, writing or reading up for a scout's badge. Phyllis was playing at mothers and Fathers with me and the younger children, Olive, Joyce and Ron; and the baby, Evelyn, was crawling over the floor in a large pair of navy blue knickers which reached up to her armpits, keeping her dress and petticoats clean with the aid of a large safety pin at the back which held everything firmly in place.

In the midst of all this activity was Father, cut-off by his earphones from the hub-bub around him (like Dr. Graham Bell, the inventor of the telephone, who was able to sleep peacefully, surrounded by a horde of noisy grandchildren, when he became deaf in his old age); inviting first one of us and then another, to listen in with a spare pair of earphones, which we politely accepted, but the novelty having worn off, were glad to get back to our games as soon as Father thought we had listened long enough.

At the table sat Mamma, by the lamp, sewing. Now and then biting off her thread and placing this and that article of finished mending in piles around her. As she sat there silently among us all, the fire-light threw our moving shadows about the room, over the walls and ceiling and into corners, whilst homely noises accompanied our moves. In a lull in the noise, the sound of coal falling through into the grate could be heard, and then the poker chasing it, riddling the ashes through; the coal hod rattling nobs on to the fire; the shovel scraping its bottom; the fire-irons clatter onto the hearth; the door being opened and shut. All winter long Father spent his breath on, "Shut the door behind you." And all through summer it was, "Leave the door open, there's no need to shut it."

When Mamma was up to date with the mending for a brief while, she relaxed by crochetting gloves or doilies. She could follow the most intricate patterns to make baby shawls, or tablecloths but chose small things to fit in with the small amount of time she was able to afford. Her gloves were lacy, dainty things and we marvelled at the minute hooks, the delicate cotton and intricate designs. If she were sewing, Father with the eyes of a hawk, intent on regulating all our doings, singled out one of us now and then to re-thread her needle. And licking the cotton a few times to help it through, we did so, some of us being more adept at it than others.

With Father out of the room for a few minutes an argument might start up. Then our heady dialogues were interrupted by Mamma's pearls of wisdom:

"Speech is silver, silence is golden."

"A still tongue makes a wise head."

"A soft answer turneth away wrath."

"People in glass houses shouldn't throw stones".

These were said together with quotes from the good book about turning the other cheek and two wrongs not making a right, until we were all feeling guilty as each remark applied to us equally.

The baby was always bathed in the morning directly after breakfast. There on the carpet in the dining room, before the fire, was placed a large zinc bath with a handle either end. The baby went through the routine Mamma must have learnt from her own mother, helping the sick cottagers with their new babies.

First the water was prepared, Mamma testing it with her elbow as she added hot water to the cold. Then the swaddled baby was lifted from the cot, previously carried in for the bath. Mamma sat on a low chair before the bath with a large white towel over her lap. On this the baby was laid on its front, as all the gowns, fastened at the back, were untied, and removed. First the embroidered top gown and then the flannelette; then the crossover viyella vest and then the belly-band which kept the navel, sometimes protuding after the severing of the umbilical cord, firmly in place. This avoided chance of hernia, often brought on when babies were left to cry a lot. The belly band was soft fine material but Mamma never left her babies to cry. She maintained that crying babies became miserable and discontented and so cried more, and contented babies slept well. She often said:

"The more a baby sleeps, the more it wants to."
And this was true of Mamma's babies that were born after I was.

Lastly the nappie was removed together with the muslin lining and dropped into a bucket of water. Now the baby lay naked on the towel which was wrapped around it firmly, the baby's arms inside and only its head uncovered. Crooning sweet words, Mamma supported its head from behind with one hand, the baby's body on her lap, and gazing into the delighted face, she soaped the round head with the other. Lowering it near the warm water, it was rinsed off with a soft flannel and then towel-dried with a smaller white towel. Tiny spills of cotton wool cleaned its nose and ears; the large towel was unwrapped from around its body and left across her lap. Then the baby was lowered to the bath, where, supported at the back of its head, it was cleverly soaped all over with the other hand. There in the warm water, it was gently floated up and down, gurgling with pleasure as Mamma crooned,

> "Bye Baby Bunting, daddy's gone a-hunting,
> Gone to fetch a rabbit skin to wrap his Baby
> Bunting in."

Several of us little ones enjoyed this ritual as much as the baby, putting our hands into the water to help splash it all over, until, with a cry of disappointment, it was lifted out protesting and dripping on to the towel, to be quickly and gently dabbed dry and stroked with the soft towels kept strictly for the baby.

Lying there on its back on Mamma's lap, chubby and pink, clean and dry, it was powdered, turned over and powder-puffed again, whilst we all admired and joined in with "This little piggy" and "Bye Baby Bunting". We little ones watched the baby clutching at Mamma's hair as she bent to kiss it; grasping at her frills and bows; chuckling and gurgling as it was tickled, and tried its feet out on her lap, pushing up on its tiny toes between hugs and kisses.

Then it was dressed for the day. Over its soft powdered body went all the clean things laid out beforehand near the baby basket which held the powder and the puff; safety pins; cotton wool; a spare belly band; zinc and castor oil ointment; small nail scissors, the baby soap in a dish, a clean bib and perhaps a ribbon or two. The baby basket was lined with white organdie, pleated and frilled and padded in one corner to hold the safety pins. Made by Mamma it was always clean and as hygenic as the white swing cot, as was the soft baby brush used on the soft downy head.

Now the baby was dressed with first the nappie with its muslin lining which was crossed over neatly and tucked round the baby's thighs to avoid any lumpiness and pinned. Then the vest was manoeuvred on to the powdered body and tied at the side. The long flannelette petticoat followed, the ribbons slotted through the sides and then the white, embroidered day gown, at which point, the baby was rolled over on to its tummy for the gowns to be tied at the back. With all the ribbons tied securely, a quilted satin, or silk embroidered, or woolly matinee coat, was wriggled gently over the baby's arms as it sat cradled in the crook of Mamma's elbow, on her knee. Then finally with its little coat on, clean and comfortable, it was feeding time and we watched as the baby snuggled up closely to Mamma, and with a bib protecting its fine clothes, a few gurgles and contented sniffles, it tucked into its breakfast.

We watched this routine many times, the well-fed baby up on Mamma's shoulder, being gently patted to expel its wind. Its fine white bonnet, pleated and beribboned, one of Mamma's creations, was slipped over its soft, downy head, the ribbons tied, and then into the clean covers of the bassinet to sleep, outside on the porch or in the garden, dependent upon the weather, until it made its wants felt after a long, contented sleep.

Before the family was complete Mamma was able to bake bread twice weekly in the kitchen range. But when the last three arrived one after the other, there was so much for her to do with all the washing which was a whole day's work, together with shopping, cooking, housework, and so many little ones, that she baked bread only occasionally, although she still made all the puddings, pies and cakes and preserves as before, and still 'kept a good larder'.

So we who were old enough went out for the bread, and brought back thirteen loaves at a time, in the pram. We also bought two or three dozen eggs at a time, getting the not too badly cracked for half price. Sitting on a low easy chair in the kitchen, Mamma held a large bowl in her lap and mixed the cakes. Twenty four eggs went into the mix. We watched her break them one by one into a large china basin and whisk them into a froth with the egg beater. Then sitting down she flicked the soft marg and butter, the beaten eggs and sugar, through her fingers in the large bowl until the creamy mix became light and fluffy. Then the rest of the cake went in: nuts and raisins, essence and lemon or orange zest, a grate of nutmeg, mixed spice or cinnamon, currants and chopped peel, a few maraschino cherry halves, all mixed thoroughly together before the flour was sifted in; milk and water or a drop of home-made wine, keeping it all to the right 'dropping' consistency. Then it went into the large, round cake tin and then into a smaller one, with the remainder of the mix filling as many patty pans as it could. Then one of us wiped our fingers round the bowl and licked them clean. I never liked uncooked cake and preferred to wait knowing that Mamma would always find some small cakes that had 'done' too well in the patty pans and these we would eat, the smell and taste being delicious beyond description when just baked. Mamma's carroway seed, chocolate, ginger, madeira, coconut and sponge cakes, were equally delicious and 'never went begging' as she expressed it.

With the cakes in the oven, a delicious smell of baking soon filled the house. How we hoped that some of those cakes on the tray edges would be too brown so that Mamma would say, "Here you are, you children, you may as well eat these." There were so many that half a dozen were not missed. Out of the oven she lifted mouth-watering pork pies made specially for the boys when they started work. Graham was well built and needed substantial meals.

"These will fill a hole in his stomach," said Mamma, placing them on a rack to cool.

Sometimes, hot and bothered, preoccupied with the batches of cakes, tarts, sausage rolls and pies, she said the wrong name.

"Go and give this one to Gilbert," she would say. "I mean Stanley, Graham, Ralph, Phyllis, Dorothy, Olive – oh bother it – I mean Ron," with a small ginger-bread man she had baked for him. Wiping her hot brow with the back of her hand she declared,

"I have to go through all the names until I get to the right one." Then pulling the last tray from the oven it was added to the vast pile to be cleaned, in the sink.

One of our friends one day, entering the kitchen and hearing Mamma going through a long string of names before she hit upon the right one, became very concerned.

"What is the matter with your mother?" she asked anxiously. "Is she ill?" and then lowering her voice to a whisper, "Is your mother drunk?" which made us all feel highly indignant.

Mamma's constant battles to save ha'pennies meant she had to budget skilfully, which she did. There was always plenty of good plain food as she termed her home cooking, but which people now might regard as 'eating well'. There were never any 'bought' pastries, petit fours or shop iced cakes, but anyway we didn't like them as they were too sickly. We all stayed fit and well eating Mamma's blackberry and apple pies, tarts and cakes, spotted dog, meat pies and meat loaf, paté and brawn, stews and bakes, fritters and pancakes and a thousand and one ways of using left-overs in tasty dishes. When asked how she managed to keep such a good table she said simply,

"It is a matter of working one week in with another."

There was nothing that Mamma did not make better than anyone else and yet she always said how much better at cooking her mother was.

Mamma spent a great deal of her time sewing and making our clothes on her Singer sewing machine. There in the corner of the dining room over by the French doors she sat treadling the machine, whilst we hovered around watching and worrying, especially if the garment was for the worrier. Going to a party called for a special dress. Sometimes it was something to wear for school. Mamma made Olive a clown's outfit in silk. One half was in red and one half in green. Even the little round cap with a bobble on the side was in both colours. I had a school party dress with tinsel brocade around the arm-holes. How excited I was as I saw that it was almost finished. Then I tried it on. It was a pretty blue gathered at the waist. But this exciting dress spoilt my party as it scratched me wherever the tinsel brocade touched my arms and shoulders and that no doubt, is why I remember it and have forgotten other, more comfortable dresses.

Always busy, Mamma turned Father's collars, put new seats in trousers, made small coats out of large ones, turned the cuffs on shirts, and complained gently.

"I never have time to do a stitch for myself."

Only when she was 'expecting' did Mamma find the time to make the necessary garment which was to be worn for the next few months. It was yoked and pleated or gathered and smooked, suiting her far better than any of the things she could not afford to buy.

Father sometimes became irritable if the machine was 'out' too often. Then he complained saying of the sewing,

"Put it away. Have a rest. It can wait," brooking no arguments, whatever 'it' was.

Then Mamma would say to us, having packed it all away:

"Yes, 'it' can always wait until he wants 'it' and then he can't wait and wants 'it' immediately," which of course we all knew.

Father was in the habit of telling Mamma to "Sit down. Leave 'it'. To do 'it' later. 'That' can wait" was his dictate and Mamma was forced to comply for the sake of peace. He liked to see her at rest and it was as well that he did as we all pestered her for everything. If Father heard us question, "Mamma, have you seen my gloves?" he fairly bawled our heads off.

"Dont't ask your Mamma, LOOK for them," and Mamma dare not utter the whereabouts to us.

There were days in the 1920s when there was literally nothing for our lunch and hearing the ragman's bell approaching, Mamma sent one of us running to call him before he passed by. Offering him a few unwanted articles she collected a few coppers in exchange.

"Now run to the top of the road and get some faggots, they will do for us, and get some chump ends for Father."

The faggots were soon made into a tasty meal with pulses and vegetables in a stew, whilst Father's chump ends were baked in a batter to make toad-in-the-hole with jacket potatoes. The chump ends were four pence a pound whereas a dozen or more faggots could be had for eight pence.

We knew the ragman as 'Old One Eye' because he had only one, the other being just a screwed-up hole. He often came in useful when Mamma was short of money; when Father was out of work and the pantry out of food. One time Father threatened to prosecute 'Old One Eye' for the following reason.

Father had a friend with an art shop. Like many other traders his friend was on hard times. Unable to pay Father for a quantity of advertising he had done for the shop, his friend paid him with pictures. Father had the choice of the stock. These were hung in every room in the house, even in the outside toilet. Along the hall they vied with Raggazone's pictures of Geisha Girls in Japan; Mount Fuji from every point of view; waterfalls in moonlight and glass covered cases of huge butterflies from the far east. In our bedroom, families, dogs and children, stared down at us as we lay in bed at night, telling our saga of the 'Bare Family' which evolved as a reflection of the times we were in at that stage in our lives, the great depression.

Looking for something to give 'Old One Eye' one day in exchange for a little cash, Mamma's eyes alighted on a picture hanging alongside the staircase, which had at one time hung in the outside toilet. As soon as his bell was heard he was invited in to look at it. In no time at all, he was going out in the reverse direction with the picture under his arm. Later that day when Father was back home and told about it, he exploded like a volcano to find which picture had gone. Mamma promised to get it back but the ragman said he had sold it and nothing Father said made any difference. For some time, 'Old One Eye' vanished from our street and his bell wasn't heard.

Mamma waged a constant battle to stretch every halfpenny as far as possible. When we asked for an extra copper or two for school things, scouts, swimming or anything, she went into a routine refrain with,

"A ha'penny here, a ha'penny there
And a penny somewhere else.
Tuppence here and tuppence there,
And sixpence somewhere else ...."

and so on until we who were old enough joined in as usual and the lament was ended. Poor Mamma. what marvels of management she carried out to see us through those hard times; day after day, week in and week out, covering the larder shelves with conjurations from so little.

"I'll have to try to get something out of thin air," she often lamented, looking into the pantry to see if there was anything left over to make into a meal.

As she was a very good whist player, she often went to whist drives to try to win the 'top' if she was able to afford a ticket. Once, when I was still the youngest and about two years old, I went with her. I held on to the back of her chair, and as she moved from table to table, sitting in a differently-facing direction each time, I clung to her skirts. There was a great confusion when the players changed tables and I was jostled about below a forest of grown-ups. Then there was a grim silence after the card-cutting, as play was resumed. Suddenly the banging down of cards, noisy arguments amidst the scraping back of chairs, the rising of tall bodies above me, presaged another eddy of chairs being seized like partners for a polka, twisted into place and sat upon, then the noise of cutting the cards clipped the tables, and the heavy breathing and snorts as cards were laid, took over in the relative stillness after the brouhaha of the chairs. At last, with great commotion all the people rose from their chairs. I hung on to Mamma's skirts as she walked towards the door with crowds of people.

"I just missed the 'top'," she was saying to Mrs. Braithwaite who went to the whist drives very often. "If only I had a decent partner at the last table."

Often she came home elated at having won enough to pay a bill. It was now that all the pipes became furred up, so that we had to carry the water from the copper in the wash house, upstairs for our baths. It was now that many things needed doing in the house, but there was no money to do them.

The whist drives became a life-line almost, for Mamma, in the 1920s. They provided the only Easter eggs we had. Large, beautiful, expensive eggs they were, in fancy baskets tied up with huge ribbon bows. Sadly she placed them on the table as we crowded around to admire. She was happy for us but bewailed the fact that money was not given for the lesser prizes instead of Easter eggs.

Our parents liked walking and often walked long distances so that we had to do the same when out with them.

It was a rare treat to go with Mamma to Wanstead Park, usually to take us out of the house, out of Father's way whilst he had a sleep before going to work somewhere or other in the evening.

Then after school occasionally, she walked us all, with the pram; the two youngest in the big bassinet and the rest running and skipping alongside. Some of our friends might come along as well. Once there in the park, how wonderful it was to be with Mamma.

"Go off and play," she told us, "and I will call you when it is time for you to have your tea."

Off we ran into the woods to play 'Release'. There on top of the hill we stood awaiting release. Only the fastest runners were able to dodge the catchers and release us. Now and then we ran back to where Mamma sat on a large chest on the green; a tennis or cricket locker. There she was, knitting long navy blue scout socks which hung down in front of the locker, beside her skirt, as she knitted the green circles at the top, stopping to hand out drinks. In the well of the pram, Mamma had packed a picnic and plenty to quench our thirst. Soon she called us all to have our tea. On a cloth laid out on the grass were sausage rolls, sandwiches and cakes, biscuits and fruit. When we were all tired out and the evening was advanced, we walked the three mile long way home, where, washed and exhausted we were soon all fast asleep in bed.

If Mamma went out without us all, there were always some who wanted to go with her and couldn't for some reason or other and she tried to be fair and treat us all the same. Sometimes we were all left behind and to our chorus of,

"Can I come?" and "Where are you going?" the answer we received was:

"Oh, I am going to Halifax", or "There and back to see how far it is", or "I am only going to Timbuctoo."

These answers left us puzzled and silenced whilst Mamma escaped.

It was a good thing that Mamma was a good walker for Father liked walking fast, swinging his arms with great gusto. When they were first married, he entered her in a walking race at Brighton against her protests that she would be no good. He was very proud of her when she won against people who had been training especially for the race.

Going shopping for Mamma was quite a business. First she spent ages writing out a list of all she needed, whilst we sat or knelt on chairs, leaning on our elbows, watching. The exact amount of each item was there with the price. Then she counted out all the money from her purse to see if she had enough, and how much she could afford to spend. Then the list was totalled and examined closely to see what could be crossed off. Cutting down an amount here and crossing out something else, she at last whittled the total to whatever she could afford, exact to a half-penny or farthing. Farthings were on many articles, usually reels of cotton, elastic or material, often one and eleven three a yard, which was one shilling, eleven pence and three farthings a yard. Having trimmed the list to suit her purse, Mamma sent two or three of us out together with the list to fetch the goods.

Shopkeepers and their assistants understood the hardship of their customers and knew that things had to be exact. Seldom were we sent back to the shop for something to be put right and then, amazingly, it was for a mere half penny usually, when the weight was slightly out.

There were bags of potatoes to be lugged home and lugged they were by two of us at a time, struggling with fourteen pounds in a bag and sometimes twenty eight pounds in a sack, most difficult things to get hold of at the corners when they are bulging tight with potatoes. What a relief to reach home and how some of us grumbled.

The paraffin was fetched from Willie Wheatley's shop, just around the corner and much nearer. We needed it for the oil lamps and the Valor stove which gave out a good heat. The paraffin was in a large drum just inside the shop door where it stood on the warped wooden floor which was almost entirely covered. Boxes and bins, shelves and trays stood about and on each other, holding everything that any household could possibly want from mouse traps to mustard pickle. There were loaves of bread, fire-lighters, pickled cabbage and pokers, rope, wire and string, hanging wherever they could lodge, in coils and loops; bicycle pumps and crockery, soda-water syphons and groceries; tins of cocoa and mustard, jars of jam, lemon curd and pickled onions. Anything that could be eaten, used as fuel or classed as being of use, was there all choc-a-block with toilet roll holders, chamber pots and coal scuttles. The stock was endless, the shop was small, and there was just enough room to spare for one of the Wheatleys to thread his or her way through the maze into the small space by the door, to measure out the required amount from the vinegar barrel or the paraffin drum. Usually three pairs of eyes watched the funnel in the can or bottle, depending whether it was paraffin or vinegar, directing the flow of the liquid. The eyes were either Mr. Wheatley's or his wife's or Willie's and those of two of us.

Several of us went for the shopping when the list was very long. One of the boys would take the kit-bag and the rest of us carried baskets. Only the bread, nice and clean and fresh, was brought home in the pram. Anyway, when Mamma gave up baking all our bread, through lack of time, only the pram could hold thirteen loaves and the baker's was a long way off. One heavy item which was almost as bad as the potatoes, was the half quarter of flour that we fetched every week. This fourteen pound bag was a half of a quarter of a hundredweight and was rightly in the avoirdupois system based on pounds, known as a stone. But we were never sent to buy a stone of flour, the bakers recognising it as a half quarter of flour.

We went to the chemist's for the ingredients for the medicines and the polish. The names were difficult to pronounce and the shop-keepers went over the names on the list with us as if they were written in Chinese.

"Epicacuhanna wine?" they questioned disbelievingly, to test out if we knew what we were doing. Peering at the scrap of paper on which Mamma had written all the ingredients, they asked us to say the words ourselves. Luckily we could as Mamma always spoke out loud as she wrote, repeating each item over and over to make sure we understood even if the shopkeeper didn't.

Then it was the turn of the next item.

"Syrup of squills?" they queried again, taking as long as possible, or so it seemed to us, to make up the required amount. And then it was the turn of the laudanum.

"Do you really require all this laudanum?" and we had to explain that we needed it for cough mixture and there were a lot of us. The tincture of quinine followed and we were able to repeat all the names clearly and reassure them that the list was correct and we really did want them all.

"And salts of lemon?" asked the chemist looking over his spectacles. "What is that for?" We were surprised that he was obviously not used to cleaning panama hats as that was what we were needing it for.

Father's precipitated chalk gave us the most trouble with pronunciation. But finally we left the chemist's shop with the oil of shellac and everything else for the polish which I now cannot remember, and all the ingredients for the cough mixture, and the spirits of salts for cleaning our hats, and the laudanum and many other things like them that people are not allowed to buy these days as they are on the poisons list and too dangerous.

Father's tuppenny packet of Woodbines was sandwiched among the long list somewhere.

When the gas came to our street we never liked it. The noisy, hissing and flaring gas kept me awake and gave me nightmares. The oil lamps were soft, cosy, quiet and friendly and didn't blacken the silver as Mamma declared the gas did. The cob-web-like gas mantles disintegrated in holes bringing Father's wrath upon us, but Mamma declared that they broke themselves. The new iron electric cooker freed us from gas and with it all the gas lights with their mantles and we moved into the electric age with light bulbs which lasted so much longer than the abhorred gas mantles.

When we no longer used the oil lamps, it was astonishing how often we sat and played by firelight preferring it to the electric light if we were not writing. Father agreed with this. He relaxed and dozed in the easy chair whilst we enjoyed ourselves in a subdued hubbub of play. Events moved rapidly. Days and weeks and months passed. We followed each other rapidly from Infants to Juniors and on into Big School. Nothing stayed the same except for Christmas.

This was the highlight of the year. Mamma was at the helm at this time. As the organiser, the buyer of nearly all the presents, the chooser of the provisions, the chef responsible for the splendiferous Christmas puddings, the mince pies and rich cake with its home-made marzipan and snowy top, the turkey, stuffings and sauces, Mamma was totally in charge, the director, the producer and the star. Father for a change was in the supporting role: keeping us all occupied and out of Mamma's way: helping wherever possible – with the stuffings, whether chestnut or sage and onion: checking on our behaviour where we played in the front room, well away from the kitchen: giving out small jobs to be done and thinking up games and competitions with small prizes until at last, the very late meal was ready and he ushered us into the dining room himself, making sure that everything was just as it should be; the crackers and holly and mistletoe all in the right places and that we all were too. He was determined that nothing was going to spoil this time of great enjoyment that meant so much to him after his lonely boyhood. He was the master of ceremonies at Mamma's side: carving, organising, serving and waiting: lighting the pudding: sharing the wishbone with Mamma: sorting out the turmoil with the crackers which fell into other people's puddings: helping us find the silver in the lucky portions and finally giving us permission to leave the table without orders about the washing up. When at last he considered himself off duty and able to have his port and cigar in peace and quiet, he joined his off-spring who were all in the front room, bouncing about with their toys. After he had relaxed for a while, he joined in and it was musical bumps or heading balloons to his quick lively piano playing: or oranges and lemons or nursery rhymes as we skipped about or sang.

In the busy round of family life, Mamma did make the occasional visit to her two sisters, Dolly at Battersea and Aggie at Chichester, when I was two, before Olive was born and the great depression was upon everything and everyone.

I remember the cottage garden at Chichester. By then Aunt Aggie was widowed. Mamma was expecting Olive to be born that Christmas and took Phyllis and me on the train to visit her. Phyllis was four and I was two, and we were not to see Aunt Aggie again until I was eighteen and Aunt Aggie was into her seventies and still climbing her apple tree for apples which she still did when she was over eighty; and no doubt would have done into her nineties if her daughter Ivy had not taken her out of the cottage into her own home to make sure she did not have any more tumbles.

Wallace, the husband Aggie idolised, worked for the railway. One foggy day he stepped aside, as he thought, to avoid an oncoming train, but unable to see as he crossed the lines, he stepped in front of a train and was cut to pieces. They never did find his head Mamma was told, but Wallace was never mentioned in Aggie's presence. For a long time she was ill only wanting to die, but time gradually healed the grim tragedy, scarring over the wounds of loss, and Aggie went on tending her garden, growing all her own vegetables organically, scorning the chemicals and fertilisers increasingly used, declaring the fruit and vegetables would never taste the same again until the farmers went back to organic farming.

The cottage garden was a sea of nasturtiums, sweet scented stocks, lupins and lavendar, poppies and scabious, Sweet Williams and wall-flowers, right along to the apple tree at the bottom. The garden was long and narrow with a straight path down the middle. Phyllis and I wandered along the path; we could hardly get among the flowers so close together they were; we picked the lavendar and put it in our pockets and pulled the bunny rabbits off their stems then squeezed their mouths open, whilst Mamma and Aunt Aggie sat inside by the large low window and talked. They talked and talked and caught up on all the news so longed after. News of the families in Chichester, Lower Beeding, Lewes, Ditchling, Horsham, Tunbridge Wells, Sevenoaks and London, and of Father's latest exploits and of his mother's too, told in detail. A brief stay only it was, perhaps for the day or perhaps we stayed the night, then back home to Father and busy family life. Olive's advent later that year, in December, as Mamma put it, "Put the kibosh on any further visits." "With one you can run: with two you can walk, but with three you must stand still," she stated.

Mamma's endless sayings were a short cut replacing long conversations, a kind of verbal shorthand. There seemed to be a 'saying' for everything.

"Watched pot never boils," she affirmed, fork in hand, when the greens were not quite ready to be poked down.

"There's not enough room to swing a cat," which made us all step back a pace as we jostled to be near the pastry board.

"You don't look a gift horse in the mouth," tipping out a bag of Annie Alcock's stale bread into a bowl of water for bread pudding. Then unwrapping Annie's old shoes, sent over with the bread, "Beggars can't be choosers."

Quotes from the bible flowed from her naturally and took the place of the chapel going that she once loved. Following her everywhere as I did, until old enough to run about with my brothers, the words flowed about my ears.

"In my Father's house are many mansions," stated Mamma perhaps speculating on my question as to the possible dwelling of Father and Raggazone in heaven.

"Cast thy bread upon the Waters for thou shalt find it after many days," she said, firm in her faith that all was well with the universe if only we would believe.

"It's a long lane that has no turning," she told worried folks telling their troubles to her, adding, "every cloud has a silver lining". And, "Nothing venture, nothing gain, to the boys", apprehensive, about to start a new job. Every occasion prompted one of Mamma's wise remarks so that they seemed part of our every-day language. Out of the three hundred and eighty or so idioms and proverbs printed in the Oxford English Book of the Written and Spoken Word, over one hundred and seventy were used by Mamma as ordinary every day language when she chatted to us. Stanley and Ralph counted them. There must be many other excerpts that we heard over and over setting us guiding lines and principles to last our life-times and proving the adage, as she often said – "the hand that rocks the cradle rules the world".

Many a sermon could be written by stringing Mamma's sayings together and that is just what they were, short sermons. 'Man shall not live by bread alone': 'it is more blessed to give than receive': 'ye are the salt of the earth': and the hundreds of other wise words that came to us from her, all flowed over us like a Gregorian chant and filled our ears and took root with the nursery rhymes and proverbs. We considered ourselves 'lilies of the field'.

We hoped our 'light would shineforth' and felt that we were 'the salt of the earth' and knew it was true that it was 'more blessed to give than to receive', and that 'pride went before a fall'. The recent war with its indelible damage, reinforced opinion that good men, 'should beat their swords into plough shares' to bring eternal peace, 'the wolf dwelling with the lamb'. We knew all these things from Mamma as she sang her daily theme, the melody of life that came with our daily bread. "For," she declared "The price of wisdom is above rubies."

Chapter Eleven

Father

Father went at everything like a whirlwind. If Mamma was the sails of the ship which kept us all safely aboard, Father was the wind in the sails. Occasional squalls blew up with Father being so hot-blooded, but Mamma, knowing the futility of reaction, let it all blow over her head. She viewed him rather like the weather.

"If one is fire the other has to be water," she calmly said and that settled the matter; summing up her philosophy of her life with Father.

When Father was finally in a regular job with the government, he kept up his whirlwind ways, allowing no time for dawdling. Every morning he shaved with his cut-throat razors which did not lend themselves to short-cut tactics, so that nine times out of ten, he appeared at the breakfast table with blood on his face somewhere. As soon as he began to shout, "Clariss!" from the bathroom, Mamma ran to give him the alum which was there in the bathroom, but he couldn't wait a second to find it and had to have a fuss made, usually by himself. So Mamma ran upstairs, calling as she went, "Alright, George, I'm coming, George", handing him the alum as quickly as she could.

With the alum pressed to the cut, Father tore downstairs straight into the dining room to the breakfast table. There he speedily sat down before a very large cooked breakfast, placing his pocket-watch upon the table by his plate he tucked a large white serviette over his front, and polished off a meal of bacon and eggs, mushrooms and tomatoes (no skimpy kippers for him), or a steak. Then a half slice of toast with honey or marmalade afterwards. Followed with one or two cups of strong tea with the cream off the milk. These were usually poured into the saucer as there was no time to sip hot tea from the cup. Then pushing back his chair and pocketting the watch, he ran into the kitchen where Mamma had his tooth-brush ready with the toothpaste on it. There at the sink, elbows wide, he vigorously scrubbed his teeth making a thorough job of it. Behind him, Mamma hovered, holding his shoes which she had polished, ready to thrust into his hands to save him a precious second. Then it was into his coat whilst Mamma hurried to the front door with his briefcase, holding the door open. Father grabbed his trilby from the hall-stand, donning it as he flew out of the front door, snatching his case and a kiss at the same time. Once gone Mamma complained to us about his departure.

"Our lips never meet," she declared with a sigh, sending a long wistful look after Father's departing back, rapidly disappearing towards the station, with his quick, forceful strides, coat tails flying. Then closing the door, peace descended over the house and all was calm.

Activities of every description interested Father, whether it was showing us children how to build card towers on the dining room floor, or going to play billiards or bowls, tennis or rummy, with his friends from the Conservative Club. His range of friends was wide like his interests.

Mamma told us of the bad behaviour of his football club when they were first married. They were known as the 'Preston Boys' and wore striped jerseys as we saw from a photograph of Father with them. He invited them home for a celebration party. The newly-weds' home was luxurious with deep-piled expensive carpets. They all drank too much apart from Father who was partial only to port. Soon they were playing practical jokes, spilling drinks and competing in spitting cherry stones at each other. Mamma, upset at spills on the pale green carpet, cherry stones being trod about and the din they were making, went to bed.

When the party broke up in the early hours, they played a practical joke on Father leaving him locked in the front room. Not amused, he punched through the door panel to reach the key in the lock. The next day Mamma went home to her mother where she stayed until Father had the door repaired and went to fetch her.

Father's habit of playing practical jokes on his friends back-fired one day. His friend Billy Cummings, from whom I always hid, usually behind a chair, called one day. Billy was red-faced, with ginger hair which went with his disposition. Father offered to cut Billy's hair. He sat him down in the conservatory with a large sheet tucked round him. Father got down to the scissoring, feet apart, fully intent on the operation. Contentedly Billy kept up an amicable conversation, unusual for him, being notoriously bad-tempered. Suddenly we were all startled as Billy began to swear and shout. He jumped up and throwing off the sheet, rushed to the hall mirror. Then with Father bursting with laughter and Billy calling him names, he went off home in a rage.

Some months later when we had forgotten all about it, Father was foolish enough to let Billy cut his hair. This time the same thing happened in reverse. It was Father who sprang around swearing and the red-faced Billy bursting with laughter. When Father had cut Billy's hair, he had suddenly run the clippers up the back of his head and over the top in a wide swathe to his forehead, not at all the fashion with their sophisticated Edwardian sideburns. Now his friend did the same for him.

Mamma sometimes dispaired of Father as he could not resist a dare, often attracting attention. She told us how he staggered out from a public house, carrying a huge potted fern which he could hardly lift – all for a dare, and how she had made him take it back. And how upset she was when, holding his arm on an afternoon walk, he potted a few eggs outside a shop, with his stick. Not the thing expected from a dandy in fancy waistcoat and boater. This would be in 1906 or soon after, when he was eighteen to twenty, holding his own at Billingsgate with veteran traders from generations of fish merchants, and keeping up the style with the London dandies.

The porters working in Billingsgate Market carried the baskets of fish, stacked one upon the other, high above their heads. As Father was a keep fit enthusiast they took bets on the number of baskets of fish he could carry at one load. He did not disappoint them and over-did it. He strained the muscles of his heart and Mamma said it took him a long time to get over it.

For nine hundred years Billingsgate was a fish trading centre. The name is thought to derive from Beling, a Saxon, owning wharves east of London

Bridge. Ethelred the Unready collected tolls on vessels arriving at 'Blynegate'.

On Saturday 16th January 1982, Billingsgate moved, after nine hundred years of trading near the Monument in London, to a new fish market on the Isle of Dogs. Old Billingsgate was regarded with affection and the move attracted a lot of publicity. Crowds went to have a last look round. The cavernous basements below were several feet thick with ice, built up over years. A Roman constructed wharf with a bridgehead was discovered. This was London's noisiest market; where Father developed his voice. In the early hours of the mornings, porters bellowed abuse and anecdotes, and steel-rimmed carts trundled over the cobbles, added to the din. It was renowned for foul language and bawdy talk even in Shakespeare's day and was referred to by him in King Lear.

Early on Sunday mornings at about five o'clock, Father went to the Hollow Ponds at Leytonstone where many other boys and men were swimming. None of them wore anything in the water and it was strictly for males. As they grew older, my brothers went on these early morning dips and listening to the excitement as they set off, we girls wanted to go. I often pestered to be allowed to join them.

"No girls are allowed," they said. "It's for men only, swimming in their birthday suits."

When the ponds froze over in winter they still went there, to skate.

One Saturday, on a bitterly cold afternoon, Father fixed us all up with ice skates. They were all old skates he had bought somewhere, being an opportunist, and he was determined we should use them. What a to-do it was as he screwed and unscrewed pairs of differing sizes to clamp on to our boots; ordering us all around to try them on over and over, put us all off out in that cold censervatory.

However at last all were fixed and the small crowd of us, took the walk to the tram stop at the station. It was icy cold but strangely exhilarating on top of the tram right up at the front. The overhead cables whined accompanied by the grinding of iron wheels on rails. Into the darkening leaden sky, the cables spat huge showers of sparks in noisy staccato bursts, spluttering and crackling. At last we saw our arboreal armchairs slowly approach, and ourshivers focussed on the pond, unfamiliar in the icy mist which clung about it. Crowds were standing and skating, running and walking in every direction on its surface like confetti, shaken out from the misty bag above.

Although still afternoon it was nearly dark and over the pond hung that strange half-light that comes from the ice itself. We sat down to fix our boots on. The pond was covered with people; pushing and pulling prams and toboggans pieces of wood and each other over the ice, with here and there a few fast skaters. We all scattered. Those of us who could skate soon disappeared. The north wind was bitter cutting across the Flats. I found some bushes by the fringe and hung on to stand up on the blades. I looked around for my brothers and then I saw Father in his thick over-coat, flinging his arms about with the movements of his feet. Travelling quite fast he was, until he suddenly vanished through the ice. The pond was never deep and he was soon at the bank.

"I am going to run all the way home;" he said, "you must all come home together, on the tram," and off he ran very fast indeed, in his bulky overcoat stiff with freezing water, and soon vanished once more.

He never took us on the ice again and neither did he catch cold that night after the three miles or so run back home.

As soon as Father thought of something he wanted to do he did it, like the time he decided to make a Mahjong set. He wanted a set but it was the 1920s and he had no money.

At ten o'clock in the morning he went out and bought the wood. Then he and Graham, nine at the time, worked together so that the set would he ready for use that evening.

Father cut all the one hundred and forty four tiles as they are known, and Graham smoothed all the edges with glass paper. When they were all smoothed and of equal size, Father began to paint the unique characteristics on each tile, as on those that have been used in China since the days of Confucius. There were thirty six bamboo; thirty six circlets; thirty six characters; sixteen winds – four each of North, South, East and West; four each of Red Dragon, Green Dragon and White Dragon, not needed; and lastly the four Seasons and the four Flowers. Usually the tiles are of ivory, bamboo or bone, engraved and painted, but Father's were, of necessity, from wood.

Each tile was skilfully painted with its suit and numbered where required. All the Ones and Nines were colour-fully decorated as were the Dragons, the Winds, the Flowers and the Seasons. With Father's skill in designing and advertising, he had the whole set bought and cut, smoothed and painted, varnished and dried (in the oven), in four hours. Mamma told us about this many times.

That evening Father sat down to use the set with his friends. We all learnt to play but the grown-ups games often went on far into the night for small stakes of money that caused some argument. Annie Alcock was known as a 'bad loser' which Mamma said spoiled the game, especially if it was Whist.

One Sunday morning Father went out early to play tennis. We small girls were sent to the tennis court in the park to ask him to bring us all back with him at lunch time. There was a small low gate by the tennis courts which we were able to open. We soon lifted the wire loop from over the gate and ran on to the tennis court. Suddenly Father was surrounded by several small children. The young ladies playing with him, laughed to see all these children appear. Shepherding us all back through the gate, Father put his hand in his pocket and gave us sixpence to spend on our way home. Off we ran to buy sweets, feeling it was not quite right to have sweets before our Sunday dinner. Arriving home, Mamma did not seem too put out about our sweets.

"I don't suppose he will be long now before he is home," she said. "He is bound to follow".

You never could be sure what Father would do next. One hot summer's day my nose started to bleed and wouldn't stop.

"Go and lie down quietly on the gardern seat," said Mamma, "until it stops, and hold this wet sponge on it."

I held it there feeling like a martyr as I lay on my back gazing up at the pear trees. Up at the bathroom window, behind the frosted glass I saw Father shaving. He shaved twice daily as his beard was so dark and stiff. I closed my eyes in the warm sun. The sponge on my nose was warm. Suddenly a bowl of cold water descended from the bathroom all over me. I felt very aggrieved. Father thought it was very funny. When Mamma showed him my wet clothes he laughed.

"It stopped the nose bleed," he said. "That's the quickest way to stop a nose bleed."

We were never left in any doubt as to what Father expected of us. He made everything crystal clear so that there was no excuse for not doing whatever it was you were supposed to do. Although he came to work for the government later, there was no red-tape nonsense where he was concerned, with lack of communication (as someone put it, 'like a maze, surrounded by a wall wrapped in fog'), Father's orders were the complete opposite, clear-cut and everything, explained in detail, with a vigour, that waived aside any nonsense about not understanding the exact plan of action he had mapped out for you.

As he went on at length, sheer exasperation compelled us to utter a plaintive, "I know", to be immediately stopped by:

"You think you know, but you don't know." He then reiterated all that he had told us until he had said all there was to say on the subject.

"A still tongue makes a wise head," was the only comment from Mamma when we grumbled to her about the long time he took to tell us something.

A loose tooth soon attracted Father's attention who was very practical in many ways. Fear of eating a crust because of a loose tooth set him trying to persuade the unfortunate to let him see how loose it was. The unwary opened their mouths wide for Father to wiggle the tooth. He was canny and never pulled it out straight away. But seconds later at another look, it was suddenly out. Sometimes he used his small pliers but there were some members of the family who made a fuss and put up with the misery of a tooth hanging on a thread, until it fell out by itself.

Like Mamma, Father had his own sayings like the 'Wiffle Woffles'. When we were in bed with measles, mumps or other painful things, he'd come to see us. "You've got the 'Wiffle Woffles'," he'd laugh, trying to make us feel better.

As he rested with his feet up after a very long walk, one of his favourite past-times, we little ones pestered him to play with us.

"I can't. I've got a bone in my foot," he'd say. "You find the comb and comb my hair." This we did, scraping away, hoping the bone would be gone by the time we had all had a turn and forced his slippers on his feet. But the bone, always defeated us so we went off finally and left him asleep in the chair with his feet up on another.

Father loved teaching anyone anything and he taught the boys to wrestle, showing them locks and falls so that we were glad he didn't teach us. We kept well out of the way, climbing up on the table, which was pushed against the wall whilst this was going on, as it all seemed rough and dangerous.

Playing about around Father whilst Mamma was busy in the kitchen kept him well occupied finding things for us to do. After finding his slippers and putting them on him which he made as difficult as possible, wriggling his toes and crossing his feet, we ran to find the newspaper. He sent us back and forth with messages for Mamma, for his cigarettes or a match, or climbing up to reach a spill from one of the big, brass shell cases from the war, which stood at either end of the mantelpiece.

With his feet up he relaxed after a busy day. We combed his dark hair until he fell asleep and then we woke him up, knocking with the brass handles on the book-case drawers, as we played at 'mothers and Fathers' . Then Father barked at us to play something else. And then something else became too noisy and we were shouted out of the room, Father having had less than his forty winks. Then it was into the passage or conservatory trying to avoid arguments and noise as we knew too well that it would not take him long to find 'jobs' for us all.

When Father came home to idle children he quickly had us all seated around the table where he gave out paper and pencils and instructions, and before we knew it we were all playing at schools and vying with each other to carry out his instructions.

Father had the knack of dealing with several people at the same time, especially if they were his own children. Some days we were packed off to the park for fishing with the boys. Mamma's bamboo curtain pole served as a fishing rod and we spent long hours unsuccessfully trying to catch fish. One stormy day we were caught in a downpour. The road we were returning along was the never-ending Wanstead Park Avenue and the only shelter was somebody's porch. Three or four of us crept into the front porch of a large house. Here we stood out of the heavy rain. Suddenly the door opened and the gentleman there demanded that we give him the bamboo pole. We protested that it was Mamma's curtain pole but he took it and went inside and closed the door. We were left with a dreadful sinking feeling knowing that Father would be very cross if we returned without it. The minutes dragged by as we racked our brains trying to think how we could get it back. Suddenly the door opened and he was back. In his hands he held the pole. He handed it to Ralph, the eldest, with an apology. 'Please forgive me," he said, "but only last week my bamboo pole which holds our sun-blind, was taken from this porch, but I now see that this isn't the one."

One of Father's friends was Mr. Barnes the secretary-cum-care-taker of the Conservative Club. Now and then either Mr. or Mrs. Barnes went away somewhere or other and asked Father if one of his children could stay there to keep the other one company until their return. Ralph went to keep Mr. Barnes company when Mrs. Barnes was away and I went when Mr. Barnes was away. When Ralph went he described to me what happened. Mr. Barnes, thin and tall climbed into bed alongside Ralph, aged twelve. "Now, Ralph", he said, this is what you do when you get into bed. Lie on your back and stretch your legs right down straight towards the bottom of the bed. Then start counting slowly, once every second, up to a hundred, like this: one – two – three – four. When you get to a hundred turn on your side and you will go straight to sleep. If you do this every night, you will grow up and live to be an old man like me."

When I went to their flat over the Conservative Club to stay for a week I didn't enjoy it. It was deadly quiet. No wonder Mrs. Barnes, a tiny, sharp-featured, reticent old lady was afraid to be alone. The flat was large. Their little black terrier dog, like the one on the gramophone adverts, was as sharp as a fox. At the slightest sound he stood up, his ears pricked, head on one side at the alert, a soft growl starting at the back of his throst. Then Mrs. Barnes pushed back her chair and looked out of the windows. Reassured that all was well we settled down in front of the coal fire until it was time to have our cocoa and go to bed. I went first, climbing into the large strange bed and lying quite still in the silent room so different from home. In the darkness I lay awake; was Mrs. Barnes in bed or not, I did not know and unable to go back to sleep until I knew, I finally screwed up the courage to put one finger out, tentatively and slowly across the bed. At last my finger tip touched the body of Mrs. Barnes and once more, lying so still afraid to move, I finally fell asleep.

The dog whose name was Spot was an excellent house-dog, growling at visitors and instantly quiet when told by his master or mistress. This tiny terrier, part mongrel, of impeccable behaviour, nevertheless had the cane one day. I stupidly looked on not knowing why, or what he was being punished for, until it was too late. The old lady had seen three or four lumps on the carpet and calling Spot to her and fetching the cane, gave the dog two or three sharp whacks with it. The obedient dog stood quite still whilst being hit and then went to its bed as told. Mrs. Barnes fetched a brush and shovel and brushed up the black lumps. "Oh dear", she said, "it is only coal", and put it into the coal scuttle. I realised too late that she was unable to see clearly and had punished Spot needlessly as she had spilled the coal when bringing it in.

On returning home from this visit I was very upset when Mamma told me that the youngest, Evelyn, had nearly died from pneumonia. How dreadful to think I was away from the family whilst this crisis was on and nobody had told me. It was bad enough having to leave home to stay with Mrs. Barnes, but now I felt left out, almost abandoned. I crept away to think it over, overwhelmed with the shock of it all. Not being told – that was the worst of it. I am sure Mamma would have been surprised had she known how much I took this crisis in my absence to heart.

Thunderstorms at night seemed terrifying and when they were bad, our parents came into our rooms with a lighted candle in a candlestick. We all got up out of bed and went downstairs into the passage where we clustered together, away from the windows where vivid lightning flashed through the curtains. As the storm abated Father made us all a very sweet, hot drink, and back we went to bed. Sometimes the storm returned so that we once more gathered together as thunderbolts seemed to be crashing all around and indeed one fell in Shakespeare Crescent, near the Old Iron Bridge. "Like a ball of fire," one onlooker stated.

Weather, then, was all important as everyone walked or went on the tram or bus or by bike. People dressed for the weather, wearing mackintoshes and taking umbrellas. As we went out Mamma would call, "Have you got your mackintosh on?" or "your wellington boots?", or "your umbrella?" to the older ones. Getting soaked through was a common occurrence. Wet days we spent most often playing in the conservatory, but as it fell into disrepair and the carpet wore away, all the former air of luxury faded and there was no money to put it back into its former state – when Father and Mamma had first moved in and all was new.

It always seemed to be raining when Father went fishing and we had to take his sandwiches and flask of tea to him. It was a long way from our house to the lily pools at the back of the woods in Wanstead Park. Always quiet and sinister along by these pools under the overhanging trees, it was even more so during the week when few people were likely to be there. Hurrying through the bushes with the rain dripping off the trees overhead it was still and lonely, the only sound from twigs underfoot and the slow dripping rain. And what a relief; suddenly there was Father fishing for carp; sitting on a small stool; all alone; daring us to make a sound. There never seemed to be any other person fishing there. It was a long way to carry the sandwiches and tea from our home to the lily pools. There was the walk to the tram and the ride to the ponds. Then the long walk down Wanstead Park Avenue into the park. The trek by the boating lake, over the cricket field into the first woods. Then across the forest glade into the second woods. Then through that, past the hill and down to the quiet lily pools, where there was nowhere to go except along the path. One day I dropped the flask and broke it but to my surprise Father was not cross. I think he was so glad to see me that he dismissed the broken flask from his mind. I was alone that day like Father and we were both glad to share the meeting on this overcast April afternoon; rather like Stanley and Livingstone I suppose.

The horse manure that we so reluctantly tracked down brought forth excellent results, so that Mamma always had splendid rhubarb for pies and Father a fine rose for his buttonhole, for the best part of the year. Memories of those days come crowding back. Father seemed indestructible, strong and virile like a Roman centurion in charge of a fort with a legion to look after. We came in to find him boiling up mussels he had brought back from the market or from the sea; cooking whelks as tough as old gum boots; spreading winkles on our plates as we all set to with a pin to remove the eyes; or handing out a ration of shrimps or prawns as he enjoined us to "Wait!" quite needlessly as we all knew better than to pick up a pin, shrimp or winkle, until told we could by Father. This sort of diet kept us all well-occupied for some time according to our individual skill and experience.

As soon as we were all started on the task of transferring the contents of any shellfish to our mouths, Father, busy with his own feeding, nevertheless always found time and energy to keep up a running stream of advice and instructions on improving our techniques. Removing the lid off a winkle here and separating a shrimp from its outer coat there, he deftly reached about him, breaking the rules he set for us, such as not talking whilst eating and not stretching across the table. Not a move escaped him and woe betide anyone who professed not to be enjoying these treats.

Eating with Father was a ritual that we were all well aware had to be followed through according to Father's rules. Whether it was a late enormous Sunday dinner, a shovelful of chestnuts we were told to roast over the fire, a couple of toasted muffins or half a pomegranate, we each received instructions as to the best and proper way to go about it. Needless to say we were all very clean and careful both at table or by the fire in winter, with Father's eagle eye not missing a move.

When Father came home from work he often brought fruit with him, the largest juicy oranges or pineapples, pomegranates for us and grapes for Mamma, never chocolates and never sweets. Only on Sundays did he pay for our coconut toffee. He took care to see that Mamma was sitting down whenever possible, warming a cushion in winter to put at her back. He liked to make a fuss of her which Mamma never reciprocated. It was his disposition to show his feelings in this fashion, which Mamma, quietly reserved, accepted. But she put him first before everything and all of us, giving him enough food for two men. That was her way of caring.

Father took great care of his possessions and was never clumsy. He treasured all Raggazone's souvenirs as well as his own antiques and we were careful not to spoil anything through carelessness. The large Edwardian furniture was set off by the deep-pile green carpet in the front room, which lasted until we were grown up and leaving home, by which time it was very thin, but we still rolled it back for parties. Raggazone's curios were intermingled with Father's and alongside the cases of butterflies hung pictures of Japanese geisha girls in their various poses, displaying their arts in their immaculate costumes and make-up. The water buffalo horns over the front room door seemed to be on guard, reminding us to keep out and that the front room was for special occasions. Small bamboo furniture stood here and there, so tedious to dust together with Father's huge copper vases from Burma, intricately designed and moulded which added to the dusting. Everything surrounded us in a seemingly impregnable world, private and strong, where visitors were welcomed and duly impressed.

The family Birthday Book was kept by Father who must have spent hours whilst babies were being born, thinking up all their names and writing them into the book as soon as possible. He started off the eldest with three names each, but by the time Olive was born he made do with two, so that the four youngest had just two Christian names. In fact we believe that by the time the last two arrived he had so many hobbies that he left these two for Mamma to name.

Pearl was Father's first daughter. Born in 1917 during the war, she developed a dry cough. She was five weeks old when Mamma took her to Doctor

Collins. He was absolutely worn out with many people sick. He told Mamma to let the baby have plenty of fresh air. "Put her outside," he said, "she has whooping cough". Mama knew all about whooping cough. She had had several children with it at the same time, making paper dishes for them to be sick in, and up all night when they had choking fits and nose bleeds. She tried to remonstrate with the doctor that it was something worse. To her disagreement with his diagnosis, he said, "Look at these", and showed her a large bunch of keys.

"These are the keys to houses where the people are too ill to open their doors. I go in one day and find two people in bed ill, together. The next day I go in and find one is alive and the other dead. There is nobody to nurse them and I have patients dying by the dozen. I have not had my clothes off for many nights. You must do what you think is best for your baby". So saying he wearily showed Mamma to the door.

Father was due home on a short leave from France. Mamma walked home with the baby in her arms. Father was standing in the kitchen weary and dirty in his khaki uniform. Mamma cried that the baby was very ill. He held the baby in his arms as Mamma warmed a spoon with a little brandy and water to put to the baby's lips. Turning round with the spoon Mamma gave a pitiful cry. The baby had died in Father's arms. Named Pearl by Father as she was so perfectly formed, she was the only one to be born with Father's features, with dark eyes and black curly hair.

She was laid on the front room table, the elegant walnut, in a tiny coffin lined with white satin. With so many awaiting burial Mamma became distracted with grief whilst Pearl lay there. In the night Father found her nursing the baby, unable to accept its death. The room had to be kept locked until the funeral was over and it was a cruel stroke of fate that allowed Father home only to lose his tiny daughter. But had he not been home, I fear as to what might have happened to Mamma.

Whilst Father was serving in France with the Middlesex Regiment, he endured all the horrors of trench warfare and the long forced marches. For years he would not speak of his war experiences. Once he told me how his good teeth helped him survive. On the long marches, on roads constantly shelled, they became ravenously hungry. They all had hard tack (army biscuits) which they soaked in their billy cans. Any pieces of cheese became like rock and he swapped his biscuits for hard cheese from men with poor teeth unable to chew it. In this way he always had a store of hard cheese in his knapsack which kept him going saving him from the exhaustion which debilitated the men. Lord Baden-Powell told, in one of his books, how a new recruit who was having his teeth examined asked why the recruiting officer was examining his teeth. "Do we have to eat the enemy as well as kill him?" he asked. It was then explained to him that good teeth are essential to a soldier on the march if he is to stay alive.

Father was very hairy apart from his hair thinning as he grew older and had a very hairy chest and legs. He wore suspenders to support his socks and the hairs on his well-developed calves caught in the suspenders. The first thing he did before putting his feet up was to unclip his suspenders and take them off. Whilst he scratched his calves with relief, we went to fetch his slippers. We tried to fit them on his feet but he flexed his toes, arched his insteps and made it impossible for us to put the slippers on. Then he told us that we were no good and didn't know how to put slippers on, until at last, having had enough of the small girls vying with each other to push on the slippers with all their might, he sent us running away to perform some other task that he had just thought up to keep us busy.

"Red sky at night, shepherd's delight," quoted Mamma. When we heard her go on to say to Father, "It's going to be a lovely day tomorrow", we all grew very excited to hear Father's reply, "If it is we shall go to Thorpe Bay tomorrow". The thought of it kept us awake far too long. Early the next morning he woke us all early to start packing the large quantity of things we needed for a day at the sea. First we had a good breakfast with no hanging about. Then he issued the orders. One of us collected everybody's sand shoes which we needed for running about in on the stony beach. These filled one case and I had to carry that. Then there was a case of towels and swim wear. Mamma was busy packing food and making sandwiches. Packs of all sorts of sandwiches with sausage rolls and cakes filled another case. The spirit stove, groundsheets with various towels, cups and plates went into a third. There were lots of cases and everything was packed well so that nothing could be lost. At last when all that we could possibly require for a day at the sea-side, all buckets, spades and balls were assembled in some container or another, Father cast his eye around for suitable carriers among us. As we had the bags and containers thrust into our hands, we were sent off with our baggage to the station to await Mamma and Father. There we were, one after the other in a line like a gaggle of geese, straggling towards the station. We tried to scurry but our loads were heavy. We saw the backs of those despatched before us some distance in front, lugging their burdens excitedly along the streets. At last we were all assembled and Father had arrived with Mamma; looking us over to check that we were all there, he dashed to the ticket office to buy the tickets. Long before he reached the barrier where the ticket collector awaited, Father was shouting at us by name to go through as the train was due. Lumping our luggage with us we pushed past the ticket collector with Father following waving the tickets. "No time, no time", shouted Father at the ticket collector, who had the merest touch on the tickets and never had a chance to clip them. By now we children were all on the platform. Yelling at us all to wait for the train to stop, Father did a Douglas Fairbanks dash down the stairs to hustle us all together and open the train door where we all poured in.

At the next station we changed on to the steam train which was bound for Thorpe Bay. With the confidence of an officer directing a cavalry charge, Father had the train door open and all of us tripping through the doorway into the empty seats. We filled the carriage. With the luggage stowed on the racks above us Father contemplated the scene through the window. Anxious people still on the platform peered in looking for empty seats but on seeing none passed further along. A few decided that they would get into our compartment but Father was not going to have this. By now sitting down with the window closed and his foot on the door latch he shook his head from side to side to indicate no room and shouted through the window which he kept shut, "The door is locked!" So in this way with the carriage to ourselves, we travelled to Thorpe Bay with Father in charge of the compartment, reading the paper with all the tribe under strict control.

The journey through the countryside we all enjoyed. Cows gazed idly at the train, standing like statues, suspending their chewing; sheep stood in woolly clusters on grassy slopes; horses, heads together, communed with each other in the shade of trees; roads wound here and there with a horse and cart or two but not yet the busy traffic which exploded over the land with the motor car.

At last the old town of Leigh-on-Sea was alongside the train, which stopped. This is where the famous cockles are found and sold and where artists paint pictures of the cockle boats. These sail out at night to fish, to where the cockles are dug for, when the tide is out.

We stayed in the train to go on through Westcliff, Chalkwell, Southend and on to Thorpe Bay. Father always chose Thorpe Bay. There the beach was wider and sandier; there was shelter by the esplanade wall and shops near enough for ice cream or tea, but only one or two and not the hurly burly of busy Southend, where on a fine day it seemed, all London was on holiday.

Down the steps to the sand we went after the long walk from the station. Now we fairly raced with our cases, like pilgrims arriving at Mecca. Father's voice had us all rounded up in an instant and there he issued the orders. One or two of us were sent to find deck chairs for him and Mamma and hers had to have a sun canopy fixed so that the sun was not in her eyes. His first step was to get Mamma seated comfortably in a chair with the sun canopy adjusted over her large attractive hat. Of all of us, she was the only one not dressed for the seaside. With an elegant dress and jacket with three quarter length sleeves, dainty shoes and never bare-legged, she sat there like a queen, whilst Father saw to it that her slightest request was instantly obeyed.

Then it was off with everything and on with swim suits, shorts and sand shoes and racing away to catch the tide. Rarely did we catch the high tide, it was always either coming or going, but if it was gone we walked out after it with Father, miles it seemed; looking in muddy pools to see the shrimps, quite colourless; tiny crabs sank down away from our toes; ragworms waved at us, anchored in mud; cockles sent up bubbles to mark their hiding holes; and on and on we went until there was enough water over our ankles to sit down and cool ourselves until we found a deeper pool where we could swim on our backs. There we stayed, kicking the water as we splashed about until at last we felt the tide returning and we turned to look for Mamma on the beach. Invisible among the crowd and so far away we could not see her, she was there somewhere, one of the dots on the crowded beach. Unless we could see her we might return to a spot far from her in the long walk back. If Father were still with us there was no problem, but sometimes he returned before us and left us to come back later.

Now we ran back to race the returning water, skipping over the mud flats with their hard tide-rippled surfaces, every now and then slowing to scan the beach for Mamma's whereabouts. At last there they were and racing back, we were soon eating lunch with the rest.

Many small boats were moored all along, just off the beach there. If the tide were out we climbed in and all over these small craft a small distance from the shore so there was little chance of the owners happening along. One day, playing on a boat with a young lad I met on the ebb tide far out, the time flew by. With a pair of shorts over my swim suit, we shinned up the mast, jumped and chased and captained the ship for several hours. At last Stanley, one of my brothers, was sent to fetch me back to eat some food. As he approached he called, "Dorothy, you have got to come and have your lunch. We have all had ours. Mamma says you must come at once." To my amazement my new-found companion looked astounded. "Dorothy" he echoed in disgust. "Dorothy! I thought you were a boy." I was amazed. What difference did it make. We'd had a wonderful morning! When the tide was in we could swim to a small ship lying at anchor which made a good trip there and back. But whether the tide was in or out Father organised games on the beach. He co-opted people into joining in. There in a large ring they threw balls back and forth, two or three going together in every direction. Cricket with a piece of wood sent folk scurrying after the ball into the sea or among a party of onlookers. If they were annoyed Father invited them to join in. Leapfrog had strangers leaping over each other and us. We were lucky as we all wore sandshoes protecting our feet from stones and shells and could race those not so lucky. In the water it was the same. Father always had a ball and threw it at the most unlikely people. In this way he kept himself fit and everyone active. Only Mamma never joined in. She was quite content in the deck chair looking relaxed and contented surrounded by towels food and all our things, and making sure that we left as much sand as we could behind before returning home with a small crab or two in a bucket.

Some time in the afternoon, our parents went for a walk when they had tea in the Willow Tea Rooms. We hated this time, feeling the miss of them. We felt lost and kept a look out for any sign of their return. At last we could see them, strolling casually along the esplanade in the hot sunshine. Mamma with her large shady hat and Father tanned in his shirt and flannels. Sometimes he had as many ice-cream cornets as he could carry and if more were needed, the bigger children went to buy them. Then we all resumed our activities as before until Father decided that it was time for another pot of tea.

The older children went to get this from the same tea rooms, carrying it all back carefully on a tray, along the esplanade to the steps, then down to where our parents were in the lea of the sea wall, in deck chairs; and then Father sent us all to buy ice creams for ourselves.

We built sandcastles and buried each other. The tide demolished our forts and bridges as the sea lapped in and out, but there was nothing organised as at other seaside resorts, only games organised by Father.

We all urged Mamma to take off her shoes, but she wouldn't. Father was the opposite.

He walked about in swimming trunks or shorts looking more like an older brother, which school friends often took him for.

There were times when we paid for our day out with sun-burn which kept us awake half the night; our shoulders burned from hours in the sun and salt water. Then it was a painful night of it, with tossing and turning and Mamma putting bicarbonate of soda on to ease the pain. A new surface layer of skin appeared some days later when all the old sunburnt skin fell off.

These days at the sea were few and far between but they were like a week, so early did we leave, and so long did we spend there, and so much did we do.

In Wanstead Park, everything was different when our parents came. Then we all took everything, except fishing things. Everything meant the pram, loaded with food and drinks, the primus stove and all the picnic things. The two youngest came with Father and Mamma and the pram whilst the rest of us were sent on the tram with the bats and balls and skipping ropes to await their arrival on foot. We awaited them by the park gates. It seemed they would never come. In and out of the gate we went; having a rest on the grass only to dart out once more to scan the long avenue for any sign of their coming. And then when we had given up hope and were feeling downcast, feeling sure that something had happened and we should never see them there, suddenly Father was giving orders and Mamma was patiently answering a thousand questions as to why they had been so long.

Finally we were all in the forest glade with our tea laid out on a large table cloth. There everything was displayed and we all helped ourselves after asking for this or that first. Mamma sat on a seat by the pram where she handed out lemonade or water. As soon as all the sausage rolls and most of the food had been eaten, the picnic was packed away and Father took charge. There, king of all he surveyed, with no competition from the the sea or sand, he organised games. A long line of people joined in with the skipping or running through the rope after a skip along it, as it was many yards long. Snakes caught many of them out with Father at the end of the rope. The tug o' war had the men rolling on their backs. Father's voice dominated everyone and everyone seemed to be enjoying themselves. Then it was time for cricket and a small crowd joined in getting everyone out quite quickly so that all had a bat. The boys put the stumps back into the ground, knocking them in with their cricket bats. We played with a soft ball and spent plenty of time searching for it in the edge of the forest. Father knew just when to change the game to keep as many people as possible in the game. Soon he would switch to throwing the ball or two or three balls between people so that you never knew from which direction it would come next so that we had to be wide awake.

So with football, cricket, skipping, catchers and any game he could think up, with the general public joining in, Father enjoyed the days' outings and in this way, we all did too. Then as the evening wore on we all returned home; Mamma and Father with the pram and the youngest, and the rest of us on the tram. The long wait by the entrance gate when we thought they weren't coming; the joy when at last we saw them sauntering with the pram towards the park gates, were all forgotten and we were once more back at home whilst Father and Mamma walked the return. Past the Earl of Essex public house, a reminder of Queen Elizabeth's favourite who lived at Wanstead Manor centuries before; through Manor Park; past Sheridan Avenue after the playwrite Sheridan who lived in the area; on towards Plashet Road, a reminder of the great prison reformer Elizabeth Fry, who lived at Plashet House and founded a girl's school there, and then they were at East Ham Station and soon home.

Our games of shops in the conservatory helped us when it was our turn to run to the shops for a blue bag or a bar of sunlight soap. Mamma always wrote everything down no matter how trivial but Father believed in training our memories and sent us for one or two things at the most. Before we went on Father's missions there was a lecture and then a rehearsal. "I want two pennyworth of precipi-tated chalk," he enunciated carefully. "*Two* pennyworth of precipi-tated *chalk*. Two pennyworth of *precipitated* chalk." He repeated this emphasis on the precipitated three or four times. Then he repeated the whole lot over again and woe betide you if you tried to say it before he had finished talking. Having repeated the phrase to his satisfaction with the emphasis first on one word and then another, he now tested you out to see if it had sunk in. "Do you think you can say that?" he demanded. Of course we could. "Two pennyworth of precipitated chalk", we repeated. "No, no," Father corrected, "precipitated; precipitated; precipitated", the more he said it the less likely we were to repeat it to his satisfaction. At last we were sent out unless in sheer exasperation he rounded up an older member of the family to be pressed into service. Finally one of us ran off to the chemist to buy the powder; weighed out carefully first and them folded and tucked into a neat packet. Running home to Father we were greeted with, "Do you know what this is for?" as he opened the packet. Of course we knew and said so but that didn't stop Father from explaining at length what it was and why he used it to clean his teeth. Those early days, when as a lad of thirteen he had worked at a chemist's, left an impression all through his life, and he studied the British Pharmacopoeia and used his common sense, in the same way that Mamma used her knowledge of her own mother's remedies in order to keep us well and save doctor's bills.

Early on summer mornings we watched Father admiring his tiger lilies and then we slyly touched the pollen as he turned to cut a rose for his button-hole. These were those halcyon days when Father's voice floated down from the bathroom singing,

'When you and I were seventeen, and love and life were new', or 'The Lily of Laguna' reached us from the hall as Father admired his button-hole in the hall mirror and, adjusting his trilby, strode to the front door. There on the door step he preened himself for a second before stepping off down the path, where, on the pavement, he twirled his walking stick as he set off at a fast pace to meet Harry Keckwick or Billie Cummings at the Black Lion for a game of shove ha'penny. Other days the routine was almost the same. There in the hall mirror he admired his button-hole and flicked a brush over his shoulders. Then adjusting his watch and chain across his fancy waistcoat, he shrugged his shoulders as he dropped his boater on to his head. Again he stood for a second on the doorstep, perhaps wondering which of his friends to visit; then off he went, tipping his boater just a fraction and setting off at a cracking pace, in rhythm with his walking stick to see Harry Manning for a cigar and a game of billiards.

Those were the days when Mamma did the Charleston and wore short dresses with hems shaped like petals. And Father seemed to be always decanting his port into the fine wine-coloured glass decanters, never spilling a drop. When we saw him in the hall ready to go out we asked, "Can we come with you?" "Not this time," said Father, "I am going to see a man about a dog." The man, one of his friends, often returned with him for discussion over a glass of port and a cigar but we saw no dog with them. As the blue smoke curled up towards the ceiling Father remarked, "Did he, by George?" and we wondered who this George was as it clearly wasn't Father, although he often mentioned him.

In the 1920s the depression hit hard at everybody. One of our cats, 'the Old Cat', that we had for about fourteen years, almost died one bitter winter. The poor animal had its eyes glued up, its nose streaming and lay under a chair unable to move. It had cat flu. We could not afford a vet. Father emptied his bedroom cupboard and smothered the inside with eucalyptus oil. In there he shut the cat away from all of us. After a few days the cat was able to eat again and picked up strength and recovered to live on until it was fifteen or sixteen.

In the post-war 1920s the depression hit everybody so that though men were not in the army fighting, they were now in the unemployed army instead. In many ways they were worse off. Now they had no money for food whereas their food had been supplied when they were away at war and their families given an allowance. Everybody was in the same boat. There followed years of Father trying everything he knew to support his family. He hired the Town Hall and ran dances, but after a time, what with 'spot prizes' and lucky ticket numbers, he was finding it difficult as it was a great deal of work for a very little profit.

Then he decided to run whist drives. Once again he hired the Town Hall. Mamma ran up huge banners on her Singer sewing machine, stitching on them details of the event. COME TO GEORGE PARKER'S WHIST DRIVES with the first prize in money stitched large and clear. This attracted the people who were desperate to earn money somehow. These banners were run up on a flag pole above the Town Hall, with huge scarlet letters. Father printed his own cards. He had a set of small and large type which he set up and used.

The whist drives were quite a success and all went well until Father was sued for the cost of a new fur coat which a woman said had been stolen from the cloakroom during the whist drive. The case went to court and against Father who could not disprove the story, although Mamma declared that the claimant had not handed her the cloakroom ticket. The woman said the opposite and Father was ordered to pay for the coat. He was well out of pocket.

Father took to many things one after the other. At one time two Dutchmen came to the house. They and Father were working on some inventions about which we knew nothing and then they spent their efforts on taking out a patent or patents. Then he took up advertising and he was very good at it, setting up his own magazine for shopkeepers which he entitled *Who's Who*. In it were all the local traders with their adverts. But he found it difficult to get the advertisers to pay because of the depression. None had money to spare for advertising. It was a popular magazine but without capital or income he was hampered at every turn and finally he sold it out to some other entrepreneur.

Now he turned to the fish market, not to work there as it was impossible to get back in, no pitch being available with cut-throat competition for trade, but to set up a register for the traders to use. This was in the form of a magazine again, for retailers. It was entitled *The Fish Trade Record*. I know little about it except that the paper was squared and I think it must have been for the retailers to keep tally of their accounts. But in spite of all Father's drive and efforts it failed to make enough for him to keep it going; the reason being that the worst depression in history was killing off both business and men. There were many sad suicides adding to the death toll of the war and influenza, in the post-war years.

As he was so good at setting up type and the lay-out of bills and posters, he found work here and there among the business fraternity. They, however, were equally struggling with hardship and were often unable to pay him what they owed.

He had a beautiful form of script which flowed in neat and artistic rhythm. He became skilful at putting gold leaf on lettering and embossed his own large gardening volumes with his own name and the titles of the books in gold leaf. He placed the fragile gold leaf with a fine sable brush. Waiting until he was out, Phyllis and I went to Raggazone's lacquered Japanese cabinet with the nest of tiny drawers inside, and took out some of Father's gold leaf books and, fascinated, pressed it on our fingers, so smooth and fine it was.

Father finally began regular work for the authorities in Poor Relief as it was known then. He travelled about London in some very poor areas; Kentish Town was one of them. He visited people in needy circumstances to assess their entitlement to 'relief' and came home to Mamma with sad tales of the plight of the poor in the homes he visited. These were the days of the early rise of Hitler in Germany where he was promising the people that he would put them on the road to economic prosperity within five years.

Mamma told of Father's own early days, sitting on the steps of a public house waiting for his mother to come out whilst his Father was away on one of his voyages. She said, he recalled his long black curls, his short petticoats, and being carried inside by one of the men. For a penny he sang, up on the tables, standing, one foot on each hand of one gentleman whilst all the rest laughed, clapped and cheered at his songs and answers to their questions. He was a precocious child; quick witted; learning how to earn pennies by making the hardened drinkers laugh, and wary of how he handled his quick-tempered, generous-hearted mother. In the pubs, he was passed along the tables standing to sing on their hands; knowing the words of all the songs they shouted out for him to sing, and acting accordingly; pretending to cry singing, 'Don't go down the mines daddy'; and 'The Old Bull and Bush' and all the music hall songs of the day, long before he was old enough to wear breeches or go to school. Father never spoke about this to any of us. We knew only from Mamma. He knew very little about his Father's voyages and could remember only that his Father spoke of the great explorer, Nansen.

This Norwegian explorer, Fridtjof Nansen was a clever scientist. He wrote an historical account of early Norse explorers who discovered America long before the days of Columbus. He was a scholar who lectured to school children on his adventures in the Polar Seas. It was this clever Norwegian who solved the riddle of a short cut across the Arctic Ocean by way of the Pole itself. He had a small ship built, the *Fram* (which means onward), and set sail in it in July 1893. He set sail from the New Siberian Islands and moored the *Fram* to an icefloe which kept it fast for the next thirty five months. After twenty months, Nansen set off with a companion, a dogteam and a sledge for the North Pole, leaving the *Fram* in the hands of a very great Norwegian sailor.

After 150 miles Nansen was forced to turn back as they hadn't the strength to cross the great ice ridges, returning safely after astounding adventures. As for the *Fram*, she reached the furthest north of any vessel;

carried by unknown currents; she finally was free of ice and sailed into Spitsbergen thirty five months later, having been carried from northern Siberia to northern Europe through the polar ice.

Father told Mamma how his Father brought a Great Auk's egg back from one of his voyages. He said he gave this to my grandmother to keep safe. One day when she was entertaining some friends, showing them her husband's souvenirs from his travels, in the midst of her chatting and laughing, she suddenly burst into tears. They wanted to know what had happened. In the pocket under her bustle she had put the Great Auk's egg and in the excitement had sat down on it and knew that her husband would never be able to bring back another one.

Father remembered little of his own Father, often away at sea, but he recalled the last time he saw him. He had gone with his mother to see his Father off on his ship the *Garry Owen*. "It was cold at the dock-side," said Father. "Waiting with my mother to wave 'goodbye' to Father, up high on deck above the quay side, I stood there shivering. Looking up he saw his Father wave again and again as my mother wept at my side." Looking down at the small boy standing with his mother in her long ground-sweeping skirts and bustle, he saw his Father, take off his thick naval coat, and, leaning over the side, threw it down to them both. "Here," he shouted, "put that around you, it will keep you both warm." Those were the last words his Father ever spoke to them and the last time they saw each other. His Father was off to the Klondike to seek for gold. Gold fever had hit Europe and thousands were embarking from ports all over the world to seek their fortunes in northern Canada.

In the far north of Canada the Yukon Territory is seven times as large as Britain. There close to the Arctic Circle, Dawson City and the Klondike were sparsely populated and no doubt still are, but in the mad rush for gold, hordes of people went there, travelling as best they could and the population in Dawson and the Klondike went up to over 30,000 with rogues of every description. The genuine prospectors were preyed upon by hordes looking for easy pickings.

They travelled by every means possible but only the toughest and luckiest and most determined, reached the Klondike on the Alaskan border in the far north. Rich deposits of gold had been found, first in Bonanza Creek and then Eldorado. Klondike City stood where the River Klondike entered the River Yukon and Dawson City was half a mile away across the Klondike on the north bank. Those seeking gold here came from many countries and took various routes. Many sailed to San Francisco where the Commercial Hotel was known as the Yukoner's Home. From there they headed north for over two thousand miles, by boat, canoe, on sledge and on foot. Those who survived had to endure the hazardous darkness of the Arctic night and famine. Famine chronic with the Indians and Eskimos and now chronic with the gold-miners. Even women and children travelled from nearer towns over three hundred miles of ice to help their men scrape for gold, taking everything with them. They deserted the small town, Circle City, to search the creek beds near Eldorado. Famine grew with the population and in the winter of 1897–1898 the United States government was forced to equip a reindeer relief expedition. Writers told how a long line of gold seekers stumbled with their possessions up the steep trail. Those too weakened were left where they fell, whilst the seemingly never-ending line struggled on, each fighting for survival.

What happened to my grandFather between his arrival in America and his death, we do not know, but whilst Father was still a very small boy, his mother, one day, received a telegram. Excitedly she ran in to read it to her constant companion, Sadie. Laughing, expecting news of her husband's arrival, she gaily tore open the telegram. Father recalled what happened next. His mother looked at the words on the telegram and then giving a terrible scream, she threw her skirts over her face and head and fell on the floor rolling about in an agony of grief. Sadie told the boy that his Father was dead and would never come back. GrandFather William Parker, then a young man strong and healthy, had sailed to the Klondike to seek his fortune, but the telegram said, "His body was found floating in San Francisco Bay with a knife in his back."

Father kept his Father's one and only last letter.

My own Boy Georgie,

Many thanks for your kind loving little letter. I was so pleased with it when I received it, that it made poor daddy waggy cry, to think that I had such a dear little sonny & I not near him to give him a sweet loving kiss. But you know I would have done so if I had had the chance dont you? So to square matters, I have sent you a small present all for your own dear self. I am so proud of you, you dear little soul, for Mamma dear tells me you are such a good little boy to her, & you know God loves all good little boys, and so do their Fathers.

I am so sorry poor Tom misses me so much, but you must try and cheer him up, & buy him a halfpennies worth of cat's meat. I do so wish you were here my darling boy, so you must make haste & get your examination over & then perhaps you may come. I do hope Georgie you will continue to be a good boy & if Mamma speaks well of you, I shall send you a very nice present. I cannot stay to say more this time, but thanking you a thousand times over for your dear letter, I must conclude with a hundred thousand million kisses to my son Georgie from his ever loving & affectionate Father,

William

X X X X X X X X X X X X X A baker's dozen

Father treasured his Father's letter as he did the prize he received years later, for the best essay in the whole of East London. He was twelve when he wrote the essay and the book awarded was a leather bound copy of the *Life of King Alfred*. Together with the book, he kept the letter from the authorities notifying him of details of the presentation. It was handwritten.

West Ham School Board.
95, The Grove, Stratford, E.
November 8th. 1901.

King Alfred Prize Competition

Referring to my previous letter, I have to inform you that your prize will be presented to you at an entertainment to be given at the Town Hall, Stratford, on Wednesday next, the 13th. inst..

Please attend at the Town Hall at 7.00 that evening and show this letter which will gain you admission into the room.

Yours faithfully,
C. Carrell.
Clerk to the Board.

Mast. G. Parker.

Mamma always said that Father did marvellously well as he seldom saw his Father before his early death and afterwards, with grief and loneliness, his mother took to drinking.

Father loved all creatures and as a boy, was never without pets. He loved his pet white rat named Tootles. This was his constant companion and went to school with him, inside his shirt. This was not allowed and when the rat poked its head out of his shirt and the teacher saw it, he was sent to take it home, a few yards from the school, in Holbrook Road. On one occasion he brought it back again hidden in his pocket. The master was not amused when the rat jumped out causing a commotion. Father was ordered out to have the stick. Quickly he bit his lip until it bled. Seeing the blood running down his chin the master relented and sent him home once more to bathe his chin and leave the rat at home. When the pet died Father buried it in his garden in Holbrook Road and composed a poem, an epitaph in Latin. He wrote this on a board and fixed it by the grave. I cannot remember it but the name 'Parker Rat Tootles' figured in it and it ended with 'requiescat in pace' (may he rest in peace).

Father was very proud of being a Londoner and of being British. If ever there was an event of historical importance he urged us to go to see it. This is how I came to take those younger than myself to the Lord Mayor's Show.

We were not very old but arrived very early, somewhere near the Mansion House after a long ride on the tram. These trams made us feel sea sick if we went up front, but it was no use moving to a different seat once you felt this way, as the feeling stayed there inside you. The swaying of the tram as it swayed about along the rails was nauseating and the only refuge was to keep absolutely still and silent to fight against the urge to be sick.

At last we were installed alongside the Mansion House by the kerb. Although we were right in the front having squeezed gradually forward over a period of two hours, there was a long line of people on duty in front of us. They obstructed the view. We sat down on the kerb to look between their legs. We sat there for a long time then our younger brother Ron, wanted to go to the toilet. I was torn between taking him and leaving the others there in the hope of finding them again, or taking them all with me so that we could all stay together. I decided to take them all with me but I knew from the length of time it had taken to worm our way to the front, that we would never reach the front again. We ran as fast as we could to the toilet and back but could not get near to see the procession. As it all passed by the crowds moved along and followed it and many people went off about their business so that we had a splendid view of the road-sweepers and men clearing up after the Lord Mayor's Show.

In January 1936 Father insisted that we make the trip to London to see the funeral of King George V. Off we went on the tram quite early. By the time we arrived in the Mall there were already many people there installed, waiting. Soldiers and guardsmen lined the route. Barriers and stands were in position. It was a very long wait. The crowds swiftly built up behind us. The weather was sad and dreary. When the excitement and crowds were at their height, Ron once more wanted to go to the toilet. I was afraid to leave the children alone and anyway they all wanted to go, so I let our place be taken and we all squeezed our way

328

back through the press of people to search for the toilet. By the time we were ready to view the procession it was too late. There was no way to get back through the crowds. At the back of the great throng of people there was no way to see anything. Knowing the direction the cortège was taking, we ran along behind the huge crowds hoping to catch a glimpse of the Royal mourners. At last we were able to find a way through to the front and saw the slow procession as it approached. Behind the gun carriage bearing the flag-covered coffin stepped the four princes slowly, in time with the funeral march. Behind these four, the Prince of Wales, the Duke of Gloucester, the Duke of York and the Duke of Kent, walked the young, handsome King Leopold of the Belgians, stepping slowly with the funeral march, his long grey overcoat setting off his trim athletic figure, whilst beside him keeping the slow pace, equally trim and slight, we saw the regal Shah of Persia. Many others were in that procession but only these we recognised that sad morning. The image is in my mind still.

One day I happened upon a heartwrenching drama. I was then about eight years old. Father had a good friend in the Conservative Club named Harry Kekwick. He was tall quiet and friendly. His calm blue eyes would suddenly light up in a smile and widen his long moustache. His wife Betty was short plump and forceful. We never saw her until Harry suddenly died. Then she called frequently at weekends and joined the whist parties. Mama began to complain that Betty was wearing revealing dresses to capture Father's attention.

One day coming out of the passage into the hall I was amazed to see Father at the front door and Mamma distraught beside him holding onto the jacket he was wearing. He turned away from her and opened the front door. Mama cried and sinking to her knees, clasped him about the legs and begged him not to leave. Mama's words imploring, "George, George, don't leave us," cut me to my being. Father turned and looking down, closed the door, remaining inside. I surmised that Mrs. Kekwick had inveigled Father to join her and leave us all. Months later Mrs. Kekwick chanced to meet Mamma and told her she was being ill-treated by a new husband. Later I saw her at the Swimming Bath. She was employed in the ticket office. I was thankful she did not recognise me.

Many images of Father come crowding back. How he never learned to ride a bike and put his foot through Mamma's chain guard so that she wouldn't teach him and he never did learn. How he always made the Christmas punch too hot, pouring scorn on our protestations that our throats were burning. The time I ran off to bed without kissing him goodnight and he was hurt. He never found out that it was because I had been smoking a piece of rolled paper in the bathroom. How he rushed through life with never a second to spare yet exhorted us all to give ourselves time. "Everything takes time," he'd say. "You must learn to give yourself time." He was well-read and liked to pass on anything he thought of interest like the Rosetta stone, the history of the Monument and the Tower where the lions were formerly in the Royal menagerie. He liked to know about all things and expected us to be the same. He told us many things that he expected us to remember but of course we forgot half of them, such as Beef Eaters at the Tower were so named from the French Boufitier, meaning keeper of the King's buffet. And Father forever telling us these things would pour scorn on popular crazes with: "There's nothing new under the sun", which I suppose is the sentiment of Goethe who said, "Every good idea has already been thought, suffice only to think it again."

And so the long days passed into evenings with daylight fading and daytime receding; cosy evenings together and homely noises amidst family surroundings. Then we were grateful to have Father's strength and energy after the Great War in which one in three were wounded and one in seven never returned. And when the sun rose up each morning suffusing the world with rich promise, we were aware of our family heritage, and knew that the seeds of the past – all the love and country lore from Lower Beeding, and all the sharpness of Father, honed in his lonely childhood, the markets of London and the trenches of Flanders, were there for 'Us'. For 'the seeds of the past are there to create the future in everything we do'.

Seven, Going Down.

by Dorothy Parker